PROGRAMMING IN C++

Paul M. Chirlian
Stevens Institute of Technology

Merrill Publishing Company
A Bell & Howell Information Company
Columbus   Toronto   London   Melbourne

To Barbara, Lisa and Jerry, and Peter

Published by Merrill Publishing Company
A Bell & Howell Information Company
Columbus, Ohio 43216

This book was set in Century Schoolbook.

Administrative Editor: Vern Anthony
Production Coordinator: Sharon Rudd
Art Coordinator: Vincent A. Smith
Cover Designer: Brian Deep

Library of Congress Catalog Card Number: 88–63285
International Standard Book Number: 0–675–21007–0
Printed in the United States of America
    2   3   4   5   6   7   8   9—94   93   92   91   90

■ MERRILL SERIES IN COMPUTER AND INFORMATION SYSTEMS

Preface

This textbook discusses the C++ programming language. Although C++ is an extension of the C programming language, this book can be used by readers who have no experience with C. All the details of C++ are discussed, even those that duplicate those of C. The discussions of C++ are complete, enabling experienced programmers to use this book to add C++ to their repertoire of programming languages.

In addition to the features found in other procedural programming languages, C++ implements the components of an object-oriented language, including information hiding, data abstraction, and inheritance. One major new feature of C++ is the concept of a class, a user-defined type that contains both data and procedures. The implementation of classes provides the object-oriented features of C++. Additional new features of C++ not currently implemented in the C language include operator overloading, streams, and inline operations. The pass-by-reference to functions has been considerably improved. In addition, default arguments can be used with functions. The type-checking of C++ is considerably stronger than that of C. Overloading of functions and operators has been incorporated. The management of memory has been made an explicit part of the language.

Much discussion in the popular press has implied that object-oriented programming makes it possible for people with little or no programming experience to write complex programs. While some programming systems make it relatively simple for nonprogrammers to perform specific types of programming, someone had to write those programming systems. For instance, expert system development tools can greatly simplify the writing of some types of expert systems. However, writing the development tool was the actual programming task and was done by a programmer with a programming language. A programming language with object-oriented features, such as C++, can be a great help to such a programmer.

Operator and function overloading can make the programmer's task simpler. Overloading allows the compiler to distinguish between functions or operators that have the same symbol, or name, but which operate on different types or numbers of arguments. Overloading has always been used in C, but its features have not been available for programmer-defined functions. For instance, in C, the + operator causes different operations to be performed when integers are added and when floating-point numbers are added. Thus, + actually represents different operators, and the compiler selects, or overloads, the proper one based on the type of the operands. In C++, the features of operator overloading are available for programmer-defined operators and functions as well. Now, programmers can write functions that operate on different types of operands but have the same name. For example, two different routines called **average** could be written; one would take integer arguments and return a floating-point result, while the other would take floating-point arguments and return a floating-point result. In addition, the values of common operators can also be overloaded. For example, a programmer could define a + operator that adds two vectors.

The concepts of streams introduced in C++ greatly simplify the writing of all kinds of input and output statements. C++ allows functions to be inline expanded. This reduces the call overhead, especially for small functions. Pass-by-reference has been expanded, simplifying the programmer's work in many cases. Yet other new features of C++ will be discussed throughout the book.

Note that Chapter 2 is entitled "Arithmetic Operations," and Chapter 3 is entitled "Some Fundamentals of C++ Programming." This sequence permits the reader to start writing very simple C++ programs almost immediately after reading Chapter 2. The familiarity thus gained will greatly help the novice to study Chapter 3 and those following it. In addition, the elementary material on arrays can be covered before the material on pointers if the instructor feels that this sequence is desirable. Of course, the instructor can eliminate such topics as complex arithmetic and bitwise manipulations without affecting the remainder of the book.

I would like to thank Dr. Bjarne Stroustrup of AT&T Bell Laboratories for his helpful comments. Loving and heartfelt thanks are due my wife Barbara, who provided me with many in-depth discussions about C++ and who greatly influenced the book. I also wish to thank Simon Kaplan of the University of Illinois, Edmond Deaton of San Diego State University, Arline Sachs of Northern Virginia Community College, Michael Michaelson of Palomar College, and John Levandosky of Lake Sumpter College for their valuable comments.

Contents

CHAPTER 1
An Introduction to C++

This textbook will show you how to write programs in the C++ programming language. C++ is an outgrowth of the C programming language. Indeed, C programs will run under C++. However, in this book we assume that the reader does not have any knowledge of C, or of any other programming language. We shall start by discussing some simple ideas of programming and then build up to more complex ones. Although the book is written without assuming that the reader knows C, experienced C programmers can use it as well to learn C++. Because C++ is thoroughly discussed, the book also serves as a reference.

C++ is a very versatile language. It incorporates features of object-oriented languages as well as the most modern features of modern programming languages. All aspects of C++ are discussed in this book.

1–1 ■ SOME FUNDAMENTALS OF C++ PROGRAMMING

The operations of a computer are directed by a set of instructions called a program. The program that actually directs a computer is written in *machine language*. That is, it consists of a sequence of the actual instructions to the computer and the data on which the program is to operate. These are all in binary form, i.e., a sequence of zeros and ones. Machine language programs are very tedious to work with, and because of this, most programs are written in higher-level programming languages. C++ is such a language. For instance, a machine language program that simply multiplies two numbers would consist of a long sequence of instructions having no apparent relationship to multiplication. The same instruction written in C++ would be very understandable. For instance, a C++ expression that corresponds to the algebraic expression

1

$$x = a + b/c \qquad\qquad \textbf{1--1a}$$

is

$$x = a + b/c; \qquad\qquad \textbf{1--1b}$$

Ultimately, a computer is always directed by a machine language program. However, there are special programs called *compilers* and *linkers* that convert a program written in a programming language into a sequence of machine language instructions. The programmer need not be concerned with the inner workings of the compiler and/or linker; they automatically generate the correct sequence of instructions.

A sequence of commands is necessary to run the compiler and linker. These commands are given in the manual that comes with your system. The output of the compiler is not an executable program. There are other routines, such as those that perform input and output, that must be combined with the output of the compiler. Typically, these routines are stored in libraries that are supplied with your system. The process of combining your compiled programming instructions with other instructions is called linking.

There are many programming languages; each has advantages and disadvantages. Let us consider why a programmer might use C++. C++ can be used to write complex applications such as word processors and mathematical packages. However, it also has low-level facilities that make it an ideal language for systems programming tasks, such as writing operating systems. C++ incorporates various features that make the programmer's job easier. Very modern facilities, such as overloading of operators and functions, are incorporated. Not only do the object-oriented features included in classes make C++ suitable for writing artificial intelligence applications, but these features actually simplify the writing of all types of programs.

C++ Characters

Every language uses a set of characters to construct meaningful statements. For instance, all books written in English use combinations of the 26 letters of the alphabet, the 10 digits, and the punctuation marks. Analogously, C++ programs are written using a set of characters, consisting of the 26 lowercase letters of the alphabet,

a b c d e f g h i j k l m n o p q r s t u v w x y z

the 26 uppercase letters of the alphabet,

A B C D E F G H I J K L M N O P Q R S T U V W X Y Z

the 10 digits,

0 1 2 3 4 5 6 7 8 9

and the following symbols:

$$+ - * / = , . \_ : ; ? \backslash \ " \ ' \ \sim | \ ! \ \# \ \% \ \$ \ \& \ (\ ) \ [\ ] \{ \ \} \ \wedge \ @$$

The blank space, or whitespace, is also used. Combinations of symbols, with no blank space between them, are also valid C++ characters. In fact, the following are valid C++ symbols:

$$++ \ -- \ == \ \&\& \ || \ << \ >> \ >= \ <= \ += \ -= \ *= \ /= \ ?: \ :: \ /* \ */ \ //$$

Names—Identifiers

A simple C++ expression was given in 1–1b. In that expression, **x**, **a**, **b**, and **c** were all *names* or *identifiers*. Each one identified, or named, a variable. Names can be longer than a single character. This is very useful because it allows each name to describe the value it is storing. This makes the program much more readable for human readers. For instance, suppose that distance traveled is to be computed by multiplying velocity by time. Either of the following two C++ statements would accomplish the task:

$$d = v * t;$$ **1–2a**
$$distance = velocity * time;$$ **1–2b**

Note that the asterisk (*) is the C++ symbol for multiplication. Although these statements are equivalent, Statement 1–2b is much more understandable to human readers in that it clearly indicates the meanings of the variables.

Certain rules must be followed when names are selected. Names can consist only of letters, digits, and the underscore (_) character. The first character of a name must be either a letter or the underscore character. A name can be arbitrarily long. Note that a name cannot contain punctuation marks other than the underscore, a name cannot contain blank spaces, and that a name cannot start with a number. The following are valid C++ names.

> velocity
> velocity_of_automobile
> Velocity_of_automobile_on_TRACK
> velocity2
> _velocity

Note that names can contain uppercase as well as lowercase letters. C++ is a *case-sensitive* language; that is, an uppercase letter is considered to be a different character than its lowercase counterpart. For instance, the following two names are *different*:

> velocity
> veLocity

Because a programmer can easily mistake one name for another and become confused, it is poor programming practice to use identifiers that differ only in the case of one or two letters.

Reserved Words—Keywords

The C++ compiler recognizes certain words as having special significance. These are called *reserved words* or *keywords*. These words cannot be used as names for variables. The C++ keywords are

asm	auto	break	case	char
class	const	continue	default	delete
do	double	else	enum	extern
float	for	friend	goto	if
inline	int	long	new	operator
overload	public	register	return	short
sizeof	static	struct	switch	this
typedef	union	unsigned	virtual	void
while				

Note that the keywords consist of only lowercase letters. The keywords will be discussed throughout the text.

1-2 ■ SOME SIMPLE C++ PROGRAMS

In this section we shall discuss some very simple C++ programs. After you finish reading this section, you should be able to write some simple C++ programs on your own. As you progress through the book, your knowledge of C++ will increase, and you will be able to write increasingly complex programs. In the next section we shall consider some of the details of actually running C++ programs.

We shall start by considering a simple program that adds the numbers 7.0 and 9.0 and outputs the result, 16.0. The program is shown in Figure 1–1. The first line of the program is called a *comment*. Comments are ignored by

FIGURE 1–1 ■ A simple C++ program that adds the numbers 7.0 and 9.0 and outputs the results.

```
/* a program that adds the two numbers 7.0 and 9.0 */
#include <stream.h>
main( )
{
    float x,a,b;
    a = 7.0;
    b = 9.0;
    x = a + b;
    cout << x;
}
```

the compiler. They are included in programs to make them understandable to people. The compound symbol /* indicates the start of a comment, and the compound symbol */ indicates the end of a comment. Note that a compound symbol is made up of two symbols with no space between them. Thus, the line

/* a program that adds the two numbers 7.0 and 9.0 */   1–3

is ignored by the compiler. A comment can span more than one line. Once the C++ compiler encounters the /* it ignores all the text until the */ is encountered.

Note that some lines of the program are indented. This indentation makes the program more readable, but is ignored by the compiler. The indentation may not noticeably improve the readability of the simple program in Figure 1–1, but it will be very helpful when we consider more complex programs.

The second line of Figure 1–1 is

#include <stream.h>   1–4

The **#include** is called a *compiler directive*. Compiler directives cause the compiler to take some action. The **#include** directive causes the compiler to take the contents of the text file called **stream.h** and place it in the program at the point where the directive occurs. The file called **stream.h** is supplied with the C++ system. You need not concern yourselves with the contents of the file **stream.h**; all you have to know is to include it whenever data is either input or output. C++ systems come with many include files. There are many built-in routines supplied with the C++ system. Your C++ reference manual will indicate those files that are to be included when particular built-in routines are used. Note that there can be many lines of the form of 1–4 at the beginning of complex programs. We shall discuss **include** files in greater detail subsequently.

The third line of Figure 1–1 is

main()   1–5

This is actually the first line of the program. Note that it consists of the word **main** and a pair of empty parentheses. There is no semicolon following the expression. Every C++ program will *start* with the word **main** and a pair of parentheses. Although the parentheses often will be empty, this need not always be the case as shall be discussed subsequently. In this book, C++ keywords will be printed in boldface when they appear in the body of the text, to distinguish them from ordinary text. For the same reason, variable names will also be written in boldface.

The next line of the program is { , a left curly brace. The last line of the program is } , a right curly brace. The C++ program is made up of statements; each statement is ended by a semicolon. Many statements can be grouped into one *compound statement* or *block* by enclosing them in a set of curly braces. Thus, the entire C++ program in Figure 1–1, following **main()**, comprises a single compound statement.

The first line of the program following the curly brace is

$$\text{float x,a,b;} \qquad\qquad \textbf{1-6}$$

This is called a *declaration*. This statement indicates, or declares, to the compiler that the three variables called **x**, **a**, and **b** are *floating-point* numbers. A floating-point number is the usual type of number, i.e., it can have a fractional part. For example, 10.6 is a floating-point number. Floating-point numbers are also called *real* numbers. Various types of data can be used in C++ programs. The data is stored in the random access memory (RAM) of the computer. The compiler must reserve space for each item of data. Different data types require different amounts of memory for their storage. Thus, the type of each variable used by the program must be indicated to the compiler. The keyword **float** is used to specify floating-point data. We shall discuss the keywords that are used to declare other types of data throughout the book.

The keyword **float** is followed by a list of variable names separated by commas, and the statement is ended with a semicolon. Remember that in C++ all statements are ended by semicolons. Each variable's type must be declared prior to its use. The single declaration of 1-6 could be replaced by two or three declarations. For instance, we could write

$$\text{float x;}$$
$$\text{float a,b;} \qquad\qquad \textbf{1-7}$$

We shall discuss declarations in greater detail subsequently.

The statement

$$\text{a } = \text{ 7.0;} \qquad\qquad \textbf{1-8}$$

is called an *assignment*. The symbol = indicates to the compiler that the value on the right of the equals is to be assigned to the variable on the left. In this case, the value 7.0 is assigned to the variable **a**. Let us consider this. The value 7.0 will be stored in the memory locations that the compiler has reserved for **a**. If we were subsequently to have a statement

$$\text{a } = \text{ 15.0;} \qquad\qquad \textbf{1-9}$$

then the value 15.0 would be stored in the memory locations reserved for **a**. The previously stored value, 7.0, would be lost. The next line of the program causes 9.0 to be assigned to **b**.

The statement where the addition is performed is

$$\text{x } = \text{ a } + \text{ b;} \qquad\qquad \textbf{1-10}$$

The C++ symbol for addition is +. Statement 1-10 indicates the following: the value assigned to **a** (stored in the memory locations designated by **a**) is read from memory; similarly the value assigned to **b** is read from memory;

these two values are added, and the result (16.0) is assigned to **x**. Note that the values assigned to **a** and **b** are unchanged by this process, and they could be used subsequently in the program. Statements that cause an action to occur when the program is run are called *executable statements*. Such statements are *executed* by the system when the program is run. Statements 1–8 through 1–10 are executable statements.

The value assigned to **x** must be output. This is done with the statement,

$$\text{cout} \ll \text{x;} \qquad\qquad \textbf{1–11}$$

In this expression, **cout** refers to the *standard output* which will usually be the output on your console, in general, the screen of your terminal. The compound symbol $\ll$ indicates that the value assigned to **x** is to be sent to **cout**. Thus, the value 16 appears on your screen when this program is run. Note that the compound symbol does not include a space.

The requirement that a variable must be declared before it is used can prevent errors. For instance, suppose that a variable called **info** is used in a long, involved program. If you made a typographical error and, at some point in the program, typed the variable name as **infr**, an error would result because **infr** had not been declared; the compiler would spot this error, and the program would not compile. Thus, you would be prompted to correct your program. If it were not necessary to declare your variables, the variable **infr** simply would be treated as a new variable, and the program would be compiled. Although the program might run, it would give incorrect answers; this is a very bad situation. The declaring of variables is not simply an error-preventing mechanism, but that is one of its advantages.

In C++, variables need not be declared at the start of a program but can be declared at the point in the program where they are first used. For instance, in the program in Figure 1–1, if the declaration of **x** were removed from Statement 1–6, then Statement 1–10 would be in error because **x** had not been declared. This can be rectified by declaring **x** before Statement 1–10 or in the statement itself. In the latter case, Statement 1–10 would become

$$\text{float x } = \text{ a } + \text{ b} \qquad\qquad \textbf{1–12}$$

It sometimes can be very convenient to declare variables "on the fly" in this manner. However, in most circumstances, it is best to declare all the variables at the start of the program. This allows the programmer to keep track of the variables, and the danger of inadvertently changing a variable's name is avoided.

The simple programs we shall discuss in this chapter will contain only one block. Programs can be written in which one block contains another block. Any variable declared in the outer block can be used in the inner block; however, a variable declared in the inner block cannot be used in the outer block. This is actually a complex problem, and we shall consider it in much greater detail later.

The program in Figure 1–1 is artificially simple in that it always adds the same two numbers. In Figure 1–2a we illustrate a program that is more versatile in that it will add two numbers supplied by the person using the program. There are several new ideas introduced in this program. We have discussed comments and have indicated that the text enclosed between the symbols /* and */ will be ignored by the compiler. There is another way of indicating a comment. If the compound symbol // appears anywhere in a line, any text on that line following the // will be ignored. Note that although the /* and */ enclose a comment that can span several lines, the // is effective only to the end of the line on which it occurs. The program in Figure 1–2a includes both types of comments.

The program begins in the same way as that in Figure 1–1. The first difference is the line

$$\text{cout} \ll \text{"Enter two numbers}\backslash\text{n"} \qquad\qquad \textbf{1–13}$$

This results in printed output to the screen. This is similar to the output of the answer in the program in Figure 1–1 except that there is no variable to the left of the $\ll$ symbol. The text enclosed in double quotation marks is called a *string*. When 1–13 is executed, the string will appear on the screen.

FIGURE 1–2 ■ Two C++ programs that add two numbers entered from the keyboard. (a) Input and output statements as well as a new form of comment are illustrated; (b) a modification of (a) that uses a different form of output statement.

```
/* a program that adds two numbers */
#include <stream.h>
main( )
{
    float x,a,b;
    cout << "Enter two numbers\n";   //this is a prompt
    cin >> a;     //actual data entry
    cin >> b;
    x = a + b;
    cout << "\nsum = ";   // output
    cout << x;
}
```
                              (a)

```
/* a program that adds two numbers */
#include <stream.h>
main( )
{
    float x,a,b;
    cout << "Enter two numbers\n";
    cin >> a >> b;
    x = a + b;
    cout << "\n"   << a << " + " << b << " = " << x;
}
```
                              (b)

Note the **/n** symbol. This compound symbol, consisting of the backslash and the letter n, represents a *newline*. Any output following a newline appears on the next line. When the program is run, the text

Enter two numbers

will appear on the screen. This is called a *prompt*. Although experienced programmers may write programs, the people who run those programs often have little or no programming experience. Prompts are necessary to direct program users.

The actual input of data is accomplished with the statements

cin >> a;   **1–14a**

cin >> b;   **1–14b**

The **cin** corresponds to the *standard input* stream, which usually represents the keyboard of your terminal. As was mentioned earlier, we shall discuss streams in great detail subsequently. For the time being, consider the following. The **cin** indicates that input is expected from the standard input. The symbol >> is used to designate input. For instance, when Statement 1–14a is executed, a value taken from the standard input is assigned to **a**. (Note that, conversely, << is used to designate output.) When 1–14a is executed, the computer pauses and waits for input from the keyboard. Suppose, for example that the user enters **14.6**. Operation will still pause until RETURN (ENTER) is pressed. Then operation continues. The entered value, 14.6 in this case, is assigned to **a**. Expression 1–14b functions in a similar manner. We shall discuss input and output in greater detail subsequently. For the time being we are including only enough detail so that you can write and run some simple programs on your own.

Note that there are two **cout** statements at the end of the program. The first causes the text

sum =

to be output on a new line. The execution of the second **cout** statement causes the output of the value of **x**. Note that because there is no additional call for a newline, the value of **x** will be output following the equals sign. There will be spaces surrounding the equals sign because there are spaces surrounding it in the text of the **cout** statement. If the entered values of **a** and **b** were 7.3 and 9.2, then the answer would appear as

sum = 16.5   **1–15**

The program in Figure 1–2a has two adjacent **cin** statements. These two statements can be combined into a single one. That is, the two statements of 1–14 could be combined and written as

cin >> a >> b;   **1–16**

This statement is illustrated in the program in Figure 1–2b. Multiple adjacent output statements also can be combined into a single statement. This is illustrated by the statement

$$\text{cout} \ll \text{"\textbackslash n"} \ll a \ll \text{" + "} \ll b \ll \text{" = "} \ll x; \qquad \textbf{1–17}$$

Statement 1–17 is equivalent to six output statements. When it is executed the following occurs: a newline is output; next, the value assigned to **a** is output; next, a string consisting of a blank space, the plus sign, and another blank space is output; next, the value assigned to **b** is output; then, the string consisting of a blank space, an equals sign, and another blank space is output; finally, the value assigned to **x** is output. For example if, in response to the prompt, the values 9.1 and 11.2 were input, execution of 1–17 would result in

$$9.1 \;+\; 11.2 \;=\; 20.3 \qquad \textbf{1–18}$$

being output on the screen.

C++ programs do not have to be written in the form presented here. For example, we have written separate statements on separate lines. Although this is good form in that it makes the programs more readable, the compiler does not require separate lines. For instance, the following is valid C++,

$$\text{cin} \gg a \gg b; \; x \;=\; a + b; \qquad \textbf{1–19}$$

The form of 1–19 should be avoided because it obscures the program for readers.

Addition, Subtraction, Multiplication, and Division

We have considered addition of floating-point numbers. The C++ symbol for addition is +, the plus sign; the C++ symbol for subtraction is −, the minus sign; the C++ symbols for multiplication and division are *, the asterisk, and /, the slash, respectively. As an example, let us consider the C++ program in Figure 1–3, which computes the average of three numbers entered by the person running the program. The input and output statements are similar to

FIGURE 1–3 ■ A program that averages three numbers.

```
/* a program that averages three numbers */
#include <stream.h>
main()
{
    float average,sum,x1,x2,x3;
    cout << "\nEnter three numbers\n";
    cin >> x1 >> x2  >> x3;
    sum = x1 + x2 + x3;   // take sum
    average = sum/3.0;   // divide sum by three
    cout << "\nAverage = " << average;
}
```

those of the previous programs. The **sum** and **average** are computed when the following statements are executed,

$$sum = x1 + x2 + x3; \hspace{3cm} \textbf{1–20a}$$
$$average = sum/3.0; \hspace{3cm} \textbf{1–20b}$$

Note that the variable called **sum** is not really necessary because parentheses can be used to group terms in C++ just as in arithmetic. For instance, the following statement could be used to replace the two Statements 1–20.

$$average = (x1 + x2 + x3)/3.0; \hspace{2.5cm} \textbf{1–21}$$

We shall discuss the use of parentheses, and arithmetic operations in general, in greater detail in the next chapter.

1–3 ■ RUNNING C++ PROGRAMS

We shall now consider the procedures that are used to actually write and run your C++ programs. In general, these procedures vary from computer to computer and depend also upon the specific C++ compiler used. Thus, we shall not discuss specific instructions, but instead shall consider the basic concepts involved. The procedures will be essentially the same whether you are running C++ from your own microcomputer or as a user on a large time-shared system.

The actual C++ program is written with an *editor*. This is a program that, as its name implies, is used to write and modify text. You start by typing your program from the keyboard. While this is being done, the program is stored in the computer's memory. The program text must be saved in a file that is stored on a hard disk or a floppy disk. If your program is longer than a few lines, then it should be saved periodically while it is being written. This is because even a very short power interruption can result in the loss of all the data stored in memory. Thus, your entire program will be lost if it has not been previously saved to a file.

Most editors provide powerful procedures for modifying text. Using commands that vary from editor to editor, you can add to, delete part of, or modify the existing text. Blocks of text can be moved. Every occurrence of a specified string can be automatically changed. Consult the manual that is supplied with your editor to determine all the features that are available.

The C++ program that you have written to the disk is the one that is compiled. Many C++ systems require only a single command to initiate the complete compilation and linking process. In other cases, you may have to supply a sequence of commands. These instructions are provided with your C++ system manual. If there are no errors in your program, an executable program will be generated and stored on the disk. (We shall discuss errors in the next section.) The executable program can then be run.

We have not given any specific instructions for editing, compiling, and running the programs. The specific instructions depend upon your specific editor, C++ system, and operating system. However, these instructions are relatively straightforward and are supplied with the manuals provided with your system.

1-4 ■ A FIRST DISCUSSION OF PROGRAMMING ERRORS

Almost every program contains errors, or *bugs*, when it is first written. This should not discourage you. The experienced programmer knows that the correcting of errors, or *debugging*, is an integral part of programming. C++ has features that tend to reduce the occurrence of certain types of bugs. Good programming practice results in programs that have relatively few errors. We shall discuss such procedures throughout the book. In this section we shall consider some simple debugging procedures.

There are two types of errors that can occur: *logical errors* and *syntax errors*. A syntax error occurs when the program that you write is not correct C++. In such cases, the program cannot be compiled, and the compiler will report an error to you. Ideally, this *error message* shows you the offending statement and clearly indicates the error. Unfortunately, this does not always happen. For instance, suppose that you forget to declare a variable. An error message will be output corresponding to each use of the undeclared variable. All of those statements containing the undeclared variable, however, may be perfectly correct C++. The error has actually occurred at the start of the program where the variable declaration was omitted. If you forget to terminate a statement with a semicolon, a message reporting an error in the next statement may be output. As you become familiar with your system, the error messages will become more meaningful to you.

If you receive an error message that is not clear, reread your program carefully. Such a rereading, in conjunction with a consideration of the error message, will often point out the error.

A logical error occurs when the program is perfectly good C++, but it does not perform in the way that you expect it to. For instance, you might have inadvertently entered a minus sign when you should have entered a plus sign. The program will compile and run and answers will be output, *but they will often be incorrect*. Such errors can go undetected if you do not check your programs. You should always check your programs with several unrelated sample sets of data. This cannot be emphasized too strongly. *You must always check your program.*

If the logical error is simply a typographical error, then you can often find it simply by rereading your program. However, logical errors are sometimes actual mistakes in the logic of the program, that is, the program is not actually calculating what you want it to. In such cases, it is often useful to work through the calculations by hand, performing each step as if you were the computer. This process usually indicates the location of the error. In addition, you can put debugging statements into your program. Such statements usually output intermediate data. For instance, intermediate data for the program in Figure 1–3 would be the values of the three entered numbers and the value of **sum**. The process of stepping through the program by hand and comparing your results with the intermediate values output by the debugging statements usually points out the logical errors. Once the program has been debugged, the debugging statements should be removed. Some compilers provide you with extensive debugging procedures that allow you to step through the program and output intermediate values without adding debugging statements to your program. Such debuggers can be very useful.

EXERCISES

Check any programs that you write by running them on your computer.

1. Describe the functions of a *compiler* and *linker*.
2. List all the valid C++ characters.
3. List the C++ *keywords*.
4. Write a C++ program that evaluates the mathematical relation

$$x = (a + b)(a + c)/(b - c)$$

   The values of **a, b**, and **c** should be entered from the keyboard by the user of the program. There should be suitable prompts. The output should contain the text **"x = "** followed by the calculated value of **x**. Check the program with the values **a = 1.1, b = 2.4, c = 9.8**.
5. Repeat exercise 4 for the relations

$$x = (a + b)/(b - c + a)$$

   and

$$y = (x + a)(b + c)$$

   Now the two outputs should be clearly defined with suitable text.
6. Write a program that obtains the average of seven numbers entered from the keyboard. There should be suitable prompts for the entry of data. The output should contain explanatory text.
7. Write a program that computes factorial 6; that is,

$$6(5)(4)(3)(2)(1)$$

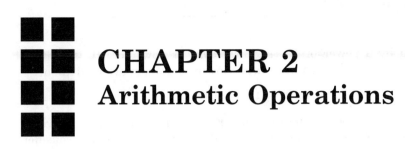

CHAPTER 2
Arithmetic Operations

In this chapter, we discuss the basic arithmetic operations that can be performed with C++. Some related topics will be considered as well. A discussion of the various types of numbers that can be manipulated with C++ is included. We begin with a discussion of floating-point numbers.

2–1 ■ FLOATING-POINT OPERATIONS

In the last chapter, we introduced floating-point numbers. Remember that these are also called real numbers. We shall now formalize these discussions. For the sake of completeness, we shall review some of the discussion of the last chapter.

Floating-point numbers are numbers that may have a fractional part. For instance, 3.23 is a floating-point number. The number of significant figures in a floating-point number varies with the compiler and/or computer. Seven is a typical value for the number of significant figures accommodated in a floating-point number. For instance, the numbers

$$0.1234567$$
$$12.21245$$

each contain seven significant figures. Most compilers provide procedures so that the number of significant figures does not limit the size of the number that can be expressed. Let us assume that we are dealing with a system that permits seven significant figures for real numbers. The largest number that can be expressed using seven significant figures is

$$9999999$$

However, most compilers allow you to deal with very large or very small numbers through the use of *exponential notation*. In this notation, the numbers

15

are multiplied by a power of 10. The *exponent*, or power of 10, is written following the letter E. For instance, the following numbers are equivalent:

$$1003 = 1.003E+03 \qquad\qquad \text{2-1}$$

Note that E+03 represents $10^3 = 1000$. E+03 can be written in several equivalent ways such as E3, E03, and E+003. As a final example consider the following:

$$\begin{aligned} E12 &= 1000000000000 \\ E{-}1 &= 0.1 \qquad\qquad \text{2-2} \\ E{-}6 &= 0.000001 \end{aligned}$$

The allowable range of exponents varies with the computer and compiler. Typically, allowable exponents lie between -38 and $+38$. Thus, very large and very small numbers can be represented.

If the number to be represented falls outside the allowable range, an error results. If the number is too large to be represented, an *overflow* is said to have occurred. Similarly, if the number is too small to be represented, an *underflow* is said to have occurred. Many systems will halt operation and output an error message at the point of the underflow or overflow. Note that some systems may continue operation after such an error without any notification. In that case, you will not be aware of the error. You should check your system to determine how it performs in the case of underflow or overflow.

The C++ symbols for floating-point operations are

+	addition	
$-$	subtraction	
*	multiplication	2-3
/	division	

Floating-point variables are declared using the keyword **float**.

Double-Precision Operations

There are times when great computational accuracy is required. A computer program may perform a great many arithmetic calculations. There may be a very small error in each calculation. For instance, consider the division

$$1.0/3.0 = 0.3333333\ldots \qquad\qquad \text{2-4}$$

In this case, an infinite number of digits is required to represent the fraction ⅓ exactly. Of course, computers, and people for that matter, can work with only a finite number of digits. Because the rightmost significant digits are discarded, a slight error, called a *round-off error*, results. If many calculations are performed by the program, small round-off errors can accumulate to produce a large total error. In such cases, the accuracy of floating-point numbers may not be sufficient. C++ provides another data type, called *double precision,* that has essentially twice the precision (i.e., number of significant figures) as does **float**.

Double-precision variables are declared with the keyword **double**. Larger exponents are often allowed in double precision. Typically, in type **double**, the exponents can range from -308 to $+308$. This number will vary with the implementation and should be checked for your system. Your system manual should provide this information. If you feel that it is possible that round-off error is creating a problem in a particular program, then replace **float** in your declarations with **double** and compare the answers. If there is a significant difference between the two answers, then round-off error is a problem. If there is no appreciable difference between the two results, then round-off error is not a problem, and ordinary **float** can be used to perform the calculations. If the difference between the two calculations is significant, you cannot be sure that the accuracy of double precision is sufficient. You should use "hand calculations" to verify that the double-precision calculations are in fact accurate.

Some calculations are much more prone to round-off errors than are others. For instance, $100 - 99$ yields the value 1. If there is a one percent error in the first number, we have $101 - 99 = 2$. In this case, a one percent error in one of the numbers has produced a 100 percent error in their difference. This type of calculation is prone to round-off error. If the two numbers in the operation were not almost equal, this problem would not arise.

It may seem as though type **double** should always be used in place of type **float**. However, this is not the case. Type **double** takes twice as much storage space in memory as does type **float**. In addition, many more machine language instructions are required for true **double** operations than for the corresponding operations in type **float**. Thus double-precision operations require more memory, result in larger executable programs, and take longer to run than do the corresponding single-precision operations.

Figure 2–1 illustrates some double-precision operations. Note that this program calculates the relation

$$x = (a - b)*(a + c)/(a - c); \qquad\qquad 2\text{--}5$$

FIGURE 2–1 ■ An illustration of type **double**.

```
/* an illustration of double-precision operations */
#include <stream.h>
main( )
{
    double x,a,b,c;
    cout << "\nEnter a, b, and c\n";
    cin >> a >> b >> c;
    x = (a - b)*(a + c)/(a - c);
    cout << "\nx = "   << x;
}
```

As far as the syntax of the C++ program, the only difference between double-precision and single-precision (**float**) operations is in the declaration of the variables.

2–2 ■ INTEGER OPERATIONS

Integers are numbers with no fractional part. For example,

$$23$$
$$-137$$
$$31000$$

are integers. In general, an integer requires less storage space than does a number of type **float**. Comparable arithmetic operations are faster when performed with integers than with floating-point numbers, and integer operations are not subject to round-off error. Thus, if an operation can be performed with either integers or floating-point numbers, it is usually preferable to use integers. Of course, there are applications where floating-point numbers must be used. For instance, if the numbers with which you are working have fractional parts, then floating-point operations should be used. Because the allowable range of integers is limited, floating-point numbers must be used when the numbers involved are very large or very small. We shall discuss the allowable range of integers later in this section.

Integers can sometimes be used in operations dealing with numbers that have fractional parts. For instance, suppose that you are dealing with numbers that have exactly two digits following the decimal point, as would be typical of financial calculations. If all numbers were multiplied by 100, then they would become whole numbers and could be represented by integers. These numbers are said to have been *scaled*.

Integers are declared by the C++ keyword **int**. For instance, the declaration

int item,count,numb   2–6

declares that **item**, **count**, and **numb** are variables of type **int**.

The arithmetic operators that are used for integers are:

+	addition
−	subtraction
*	multiplication
/	division
%	remainder

2–7

Integer operations of addition, subtraction, and multiplication proceed as with floating-point operations. The division of integers, however, requires some discussion. The division of integers results only in an integer; any remainder is discarded. For instance, the integer division 7/2 yields 3, the remainder

1 being discarded. Similarly the division 3/4 yields 0. Any fractional part resulting from integer division is discarded. The % operator is used to extract the remainder. For instance,

$$7 \% 3 \qquad\qquad \text{2–8}$$

yields 1, which is the remainder. If both the quotient and remainder of integer division are desired, the following program segment would obtain them:

```
int quotient,remainder,a,b;
```
.
.   2–9
.
```
quotient  =  a/b;
remainder  =  a % b;
```

The three dots indicate other statements that input data and perform other calculations. When the numerator and denominator are both positive, the results of the / and % operations are clearly defined. When negative integers are involved, there is no set C++ standard. With many systems, the results are such that the remainder has the same sign as the numerator, as illustrated by the following equations:

$$7/3 = 2 + 1/3 \qquad\qquad \text{2–10a}$$
$$-7/3 = -2 - 1/3 \qquad\qquad \text{2–10b}$$
$$7/(-3) = -2 + 1/(-3) \qquad\qquad \text{2–10c}$$
$$-7/(-3) = 2 - 1/(-3) \qquad\qquad \text{2–10d}$$

Note that the quotients are 2, −2, −2, and 2, respectively; the remainders are 1, −1, 1, and −1, respectively. Although different systems may compute different values when negative numbers are involved, the following equation always will be satisfied:

$$(a/b)*b + a \% b = a \qquad\qquad \text{2–11}$$

Figure 2–2 is a simple program that can be used to test how your system deals with quotients and remainders.

FIGURE 2–2 ■ A program that can be used to check integer division.

```
#include <stream.h>
main( )
{
    int q,r,n,d;
    cout << "\nEnter numerator and denominator\n";
    cin >> n;
    cin >> d;
    q = n/d;
    r = n % d;
    cout << "\nquotient = " << q << "\nremainder = " << r;
}
```

Long, Short, and Unsigned Integers

The range of integers is limited and varies from system to system. In order to describe the range of integers, we shall assume that we are working with a small computer and present some typical data. It should be stressed that this information is highly system dependent, so you should check your system manual to determine the actual allowable range of integers for your system.

For the system that we are considering as an example, let us assume that each word of memory consists of eight bits. Note that eight bits here are equal to one byte. (This definition of a byte may vary from system to system.) We also assume that two bytes are used to store an integer. In such a system, integers could range between –32768 and 32767. If an attempt is made to represent an integer that falls outside the allowable range, an overflow will result, and erroneous results may be obtained. Some systems will report such errors and stop computation; other systems, however, will continue computation and output incorrect answers. You should experiment to determine how your system performs under these circumstances.

There are occasions when the range of type **int** is not sufficient. C++ provides an integer type called **long** that has a much larger allowable range. Typically, **long** integers use twice as much storage as do numbers of type **int**. For the sample system that we are using, an integer of type **long** would be stored in four bytes. In this case, integers of type **long** can range between –2147483648 and 2147483647. Because type **long** requires twice as much storage space as type **int**, it should not be used unnecessarily. Moreover, more machine language steps are required to implement arithmetic using type **long**. Thus, although two programs might appear identical except that one uses the keyword **int** to declare integer variables, while the other uses the keywords **long int** for this purpose, the program that uses type **long int** would require more storage space for both the program and the data. In addition, the program using **long** integers would take longer to run.

A typical form of the declaration of **long** integers is

$$\text{long int item,data,box;} \hspace{3cm} \textbf{2--12}$$

Here we have declared that the variables **item**, **data**, and **box** are of type **long int**. Many compilers do not require that **int** be included in the declaration, in which case 2–12 could be written as

$$\text{long item,data,box;} \hspace{3cm} \textbf{2--13}$$

There are times when programs manipulate very small integers. C++ provides the type **short** that can be used for these occasions. For the sample system that we are using, type **short** would be stored in one byte, in which case the allowable range for the short integers is between −128 and 127. Data of type **short** requires only half the storage space as does data of type **int**. In addition, operations using type **short** may have less machine code and run faster than those of type **int**. Variables are declared to be of type **short** by modifying the keyword **int** with the keyword **short**. For instance,

$$\text{short int count;} \qquad\qquad \text{2–14}$$

declares that **count** is of type **short**. Most compilers permit the keyword **int** to be omitted. Some compilers do not implement **short** integers. In that case **short** integers will be implemented as type **int**.

If a program deals with integers that are known to be nonnegative, their maximum allowable magnitude can be extended by declaring them to be unsigned (i.e., positive or zero only). In this case, the declarations are modified by the keyword **unsigned**. For the sample system that we have been considering, **unsigned** integers can range between 0 and 65535, whereas **unsigned long** integers can range between 0 and 4294967295, and **unsigned short** integers can range between 0 and 255. Some typical declarations of unsigned integers are

$$\text{unsigned int item,tab;} \qquad\qquad \text{2–15a}$$
$$\text{unsigned long int book,add;} \qquad\qquad \text{2–15b}$$
$$\text{unsigned short int count,day;} \qquad\qquad \text{2–15c}$$

Most compilers permit the keyword **int** to be omitted from the above declarations.

2–3 ■ ASSIGNMENT

We have already seen the = operator in some sample programs. Let us now consider it in more detail. The = operation is called an *assignment operation*. Suppose that we have the following

$$\text{variable\_name } = \text{ expression;} \qquad\qquad \text{2–16}$$

where **variable_name** is the name of a variable that has been declared as a particular type, and **expression** represents a valid C++ expression that evaluates to a value of the same type as **variable_name**. When 2–16 is executed, the value of **expression** is evaluated; this value is then stored in the memory locations that have been reserved for **variable_name** by the compiler. For instance, when

$$\text{item } = \text{ test } + \text{ book } + \text{ house;} \qquad\qquad \text{2–17}$$

is evaluated, the values assigned to the variables **test**, **book**, and **house** (i.e., the values stored in the memory locations reserved for the variables **test**, **book**, and **house**) will be added; the value of that sum will be stored in the memory locations that have been reserved for **item**. Any previous value assigned to **item** will be lost. The values assigned to **test**, **book**, and **house** are unchanged by this process.

Although the assignment symbol appears to be the same as an ordinary arithmetic equals sign, its function is different, and there are valid, even usual, C++ statements that have no counterpart in algebraic expressions. For instance,

$$\text{ans} = \text{ans} + 1; \hspace{5cm} \textbf{2--18}$$

is a valid C++ expression. When this expression is evaluated, the value assigned to **ans** is read from memory, 1 is added to it, and the result is stored back in the memory locations reserved for **ans**. For instance if, prior to the execution of 2–18, the value 17 were assigned to **ans**, then, after execution, the value 18 will be assigned to **ans**.

C++ allows multiple assignments in one statement. For instance,

$$\text{ans} = \text{book} = \text{house} = \text{ans} + 1; \hspace{3cm} \textbf{2--19}$$

is equivalent to

$$\text{house} = \text{ans} + 1; \hspace{4cm} \textbf{2--20a}$$
$$\text{book} = \text{house}; \hspace{4.5cm} \textbf{2--20b}$$
$$\text{ans} = \text{book}; \hspace{4.7cm} \textbf{2--20c}$$

Statement 2–19 is a short way of writing Statements 2–20. We shall see that C++ provides many such shortcuts, but they must be used with care. Statements 2–20 are probably more readable to most programmers than 2–19. On the other hand, Statement 2–19 can be typed faster, and there is less opportunity for error. In simple cases, the shortcut techniques can probably be used profitably. However, the readability or clarity of the program must *never* be sacrificed for the sake of brevity.

Statements of the form of 2–18 occur often in programs. That is, the value assigned to a variable is replaced by the value of the variable incremented by some quantity. C++ provides a shortcut method for writing such an expression. The compound symbol += is used. For instance, the following expressions are equivalent.

$$\text{ans} = \text{ans} + \text{data}; \hspace{4cm} \textbf{2--21a}$$
$$\text{ans} += \text{data}; \hspace{4.7cm} \textbf{2--21b}$$

An expression can be to the right of the += symbol. For instance, the following statements are equivalent:

$$\text{ans} = \text{ans} + 3 * \text{data} + \text{sum}; \hspace{3cm} \textbf{2--22a}$$
$$\text{ans} += 3 * \text{data} + \text{sum}; \hspace{3.5cm} \textbf{2--22b}$$

Operations analogous to += can be applied to the other arithmetic operations. The symbols -=, *=, /=, and %= are used for these operations. For example, the statements in each of the following pairs are equivalent:

$$\text{ans} = \text{ans} - \text{box}; \hspace{4cm} \textbf{2--23a}$$
$$\text{ans} -= \text{box}; \hspace{4.7cm} \textbf{2--23b}$$

$$\text{ans} = \text{ans} * \text{box};\qquad\text{2--24a}$$
$$\text{ans} * = \text{box};\qquad\text{2--24b}$$

$$\text{ans} = \text{ans/box};\qquad\text{2--25a}$$
$$\text{ans} / = \text{box};\qquad\text{2--25b}$$

$$\text{ans} = \text{ans} \% \text{ box};\qquad\text{2--26a}$$
$$\text{ans} \% = \text{box};\qquad\text{2--26b}$$

We have thus far assumed that the entity to the left of the equals sign, or to the left of one of the compound signs, was a variable. Such a variable actually represents a set of memory locations reserved by the compiler. The computed value of the expression to the right of the equals sign is then stored in the memory locations represented by the variable to the left of the equals sign. As we progress further in the book, we shall discuss other ways of specifying the memory locations in which the assigned value is to be stored. Any of these ways of specifying memory locations are allowed to lie to the left of an assignment sign and are given the general name *lvalue* (left value). The only lvalues that we have discussed thus far are variables.

Increment and Decrement

Because the value assigned to a variable is very often replaced by that value incremented or decremented by 1, a special notation is used to designate such an operation. Incrementation by 1 is designated by the compound symbol **++**. For instance, the following statements cause the value assigned to **count** to be incremented by 1.

$$\text{count} = \text{count} + 1;\qquad\text{2--27a}$$
$$\text{count}++;\qquad\text{2--27b}$$
$$++\text{count};\qquad\text{2--27c}$$

Note that no space is written between the **++** symbol and the variable. Although Statements 2–27b and 2–27c both result in the value assigned to **count** being incremented by 1, they actually function in different ways when the increment sign is to be used within an expression. In such a case, a distinction must be made between the sign preceding or following the variable. When the **++** follows the variable name, the expression to the right of the equals sign is evaluated *before* the variable in question is incremented. If the **++** precedes the variable name, then the incrementation is performed before the expression to the right of the equals sign is evaluated. We shall illustrate these ideas with program segments. The following pairs of program segments are equivalent:

$$\text{count} = 6\qquad\text{2--28a}$$
$$\text{count} = \text{count} + 1;\qquad\text{2--28b}$$
$$\text{item} = \text{count} + 4;\qquad\text{2--28c}$$

and

$$\text{count} = 6;\qquad\text{2--29a}$$
$$\text{item} = ++\text{count} + 4;\qquad\text{2--29b}$$

After 2–29b is executed, the value assigned to **item** will be 11, and the value assigned to **count** will be 7. In this case, when 2–29b is executed, **count** is first incremented and thus assigned the value 7; next, **count** + 4 is evaluated, yielding 11; this value is assigned to **item**. Now let us consider a slightly different example. The following two program segments are equivalent:

count = 6;	2–30a
item = count + 4;	2–30b
count = count + 1;	2–30c

and

count = 6;	2–31a
item = count++ + 4;	2–31b

Now, when 2–31b is executed, the value assigned to **count** will be 7, and the value assigned to **item** will be 10. When 2–31b is executed, **count** is not incremented until after the expression to the right of the equals sign is evaluated and the result has been assigned to **item**. Statements 2–31 are shorter than Statements 2–30 and are thus easier to enter and less prone to typographical errors. On the other hand, Statements 2–30 clearly indicate the operations that are to be performed and are less prone to logical errors. Remember that the shortcut notations provided by C++ should be avoided unless the meaning of the statements is very clear.

A variable can be decremented by 1 with the −− symbol. For instance, the execution of either of these statements

count−−;	2–32a
−−count;	2–32b

results in the value assigned to **count** being decremented by 1. That is, 2–32a and 2–32b are each equivalent to

count = count − 1;	2–33

The use of −− follows that of ++. For instance, the following program segments are equivalent:

count = 6;	2–34a
item = −−count + 4;	2–34b

and

count = 6;	2–35a
count = count − 1;	2–35b
item = count + 4;	2–35c

In each case, after execution of the program segment, the value assigned to **count** will be 5, and the value assigned to **item** will be 9. Similarly, the following program segments are equivalent

$$\text{count} = 6; \hspace{3cm} \textbf{2–36a}$$
$$\text{item} = \text{count}-- + 4; \hspace{2.2cm} \textbf{2–36b}$$

and

$$\text{count} = 6; \hspace{3cm} \textbf{2–37a}$$
$$\text{item} = \text{count} + 4; \hspace{2.4cm} \textbf{2–37b}$$
$$\text{count} = \text{count} - 1; \hspace{2.1cm} \textbf{2–37c}$$

In this case, after execution of each program segment, the value assigned to **count** will be 5, and the value assigned to **item** will be 10.

2–4 ■ HIERARCHY—USE OF PARENTHESES

In algebra, there is a *hierarchy* or *precedence* that describes the order in which the operations are performed. For instance, consider the algebraic equation

$$x = b + c/d \hspace{3cm} \textbf{2–38}$$

The hierarchy for algebra states that division is to be performed before addition. Thus, Equation 2–38 indicates that **c** is divided by **d** and the result of that division is added to **b**. If the sum of **b** + **c** is to be divided by **d**, then the equation would be written as

$$x = (b + c)/d \hspace{3cm} \textbf{2–39}$$

Here we have used parentheses to group terms so that operations can be performed in an order other than that specified by the ordinary algebraic hierarchy.

C++ has its own hierarchical rules, and we shall consider them in this section. Before doing this, however, we shall consider two additional operations.

Unary Operators

The operators that we have considered thus far, +, −, *, /, and %, are *binary operators,* in that they operate on two quantities. For instance, in the statement

$$\text{distance} = \text{time} * \text{velocity}; \hspace{2cm} \textbf{2–40}$$

the * operator operates on both time and velocity. There are other operators called *unary operators* that operate on only a single quantity. For instance, ++ and −− are unary operators. Another unary operator is −. Note that − is both a unary and a binary operator. The compiler will determine which − operation is intended by the context of the C++ expression. The unary − is used to change the sign of a numerical value, that is, the value is multiplied by −1. For instance, when

$$\text{ans} = -\text{item} + 3; \qquad \qquad \textbf{2-41}$$

is executed, the value assigned to item will be multiplied by -1, and that value will be added to 3, with the result being assigned to **ans**. Note that the value assigned to **item** is *unchanged* by the execution of 2–41. There is also a unary + operator. Its usage is the same as the unary $-$. Because the unary + operator does not change any value, it is rarely used. It is included to allow programmers to write a + before a variable without producing a syntax error.

Now we shall consider the hierarchy of the various arithmetic operators in C++. The arithmetic operations are performed in the following order:

> First: Unary $-$
> Unary +
>
> Next: Multiplication *
> Division /
> Remainder %
>
> Last: Addition +
> Subtraction $-$

There are three levels of hierarchy indicated. Operations on the same level, such as * and /, have the same hierarchy. For the sake of this discussion, consider that an expression is scanned three times when it is evaluated. First, all unary operations are performed; next multiplication, division, and remainder operations are performed; finally, addition and subtraction are performed. As an example, consider the statement

$$a = b * c + d/e; \qquad \qquad \textbf{2-42}$$

When this is executed, **b** will be multiplied by **c** and **d** will be divided by **e**; the resulting product and quotient will then be added.

Parentheses

There are times when the rules of hierarchy must be overruled. This can be accomplished by using *parentheses* to group terms. For instance, suppose that the following equation is to be evaluated:

$$x = \frac{b + c}{d + e} \qquad \qquad \textbf{2-43}$$

The following C++ statement is equivalent to 2–43

$$x = (b + c)/(d + e); \qquad \qquad \textbf{2-44}$$

Each expression within a pair of parentheses is evaluated using the usual rules of hierarchy. The result of each evaluation is then treated as a single value, without parentheses, and the resulting expression is evaluated using the usual rules of hierarchy.

Sometimes one pair of parentheses is *nested* within another pair of parentheses. For instance, consider the following statement:

$$x = (a + (b + c)/(d + e))*(f - g); \qquad\qquad \textbf{2-45}$$

When such a statement is executed, the expression within each innermost pair of parentheses is evaluated, using the rules of hierarchy; each evaluated pair of parentheses is then treated as though it were a single value. Next the expression within each of the remaining innermost pairs of parentheses is evaluated and treated as a single value. This process is repeated until the entire expression is evaluated. For example, when 2-45 is evaluated, (**b** + **c**) and (**d** + **e**) are each evaluated and treated as single values. Next,

$$(a + (b + c)/(d + e)) \qquad\qquad \textbf{2-46a}$$

and

$$(f - g) \qquad\qquad \textbf{2-46b}$$

are evaluated. Finally, the results of the evaluations of 2-46a and 2-46b are multiplied, and the result of that multiplication is assigned to **x**.

Note that when a product is taken, the * symbol must be used. Consider the expression

$$x = (a + b)*(c - d); \qquad\qquad \textbf{2-47}$$

The * must be used here. A syntax error will result if it is omitted.

2-5 ■ MIXED-MODE OPERATIONS

In the programs we have considered thus far, all the variables and numbers in any statement were of the same type, e.g., all **short int** or all **float**. It is possible to write statements that perform operations involving variables of different types. These operations are called *mixed-mode* operations. In contrast to some other programming languages, C++ performs automatic conversion from one type to another when mixed-mode operations are performed. In addition, there are procedures that can be used to convert specifically from one type to another. We shall discuss these procedures and mixed-mode operations in this section. As we progress through the book, additional types will be introduced, and mixing of those types will be discussed.

Data of different types are stored differently in memory. Suppose that the number 6 is being stored. Its representation will depend upon its type. That is, the pattern of zeros and ones in memory will be different when 6 is stored as an integer or when it is stored as a real.

Now suppose that the following operation is performed,

$$x = b * c; \qquad\qquad \textbf{2-48}$$

where **x** and **b** are of type **float** and **c** is of type **int**. This is a mixed-mode operation. When the statement is executed, the value of **c** will be converted into a floating-point (real) number before the multiplication takes place. Let us consider this in detail. The compiler recognizes that a mixed-mode operation is taking place. Thus, it generates code to perform the following operations. The integer value assigned to **c** is read from memory; this value is then converted to the corresponding real value. That real value is then multiplied by the real value assigned to **b**, and the resulting real number is assigned to **x**. In other words, the compiler performs the conversion automatically. Note that the value assigned to **c** is unchanged by this process and remains of type **int**.

We have seen that, in a mixed-mode operation involving a value of type **float** and one of type **int**, the value of type **int** is converted into a value of type **float** for the calculation. Note that the stored integral value is unchanged by this process. Let us now consider mixed-mode operations between two values of other types. There is, in fact, a *hierarchy of conversions,* in that the object of lower hierarchy is temporarily converted to the type of higher hierarchy for the performance of the calculation. For instance, type **float** has higher hierarchy than type **int**. The hierarchy of conversions is

$$
\begin{array}{l}
\text{double} \\
\text{float} \\
\text{long} \\
\text{int} \\
\text{short}
\end{array}
\qquad\qquad 2\text{--}49
$$

When a type is converted to one that has more significant digits (e.g., **int** to **long**) the value of the number and its accuracy are unchanged.

Let us consider conversion from type **float** to type **int** in greater detail. Suppose that **i** and **j** have been declared to be of type **int**, while **w** and **x** have been declared to be of type **float**. Now consider the following program sequence,

$$
\begin{array}{ll}
\text{i} = 3; & \qquad 2\text{--}50\text{a} \\
\text{j} = 4; & \qquad 2\text{--}50\text{b} \\
\text{w} = 7.0; & \qquad 2\text{--}50\text{c} \\
\text{x} = \text{w} + \text{i/j}; & \qquad 2\text{--}50\text{d}
\end{array}
$$

The division **i/j** is *not* a mixed-mode operation; it represents the division of two integers, and its result is zero. (Remember that the fractional part, 0.75 in this case, is discarded when integer division is performed.) Thus, after the execution of 2–50d, the value assigned to **x** is 7.0.

Now suppose that **j** had been declared to be of type **float**. In that case, when 2–50b is executed, **j** is assigned the floating-point value 4.0. Now the division **i/j** in 2–50d becomes a mixed-mode operation, the value of **i** temporarily becomes the floating-point value 3.0, and the result of the division is 0.75. Thus, the value now assigned to **x** is 7.75.

The type of the value to the left of the equals sign determines the type of the result of the operation. For instance, suppose that **w** and **x** have been declared to be of type **float** and **i** has been declared to be of type **int**. Now consider the following program segment:

$$w = 7.0; \qquad\qquad\qquad\qquad\text{2–51a}$$
$$x = 2.0; \qquad\qquad\qquad\qquad\text{2–51b}$$
$$i = 4.0 + w/x; \qquad\qquad\qquad\text{2–51c}$$

The result of the division **w/x** is 3.5; when this is added to 4.0, the floating-point value 7.5 results. This value cannot be assigned to **i** because **i** is of type **int**. The number 7.5, therefore, is converted to an integer. When this is done, the fractional part is *truncated* (dropped). The resulting whole number is converted from a floating-point representation to an integer representation, and the value assigned to **i** is the integer number 7.

Directed Change of Type

We have seen that the C++ compiler automatically changes type in mixed-mode operations involving the types specified in 2–49. However, there are circumstances where, although automatic conversion is not performed, type conversion would be desirable (see Statement 2–50d). In these cases, the programmer must specifically designate that a change of type is to be made. Such specifications also clarify the program to other programmers. C++ provides several procedures that allow the programmer to designate that type conversion must occur.

One such procedure is called a *cast*. The type to which the value is to be *temporarily* changed is written enclosed in parentheses before the variable in question. For instance, suppose that **i** and **j** have been declared of type **int**, but we want to divide their values on a floating-point basis. This can be done by casting either, or both, **i** or **j** to type **float**. For example, if **x** and **y** have been declared to be of type **float**, then any of the following statements would accomplish the desired result.

$$x = y + (\text{float})i/j; \qquad\qquad\qquad\text{2–52a}$$
$$x = y + i/(\text{float})j; \qquad\qquad\qquad\text{2–52b}$$
$$x = y + (\text{float})i/(\text{float})j; \qquad\qquad\text{2–52c}$$

Note that if only one of **i** or **j** is cast to type **float**, the division will still be as if both values were of type **float** because of the usual rules of mixed-mode arithmetic involving types **float** and **int**.

There is another notation that can be used to change the type of a value temporarily. This is called *functional notation*. When functional notation is used, the type is written before the variable, without parentheses; the variable enclosed in parentheses follows the type name. For instance, the functional notation corresponding to Statements 2–52 is:

$$x = y + \text{float}(i)/j; \qquad \text{2–53a}$$
$$x = y + i/\text{float}(j); \qquad \text{2–53b}$$
$$x = y + \text{float}(i)/\text{float}(j); \qquad \text{2–53c}$$

In complicated expressions, the functional notation usually results in fewer programming errors. However, the cast operation is found in traditional C, while the functional notation is not. Thus, traditional C programmers may be more comfortable with the cast notation.

Neither the functional notation nor the cast change the type of a variable or the value assigned to it. What is changed is the type of the value that is used in the particular statement.

The automatic mixed-mode conversions of C++ are convenient in that on many occasions, the programmer does not have to "bother" with the cast or functional notation. However, automatic mixed-mode conversions can lead to logical errors that are difficult to debug. For instance, suppose that in writing Statements 2–52, the programmer forgot that **i** and **j** were of type **int**, but assumed that one or both was of type **float** and omitted the cast. An incorrect answer would be obtained, and there would be no warning. On the other hand, if the compiler did not accept mixed-mode statements, a compilation error would result, and the mistake would be detected. In such cases, the cast or functional notation would have to be used to temporarily change the type. Programming languages are classed as to whether they are *strongly typed* or *weakly typed*. A strongly typed language reports an error when it encounters mixed-mode operations, while a weakly typed one such as C++ does not. The convenience of the weakly typed languages is offset by the reduction in errors in the strongly typed ones. Because C++ is weakly typed, you must be very careful that mixed-mode operations do not lead to errors.

When a floating-point value is converted to one of fewer significant figures, the rightmost (least) significant figures are lost. If the exponent of the original number is too large to be represented by the new type, an error results. Such errors may not be reported by the system, and incorrect answers result. A similar situation occurs when a floating-point value is temporarily changed to one of type **int**, or when values of type **int** are converted to shorter values of type **int**. If the "new" type cannot represent the value, an error results, and this error may not be reported by the system. Therefore, care should be taken whenever a cast or functional notation is used to change the type of a value to another type whose allowable range is less than that of the original type.

The typedef Keyword

Sometimes it would make a program more readable if new names could be established for data types. For instance, suppose that a program to convert

English units to metric units were written. Such a program might have a declaration

$$\text{float inch,cm,mile,km,pound,once,gram;} \qquad \textbf{2–54}$$

It would make the program more readable if the variables relating to length were of one type, and those relating to weight were of another type. The C++ keyword **typedef** can be used to accomplish this. For example, to declare that **LENGTH** and **WEIGHT** are to be synonymous with type **float**, the following statement should be included *before* the type declaration.

$$\text{typedef float LENGTH,WEIGHT;} \qquad \textbf{2–55}$$

Once 2–54 has been written into the program, **LENGTH** and **WEIGHT** can be used interchangeably with **float**. For instance, we could have the declarations

$$\text{LENGTH inch,cm,mile,km;} \qquad \textbf{2–56a}$$
$$\text{WEIGHT pound,ounce,gram;} \qquad \textbf{2–56b}$$

Expression 2–55 does not introduce any new types; it simply causes the compiler to recognize **LENGTH** and **WEIGHT** as synonyms for **float**. Note that capital letters are used for **LENGTH** and **WEIGHT**. This has no significance to the compiler. It is conventional to write programmer-defined words in capital letters to alert the programmer to the fact that these words have been given special significance in a C++ statement.

2–6 ■ INITIAL VALUES—CONSTANTS

When C++ programs start executing, the values of the variables are undefined. Some C++ compilers will cause each variable's assigned value to be set equal to zero before execution commences. However, with other C++ compilers, the memory locations used to store the variables are not modified until a specific assignment is made. In this case, the values stored in the program variable's memory locations are unchanged from what they were before the program was run. Such initial values of the variables are called "garbage." This is usually not a problem because a well-written program contains statements that establish, or *initialize,* the value of each of the variables. Note that the expression "value of the variable" actually means the "value assigned to the variable." For instance, in the program of Figure 2–2, the values of **n** and **d** are entered from the keyboard. After this is done, these variables are used in the calculation of **q** and **r**. Programs that are to be *portable,* i.e., can be run on a variety of computers, should not make any assumption about the initial value of any variable. This initial value could be established in a statement that follows its declaration. However, it is often better form to establish the initial value in the declaration itself. This is done by following the variable name with an equals sign and its initial value. For instance, the declarations

$$\text{int } i = 6, \text{count} = 14, \text{item};$$ **2–57a**
$$\text{float distance} = 0.0, \text{velocity};$$ **2–57b**

establish three integer variables, **i**, **count**, and **item**, and two variables of type **float**, **distance**, and **velocity**. The initial value of **i** is 6, the initial value of **count** is 14, and the initial value of **item** has not been established. Similarly, the initial value of **distance** is 0.0, and the initial value of **velocity** has not been established.

When initial values are established in the variable declaration, the program is more readable because the programmer does not have to search for the statement in which a value is assigned to the variable. In addition, there is no chance of using a variable to which a value has not been assigned to the right of the equals sign when the initial value for each variable is established in the declaration. Note that such use of undeclared variables can lead to particularly nasty bugs. Suppose that the program is developed on a compiler that sets all uninitialized variables to zero; the resulting program might run without error. If the C++ source code were recompiled using a compiler that does not initialize variables to zero, the program might not function properly. It is important, therefore, to establish that all variables are either specifically given initial values when they are declared or are assigned values in executable statements before they are used to the right of an equals sign. Note that an executable statement is one that takes effect only when the program is run (executed). For instance, assignments are executable statements. Declarations such as 2–57, on the other hand, are not executable statements because they affect the compiler operation, but are not operative during program execution.

There is another advantage to establishing initial values in the declaration statement rather than in a subsequent executable statement, such as

$$i = 6;$$

An executable statement such as this would be executed every time the program was run. If there are very many of such statements, program operation would be slowed. On the other hand, the actual operation of establishing an initial value in a declaration is accomplished during compilation, before execution of the program. This speeds the operation of the program.

Constants

Sometimes an unchanging value is used throughout a program. Such a quantity is called a *constant*. For instance, if a program deals with the area and circumference of circles, the constant value *pi* (= 3.14159) would be used frequently. In a financial program, an interest rate might be a constant. In such cases, it improves the readability of the program if the constant is given a descriptive name. In addition, the use of such descriptive names can prevent errors. Suppose that the constant is used at many points throughout the program. A typographical error might result in the wrong value being typed at one or more of these points. If the constant is given a name, typographical errors are then detected by the compiler because the incorrect names will (probably) not have been declared. Suppose that a program is to be written which uses the value pi at many points. It might seem as though a variable called **pi** should be declared with an initial value of 3.14159. However, it should not be possible for the program to change the value of a constant. For instance, if the programmer inadvertently wrote **pi** to the left of an equals sign, the value of **pi** would be changed, causing all subsequent calculations to be in error. C++ provides mechanisms that prevent such an error from occurring. That is, constants can be established whose values cannot be changed.

A constant is declared by writing **const** before the keyword (e.g., **int**, **long**, **float**) in the declaration. For instance,

const int numb = 9,time = 15;	**2–58a**
const float dist = 7.0;	**2–58b**
int i = 6,count = 14,item;	**2–58c**
float distance = 0.0,velocity;	**2–58d**

Because a constant cannot be changed, it must be initialized in its declaration. In Statements 2–58, the integer constants **numb** and **time** are declared with values 9 and 15, respectively; the constant **dist** of type **float** whose value is 7.0 has also been declared. In addition, the integer (nonconstant) variables **i**, **count**, and **item** have been declared. Initial values of 6 and 14 have been established for **i** and **count**, respectively. Finally, **distance** and **velocity** have been declared to be (nonconstant) variables of type **float**. An initial value of 0.0 has been set up for **distance**.

Constants and variables are used in the same way in a program. The only difference is that the initial values assigned to the constants *cannot* be changed. That is, the constants are not *lvalues*; they cannot appear to the left of an equals sign.

C++ provides another procedure for establishing constants, the **#define** compiler directive. Let us illustrate its use. Suppose that at the beginning of a program, we have the statement

#define BOOK 7   **2–59**

The form of this statement is **#define** followed by two strings of characters separated by blanks. When C++ programs are compiled, there are several passes made through the program. The first step is accomplished by the *compiler preprocessor*. The preprocessor does such things as carry out the **#include** and **#define** directives. When the preprocessor encounters the **#define** directive (see 2–59), it replaces every occurrence of **BOOK** in the C++ program with 7. In general, when the preprocessor encounters a **#define** directive, it replaces every occurrence of the first string of characters in the program with the second string of characters. Thus, every occurrence of **BOOK** in the program would be replaced by 7. No value can be assigned to **BOOK** because it has never been declared to be a variable. Thus, **BOOK** has all the attributes of a constant.

Note that 2–59 is *not* terminated by a semicolon. If a semicolon followed the 7, then every occurrence of **BOOK** would be replaced by **7;**. That is, the **#define** directive is followed by two strings separated by a blank space. Every occurrence of the first string is replaced by the complete second string.

All programs that we have discussed thus far are short and usually would be stored in a single file. If a statement such as 2–59 appeared at the beginning of the file, the substitution of 7 for **BOOK** would take place throughout the program. As we shall discuss subsequently, a single program often consists of many subprograms, with each subprogram usually in a separate file. In that case, the compiler directive would be effective only for the single file in which it was written.

We have considered two procedures for defining constants, the keyword **const** and the **#define** compiler directive. In many programs, the action of each of these two procedures is essentially the same. On the other hand, the use of the modifier keyword **const** results in a "variable" whose value cannot be changed. We shall discuss the fact that variables can be declared in such a way that they exist only over certain regions of a program. The same can be said for constants declared with the keyword **const**. Thus, the **const** declaration is somewhat more versatile than the **#define** directive. The **#define** directive is found in standard C and thus is more familiar to C programmers.

Figure 2–3 is an example of a simple program that uses a constant. The program calculates the circumference and area of a circle. If a statement that attempted to change the value of **pi** were added to the program, an error would result, and the program would not compile.

FIGURE 2–3 ■ A simple program that uses a constant.

```
/* a program that calculates the circumference and area of a circle */
#include <stream.h>
main()
{
    const float pi=3.14159;
    float radius,circumference,area;
    cout << "\nEnter radius of circle\n";
    cin >> radius;
    circumference = 2.0 * pi * radius;
    area = pi * radius * radius;
    cout << "\ncircumference = " << circumference;
    cout <<"\narea = " << area;
}
```

2-7 ■ LIBRARY FUNCTIONS

There are certain calculations routinely performed in many programs that are written by almost all programmers. Taking the square root of a number is an example of such a calculation. Mathematical procedures for calculating square roots make use of combinations of the basic arithmetic operations of addition, subtraction, multiplication, and division. It would be a waste of effort if every programmer had to design and code a routine to calculate the square root and then to incorporate that routine into his or her program. Moreover, if a square root were to be taken at several points in the program, it would not only be tedious, but also a potential source of typographical error if that sequence of statements had to be repeated at each of those points. C++, like most other programming languages, resolves these difficulties by providing the programmer with libraries of *functions* that perform particular common calculations. Because only a single statement is needed to invoke such a function, the difficulties that we have discussed are eliminated. In Chapter 4 we shall discuss procedures whereby a programmer can write his or her own functions. In this section we shall discuss functions that are commonly provided with C++ systems. These are called *library functions*. The library functions usually are not provided in source form but as compiled code. When linking is performed, the code for the library functions is combined with the compiled programmer's code to form the complete program.

Library functions not only perform mathematical operations, but also deal with many other commonly encountered operations. For example, there are library functions that deal with reading and writing disk files, managing memory, input/output, and a variety of other operations. Library functions are not part of standard C++, but virtually every system provides certain library functions. In this section we shall discuss some of the common library functions that relate to mathematical operations; other library functions will be discussed throughout the book. You should consult your C++ system manual to determine which library functions are supplied with your system.

C++ systems provide a wide variety of mathematical functions. We shall not discuss all of them here, but shall provide enough information to give you a sense of the types of functions commonly provided. Because names of the routines may vary from system to system, you should consult your C++ system manual to determine the exact form of the functions for your system.

A function is invoked by writing its name followed by a list of one or more *arguments*. The items in the list are separated by commas, and the entire list is enclosed in parentheses. The function is said to *return* a value. For instance, the function **sqrt** returns the square root of a number of type **float**. Let us illustrate its use. Suppose that **x** and **y** have been declared to be of type **float**.

When the following two statements have been executed,

$$x = 9.0; \qquad\qquad\qquad\qquad \textbf{2–60a}$$
$$y = sqrt(x); \qquad\qquad\qquad\qquad \textbf{2–60b}$$

y is assigned the value 3.0, which is equal to the square root of 9.0. Note that we have written the word **sqrt**, followed by its single argument enclosed in parentheses. The argument need not be a variable. For instance, we could have written **sqrt (9.0)**. The execution of 2–60b will result in 3.0 being assigned to **x**. That is, when 2–60b is executed, the **sqrt** function is replaced by its returned value. Functions can be written to the right of an equals sign in the same way that a variable can; for instance,

$$y = x + 4.0 * sqrt(x); \qquad\qquad\qquad\qquad \textbf{2–61}$$

If **x** were assigned the value 9.0, then, after evaluation of 2–61, **y** would be assigned the value 21.0. Note that we have assumed here that the argument and returned value were each of type **float**. Library functions use other variable types as well.

Most library functions are designed to use information contained in particular files that are supplied with the system; these files therefore must be included when the library functions are used. These files are also provided with the C++ system. They usually have the extension **.h** or **.hxx** and are called *header files*. The required header files are listed in the system manual that describes the library functions. In general, different header files are required by different library functions. The required header files for a function will be listed in the description for that function. For instance, suppose that **sqrt** requires that the header file **math.h** be included. Then the following statement should be present at the beginning of the file.

#include <math.h>

There are math library functions that calculate the trigonometric functions. For instance, **sin(x)**, **cos(x)**, and **tan(x)** return the sine, cosine, and tangent, respectively, of the floating-point variable **x**. The value of **x** is usually, but not always, expressed in radians. The functions **asin(x)**, **acos(x)**, and **atan(x)** return the arcsine, arccosine, and arctangent of **x**, respectively. The functions **sinh(x)**, **cosh(x)**, **tanh(x)** return the hyperbolic sine, hyperbolic cosine, and hyperbolic tangent of **x**.

The function **exp(x)** returns e^x, where $e \approx 2.7182818$ is the base of the natural logarithm system. The function **pow(x,y)** returns x^y. The natural and base 10 logarithms are returned by the functions **log(x)** and **log10(x)**, respectively. Note that the function **pow** has two arguments separated by a comma.

The function **abs(k)** returns the absolute value of the integer **k**. Note that if **k** is positive, then it is equal to its absolute value. If **k** is negative, then **abs(k)** returns $-\mathbf{k}$. The function **fabs(x)** returns the absolute value of the floating-point variable **x**.

We have listed a representative sample of arithmetic functions here. Remember that the names of these functions may differ from system to system.

Figure 2–4 is a simple program that illustrates the use of mathematical functions. The program prompts the user for a number and a power and then outputs the number raised to that power. If you are not familiar with the details of logarithms, do not concern yourself with the details of the program. Just observe the use of the #**include** and the use of the **log** and **exp** functions. The program makes use of the fact that the log of **x** raised to the **y** (i.e., x^4) power is **y** times the log of **x**.

Note the declaration

$$\text{extern double log(double),exp(double);} \qquad \textbf{2–62}$$

Functions must be declared. The keyword **extern** indicates that the function is actually defined elsewhere and we are simply declaring it here. The compiler must be informed of both the type of the value returned by the function and of of the type of any argument(s). The functions return values of type **double**. Thus, they are declared to be **double**. The type of the function argument(s) are declared within the parentheses. In this case, the arguments are of type **double** and are so declared. If a function has more than one argument, the type of each argument, separated by commas, must be listed. The order of the list of argument types must correspond to the order of the arguments themselves.

C++ systems provide very many library functions. In general, they are very helpful to programmers. You should study the system manual to determine all the library functions that are provided. We shall subsequently consider the topic of functions in greater detail when we consider user-written functions.

FIGURE 2–4 ■ A program that uses mathematical library functions.

```
/* program calculates x to y power */
#include <stream.h>
#include <math.h>
main()
{
    extern double log(double),exp(double);
    double x,y,tmp,ans;
    cout << "\nEnter number and exponent\n";
    cin >> x >> y;
    tmp = y * log(x);
    ans = exp(tmp);
    cout << "\n" << x << " raised to " << y << " power = " << ans;
}
```

2–8 ■ COMPLEX NUMBERS

C++ commonly provides the programmer with operators and functions that manipulate *complex numbers*. Actually, this complex number facility is not part of C++ any more than are the library functions discussed in the previous section. However, the ability to manipulate complex numbers is provided with almost all C++ systems. If you do not know how to manipulate complex numbers, or are not interested in them, this section can be skipped. An understanding of the material in this section is not a prerequisite for understanding the remainder of the book. In this section, however, we assume that the reader is familiar with complex numbers.

Complex variables are declared using the keyword **complex**. For instance,

$$\text{complex x,y;} \qquad\qquad \textbf{2–63}$$

declares that **x** and **y** are complex variables. Every complex number consists of a real and an imaginary part. The real and imaginary parts are each of type **float**. For example, the complex number 3.0 + i4.0 would be represented by the pair of numbers of type **float**, 3.0 and 4.0. Exponential notation can be used for the real and/or imaginary part of a complex number.

In C++, complex numbers are written as a pair of numbers, separated by a comma, enclosed in parentheses. For instance, the complex number 3.0 + i4.0 would be written as (3.0,4.0). In addition, within the body of a program, the modifier **complex** must precede the pair of numbers. For example, execution of the statement

$$\text{x} \;=\; \text{complex(4.0,5.0);} \qquad\qquad \textbf{2–64}$$

results in **x** being assigned the complex value 4.0 + i5.0. When data is entered from the keyboard, or output to the screen, the **complex** modifier is omitted, e.g., (3,4) will be output.

The mathematical operators +, −, *, and \ can be used with complex numbers. On the other hand, however, ++, −−, +=, −=, *=, and \= cannot be used. In future releases of C++, these operators may be implemented for complex numbers.

A simple program that manipulates complex numbers is shown in Figure 2–5. Note that the header file **complex.h** is included in this program. Normally, the file **stream.h** would also be included when input and output are performed. Although it appears to be missing, it really is not, because the file **complex.h** contains the statement

#include <stream.h>

Consider the declarations. The first declaration simply declares that **x**, **y**, **a**, and **b** are variables of type **complex**. No initial values are assigned in

FIGURE 2–5 ■ A program that manipulates **complex** numbers.

```
/* a program that manipulates complex numbers */
#include <complex.h>  // note #include <stream.h> is part of complex.h
main()
{
    complex x,y,a,b;
    complex w=complex(3.0,4.0);
    complex z(9.0,10.0);
    const complex k(5.0,6.0);
    x = complex(4.0,5.0);
    y = x + w;
    z = complex(2.0,0.0) * z;
    z = z * k;
    cout << "\nEnter complex number\n";
    cin >> a;
    cout << "\nx = " << x;
    cout << "\ny = " << y;
    cout << "\nz = " << z;
    b = 2 * a;
    cout << "\nb = " << b;
    cout << "\nmagnitude b = " << abs(b);
    cout << "  angle b = " << arg(b);
}
```

that declaration. The next two declarations include initial value assignments. They are

$$\text{complex } w = \text{complex}(3.0,4.0); \hspace{2cm} \textbf{2–65a}$$
$$\text{complex } z(9.0,10.0); \hspace{2.5cm} \textbf{2–65b}$$

These statements declare that **w** and **z** are variables of type **complex** with initial values of (3.0,4.0) and (9.0,10.0), respectively. Note that 2–65a is in the usual form used to establish an initial value. That is, it consists of the variable name followed by an equals sign and the initial value. For the case of a complex number, the modifier **complex** is used. The form of 2–65b is special; it can be used only to set up initial values for complex numbers. It consists of the name of the variable followed by the parenthetical form of the complex number. Note that this shorthand form is used only to establish an initial value.

Complex constants can be established in the same way as can other constants. For instance,

$$\text{const complex } k(5.0,6.0); \hspace{2cm} \textbf{2–66}$$

sets up a **complex** constant named **k** with value (5.0,6.0). Note that an equivalent declaration is

$$\text{const complex } k = \text{complex}(5.0,6.0); \hspace{2cm} \textbf{2–67}$$

Executable statements involving complex quantities are very similar to those that are used with real floating-point numbers. Remember that when assigning a numerical value to a complex variable the numerical value must be preceded by the word **complex**. For instance, the Statement 2–64 results in **x** being assigned the value (4.0,5.0). The use of **complex** is mandatory in such statements.

Input and output are performed as with other numbers; that is, the input and output expressions are not different for complex numbers. As noted earlier, the form of the input and output is two numbers separated by a comma, enclosed in parentheses.

Mixed-mode expressions involving complex numbers are allowed. In this case, the real number will be converted to a complex number whose imaginary part is zero. Consider the statement

$$b = 2 * a; \hspace{6em} \textbf{2–68}$$

where **a** and **b** have been declared to be of type **complex**. When this statement is executed, the integer 2 is converted to the complex number (2.0,0.0). Note that the integer is converted to the real part of the complex number, and that real part is of type **float**.

Many of the arithmetic functions can be used with complex numbers. It should be noted that one of the statements in the header file **complex.h** is

$$\#\text{include } <\text{math.h}>$$

so that this header file is included as well. (This may vary from system to system.) For instance, **log(x)**, where **x** is of type **complex**, will return a complex number that is the log of the complex number argument. The program in Figure 2–5 uses the functions **abs** and **arg**. When the argument of **abs** is a complex number, the value returned is a number of type **float**. This number is equal to the magnitude of the complex number. The function **arg** returns the angle of the complex number in radians. Thus, **abs** and **arg** can be used to convert a complex number into polar form. The function **polar** takes two arguments: the first is the magnitude of a complex number and the second is its angle; **polar** returns a complex number in standard (real,imaginary) form. Check your manual to determine the functions that are available on your system for complex numbers. Note that the functions **abs** and **arg** were not declared in the program in Figure 2–5. This is because they have already been declared in the file **complex.h**.

EXERCISES

Check any programs that you write by running them on your computer.

1. Determine the number of *significant figures* and the largest *exponent* that can be used to represent numbers of type **float** on your computer.
2. Repeat Exercise 1, for numbers of type **double**.

3. Write a program that evaluates the algebraic expressions

$$x = [(a + b)(c + d) + (3 + a)]/(a - b)$$
$$y = (x + a)(x + b)/(c + d)$$

The values of **a**, **b**, **c**, and **d** should be entered by the person running the program. There should be suitable prompts, and the output should contain suitable explanatory text.

4. Determine the range of values that can be represented by type **int** on your computer.

5. Repeat Exercise 4 for type **long** and type **short**.

6. Write a program that tests the operation of your system when an integer exceeds the allowed range. For instance, you could include a statement

$$x = a + b;$$

where **a**, **b**, and **x** are of type **int**. The values assigned to **a** and **b** should lie in the allowable range, but their sum should not. Determine how your computer system functions in this case.

7. Write a program that checks how your system functions with integer division when the dividend and/or divisor are negative. Use all possible combinations of positive and negative dividends and divisors and obtain the values of the quotients and remainders.

8. Determine how your system functions when a negative number is assigned to an unsigned integer.

9. Discuss the difference between *assignment* and *equality*.

10. What is the difference between the following two statements?

$$x = (a++ * b)/(c-- + d);$$

and

$$x = (++a * b)/(--c + d);$$

Write a program that you can use to check your explanation.

11. Comment on the accuracy of **int**, **float**, and **double** calculations. Are integer operations subject to round-off error?

12. A manufacturer packs 150 computer boards into each box it ships. Write a program that inputs the number of boards manufactured in a day and outputs the number of boxes needed and the number of boards that are left over.

13. Use the *decrement operator* -- to write a program that computes factorial 7.

14. Describe the operation of the following statement. Clarify the statement for a reader by adding parentheses.

$$x = a+b*c+d/e;$$

15. What will be the result when the following sequence of statements is executed:.

```
a = 3;
b = 7;
c = 9;
d = 15;
x = ((a + b)*((a − c)/(a + b) + 5) − 15)*(a + d)/((c + d) + 6);
```

16. What is meant by a *mixed-mode operation*?

17. In the following program segment assume that **a**, **b**, and **c** have been declared to be of type **float**, and that **i**, **j**, and **k** have been declared to be of type **int**. What will be the values assigned to **c** and **k** after the following program segment has been executed?

```
i = 16;
j = 9;
a = 17.0;
b = 9.0;
k = i/j + a/b;
c = i/j + a/b;
```

18. Repeat Exercise 17, but now replace the last two statements with

```
k = (float)i/j + a/b;
c = i/j + int(a)/int(b);
```

19. Modify the program of Exercise 10 so that the *initial values* are established for each of the variables.

20. Modify the program of Exercise 12, but now declare the number of boards that are packed into each box as a *constant*.

21. Repeat Exercise 20, but now use a different method to establish the constant.

22. Write a program that accepts an angle in degrees, and outputs the sine of the angle. Note that the argument of the **sin** function is expressed in radians. (pi radians is equivalent to 180 degrees.)

23. What is meant by a *complex number*?

24. Modify the program of Exercise 3 so that it manipulates complex numbers.

25. Determine the mathematical functions that can be used with complex numbers on your system.

CHAPTER 3
Some Fundamentals
of C++ Programming

In this chapter we shall discuss some ideas that are fundamental to C++ programming. We shall start by considering the type **char** that is used to store character data. The discussions of input/output will be expanded upon, and we shall discuss streams in greater detail. In previous chapters, we alluded to the concepts of scope and lifetime of variables. Those discussions will be expanded upon in this chapter. The important C++ topic of pointers will be presented. A thorough discussion of many of these topics depends upon elements of C++ that we have not yet considered. However, we shall introduce them here so that they can be expanded upon easily at appropriate points later in the book.

3–1 ■ CHARACTERS AND STRINGS

In this section we shall discuss the variables that are used to store and manipulate *characters*. We shall also consider *strings* of characters. Many manipulations involving characters and strings make use of C++ operations that have not yet been discussed in this book. However, because characters and strings are involved in many input/output operations, we shall introduce them in this chapter. In the next section, we shall consider the use of characters and strings in conjunction with input/output operations.

A character in C++, as in other programming languages, is a letter of the alphabet, a digit, or a punctuation mark. In addition, there are other special characters that we shall also discuss. Character variables are declared with the keyword **char**. In a digital computer, each piece of data is stored as a binary number. The data can be considered to be encoded into that number. The encoding is different for different data types. For instance, the encoded number that stores the **float** value 6 is different from the encoded number that stores the **int** value 6. Characters are stored as integers; in fact, the type **char** is actually an integer type. (Each character is represented by a different integer code.) The number of bits used to store each of the data types varies with the computer. However, the following general statements can be made. The number of bits used to store a **char** is equal to, or less than, the number of bits used to store a **short int**; the number of bits used to store a **short int** is equal to, or less than, the number of bits used to store an **int**, and the number of bits used to store an **int** is equal to, or less than, the number of bits used to store a **long int**. Consider the use of the word "equal" in this discussion. For instance, how could type **long int** and type **int** be stored in the same number of bits? In general, type **long** uses more bits, often twice as many, than type **int**. However, some systems may not actually implement type **long**, although the compiler may accept it as a declaration, and a declaration of type **long** is treated as though it simply were a declaration of type **int**. In such a case, type **long** and type **int** would be stored in the same number of bits. In a typical small computer, variables of type **char** and type **short** are stored in a single eight-bit byte. In such a computer, variables of type **int** and type **long** are typically stored in two and four bytes, respectively.

There are several coding schemes commonly used to represent characters. One of the most widely used is the ASCII code (American Standard Code for Information Interchange). The ASCII code set is given in Table 3–1.

The ASCII codes 1 through 26 are called *control codes*. They are generated by simultaneously pressing the Ctrl key and the letter in question. The control codes are also represented by a two- or three-character alphanumeric symbol. (Note that these symbols are not entered from the keyboard.) The significance of these codes dates back to the time when the ASCII codes were used for teletype communication. Many of these codes still have significance today. For instance, ASCII 7 causes the bell on the computer to ring and ASCII 10 corresponds to a line feed. When the Esc key is pressed, an ASCII 27 is generated. Therefore, sequences of characters starting with ASCII 27 are called *escape codes*.

The ASCII codes from 32 to 127 represent standard characters. However, the other codes, in particular the control codes, often have special significance to the system. This meaning may differ from system to system. C++ provides special characters called *escape characters* to represent characters whose meanings could be misunderstood by the system or the compiler. The escape characters all begin with the backslash, \. Table 3–2 lists the escape characters. Note that two consecutive backslashes are necessary to represent a backslash. Because single characters are enclosed in single quotation marks (apostrophes), a special character is needed to represent the quotation mark as a character. Note that the escape characters in Table 3–2 are enclosed in single quotation marks; i.e., they are treated as single characters. In a similar way, because double quotation marks are used to delimit strings, there is an escape character for the double quotation mark. Each escape character

TABLE 3–1 ■ The ASCII Codes

Code	Character		Code	Character	Code	Character
0	null		43	+	86	V
1	Ctrl A or	SOH	44	,	87	W
2	Ctrl B	STX	45	−	88	X
3	Ctrl C	EXT	46	.	89	Y
4	Ctrl D	EOT	47	/	90	Z
5	Ctrl E	ENQ	48	0	91	[
6	Ctrl F	ACK	49	1	92	\
7	Ctrl G	BEL	50	2	93	]
8	Ctrl H	BS	51	3	94	^
9	Ctrl I	HT	52	4	95	−
10	Ctrl J	LF	53	5	96	`
11	Ctrl K	VT	54	6	97	a
12	Ctrl L	FF	55	7	98	b
13	Ctrl M	CR	56	8	99	c
14	Ctrl N	SO	57	9	100	d
15	Ctrl O	SI	58	:	101	e
16	Ctrl P	DLE	59	;	102	f
17	Ctrl Q	DC1	60	<	103	g
18	Ctrl R	DC2	61	=	104	h
19	Ctrl S	DC3	62	>	105	i
20	Ctrl T	DC4	63	?	106	j
21	Ctrl U	NAK	64	@	107	k
22	Ctrl V	SYN	65	A	108	l
23	Ctrl W	ETB	66	B	109	m
24	Ctrl X	CAN	67	C	110	n
25	Ctrl Y	EM	68	D	111	o
26	Ctrl Z	SUB	69	E	112	p
27	Esc	ESC	70	F	113	q
28		FS	71	G	114	r
29		GS	72	H	115	s
30		RS	73	I	116	t
31		US	74	J	117	u
32	space		75	K	118	v
33	!		76	L	119	w
34	"		77	M	120	x
35	#		78	N	121	y
36	$		79	O	122	z
37	%		80	P	123	{
38	&		81	Q	124		
39	'		82	R	125	}
40	(		83	S	126	~
41	)		84	T	127	DEL
42	*		85	U		

TABLE 3–2 ■ The Escape Characters

Characters	Meaning
'\b'	Backspace
'\f'	Formfeed
'\n'	Newline
'\r'	Carriage return
'\v'	Vertical tab
'\\'	Backslash
'\''	Single quote
'\"'	Double quote
'\0'	null ASCII 0

is considered to be a single character, even though it may be represented by two or more symbols. In general, escape characters are not entered from the keyboard, but are used within programs. Several of the programs that we considered previously used newlines (\n) to cause output to appear on a new line.

Any ASCII code can be represented as an escape character by following the backslash with the octal representation of that code. If the number is preceded by the letter **x**, it is considered to be a hexadecimal representation. For instance, '\40' and '\x20' are both equivalent to the same decimal ASCII code, 32. (If you are not familiar with the octal and/or hexadecimal number systems, then ignore the comments in this paragraph.)

A simple program that outputs the ASCII code for a character is shown in Figure 3–1. Note that **ch** is declared to be a variable of type **char**. When the statement

$$cin \gg ch;$$ 3–1

is executed, the system expects a character input. The data entered from the keyboard is converted into an ASCII code, and that number is assigned to **ch**.

FIGURE 3–1 ■ A program that outputs the ASCII code of a character.

```
/* a program that outputs the ASCII code for a character */
#include <stream.h>
main()
{
    char ch;
    cout << "\nEnter character\n";
    cin >> ch;
    cout << ch;
}
```

Note that if **ch** had been declared to be of type **int**, for example, the desired conversion would not take place. In fact, in that case, even if the system accepted a symbol from the keyboard, there is no way to predict what the output would be. The next statement is

$$\text{cout} \ll \text{ch};\qquad\qquad\text{3--2}$$

The C++ system then outputs the value assigned to **ch**. Note that there is no conversion here; the numerical value (the ASCII code) is output. Some systems may not function in this way and, in fact, the actual character might be output. With such a system, declare a variable of type **int**, then assign the value of **ch** to this variable. When the value of this variable is output it will be the desired ASCII code. Note that this is a mixed-mode operation, and the value assigned to **ch** will (temporarily) be converted to one of type **int**.

Character variables can be assigned values. For instance, consider the statement

$$\text{ch} = \text{'a'};\qquad\qquad\text{3--3}$$

When this statement is executed, **ch** is assigned the character value **a** (ASCII 97).

Strings

A collection of characters is called a *string*. In C++ a string is delimited by double quotation marks. For instance,

$$\text{"The quick brown fox."}\qquad\qquad\text{3--4}$$

is a string. Strings differ from the other types that we have considered in that the amount of memory required to store a string varies and is dependent on the length of the string. Later in this chapter, we shall consider string variables. In this and the next section we shall consider the output of strings. A string can be output simply by directing it to the standard output. This is the form we have been using. For instance, the execution of the following statement will result in the output of 3–4 without the quotation marks.

$$\text{cout} \ll \text{"The quick brown fox"}\qquad\qquad\text{3--5}$$

We shall extend these ideas in the next section.

Another useful C++ operator is **sizeof**. Although the usage of **sizeof** is essentially the same as that of a function, **sizeof** is actually a C++ operator and need not be declared when it is used. When **sizeof** is used, we obtain the number of bytes required to store its operand. Although the size of a byte is not defined, the value calculated by **sizeof** assumes that one byte is the amount of memory used to store a value type **char**. For instance, if **x** is an integer variable, then the execution of

$$\text{x} = \text{sizeof(char)};\qquad\qquad\text{3--6a}$$

will result in **x** being assigned the value 1. If type **int** takes twice as much storage as **char**, then the execution of

$$x = sizeof(int);$$ **3–6b**

will result in **x** being assigned the value 2.

Because **sizeof** is an operator rather than a function, **char** and **int** in the above examples are called operands rather than arguments. We have illustrated the operand of **sizeof** being the name of a type, e.g., **char** or **int**. Actually, the operand can be a variable name as well. For instance, if **item** has been declared to be of type **int**, then the execution of

$$x = sizeof(item);$$ **3–6c**

would cause 2 to be assigned to **x**.

3–2 ■ STREAMS—BASIC INPUT AND OUTPUT

In this section we shall expand upon the ideas of input and output to and from the terminal of the computer. For the sake of completeness, we shall review some of the material that has been discussed previously. C++ provides a simple and effective procedure for handling input and output, called *streams*. Streams can be used to provide input to the computer from the keyboard, disk files, or the various ports. Similarly, streams can be used to produce output to the screen of the terminal, a disk file, or any of the computer's ports. Actually, streams are not an inherent part of the C++ language but, because all C++ systems implement streams, C++ programs that incorporate streams will be portable. In this chapter we shall discuss streams as they are used in relation to the terminal. Subsequently, we shall consider how these ideas can easily be extended to other types of input/output.

C++ provides a very general type of data storage called the *class*. We shall discuss classes in great detail later in the book. For the time being, let us simply note that the two **class** types **istream** and **ostream** are defined and that these classes provide all the features needed for input and output, respectively. The data objects **cout** and **cin** are data objects of type **ostream** and **istream**, respectively. These objects are defined in the header file, **stream.h**. This is why this header file must be included whenever streams are used for input/output. (Advantage C++ names its header files with an extension of **.hxx** rather than **.h**.) Note that **cin** and **cout** refer to the standard input and output of the system, respectively. The standard input is usually the keyboard of the terminal and the standard output is usually the terminal screen.

Stream input/output makes use of two operators: >> called *get from*, and << called *put to*. Thus, execution of the expression

$$\text{cout} \ << \ \text{"The quick brown fox";} \qquad\qquad \textbf{3-7}$$

results in the string "The quick brown fox" being put to the standard output. In most cases, this string then appears on the screen of the terminal. Note that the double quotation mark delimiters are not output. The values assigned to variables can also be output in this manner. For instance, if **ave** is a variable of type **float** that has been assigned the value 4.77, then the execution of

$$\text{cout} \ << \ \text{"Answer is = " } << \ \text{ave;} \qquad\qquad \textbf{3-8}$$

will result in the output of

$$\text{Answer is} \ = \ 4.77$$

The C++ system will recognize the variable's data type and output it appropriately. Remember that the stored binary number must be decoded, and how it is decoded depends upon the variable's declared data type.

A value can be assigned to a variable from the keyboard through the use of **cin** and the >> operator. For instance, the execution of

$$\text{cin} \ >> \ \text{item;}$$

causes operation to pause until the user types in a value followed by a RETURN. That value will then be assigned to item. Because we have already used this type of input and output, additional examples will not be given here.

Formatted Output

The use of streams for input/output is very convenient and, for many purposes, suffices. However, there are times when additional control over the form of the output is required. For instance, suppose that an aligned list of integers is to be output or that a floating-point number is to be output with the number of digits following the decimal point rounded to two. The procedures that we have discussed do not provide for such format control. C++ allows the programmer to *format* the output, and we shall consider such formatting now.

Formatted output uses the C++ word **form** followed by a list that is enclosed in parentheses. The first item in the list is called a *control string* or a *format string*. The remaining items in the list are either variables or constants, and they are separated by commas. The format string is delimited by double quotation marks and contains literal text that is to be output. Embedded within the text are *conversion specifiers* that control how the variables and constants in the list are output. With unformatted output, the C++ compiler uses the declared type of the variable to interpret the coding of the stored data in memory and to convert that data into a form that is suitable for output. When formatted output is used, on the other hand, the programmer specifies how the conversion of the stored data is to be performed. Let us illustrate these ideas with an example. Suppose that **item** and **ave** have been declared to be of type **int** and **float**, respectively. Now consider that the following sequence of statements is executed:

```
item = 17;                                              3–9a
ave = 99.5;                                             3–9b
cout << form("\n%dstudents have %f average",item,ave);  3–9c
```

The conversion specifiers all start with the % symbol. When 3–9c is executed, the following takes place. All text in the format string up to the first conversion specifier, %**d** in this case, is output, then the value assigned to **item**, the first variable following the format string, is output using the specifications of the first conversion specifier. Next, any additional text in the format string up to the next conversion specifier (%**f**) is output ("students have "). Next the value of **ave**, the second variable in the list, is output using the specifications of the second conversion specifier. Finally, the rest of the text in the conversion specifier ("average") is output. Thus, the output in response to the execution of Statements 3–9 is

17 students have 99.5 average   3–10

The %**d** conversion specifier indicates that a variable of type **int** is to be output in decimal format, while the %**f** conversion specifier indicates that a value of type **float** is to be output in decimal format. Note that decimal format is the usual decimal number system. In general, the text in a format string is output until a conversion specifier is encountered. Then, the first variable or constant in the list to the right of the format string is output using the specification of the first conversion specifier. This procedure is continued until all the text and/or conversion specifiers in the format have been used. Note that there must be a separate conversion specifier for each variable or constant in the list following the format string.

The data can be specified to be output in a *field* that is a certain number of characters wide by placing an integer variable or constant before the letter in the format specifier. For instance, the conversion specifier

%15d   3–11

indicates that integer data is to be output in a field that is 15 characters wide. If the integer is shorter than 15 characters, it will be *right adjusted* or *right justified* in the field. This means that the number is written as far to the right as possible. For example, if the integer 152 is to be output using the specification in 3–11, 12 blanks followed by 152 would be output. In the case of floating-point numbers, the number of places to the right of the decimal point can also be specified by placing a period and an integer variable or constant to the right of the field specifier. For instance, if the number 19.3676 is output using the conversion specifier

%15.2f   3–12

the output would consist of 10 blanks followed by 19.37. Note that the number is rounded using the usual rules. That is, if the digit to the right of what will be the rightmost output digit is 5 or more, the rightmost digit is increased by 1. If the field that is specified is not large enough to output the number, then the field size will be increased automatically.

If a minus sign $(-)$ precedes the field size, then the data will be *left adjusted* or *left justified* in the field. Additionally, the field specifiers **o** and **x** are used for the output of data of type **int** in the octal or hexadecimal number system, respectively. For instance, the specification

$$\%15x \qquad\qquad\qquad 3\text{–}13$$

is essentially the same as that of 3–11 except that now the output will be in hexadecimal. Similarly a conversion specifier

$$\%15o \qquad\qquad\qquad 3\text{–}14$$

will result in an output in octal.

A **u** conversion specifier indicates that an unsigned integer is to be output. The letters **d**, **o**, **x**, and **u** can be preceded by either an **l** or an **h**. These specify **long** and **short**, respectively. For instance,

$$\%15ld \qquad\qquad\qquad 3\text{–}15$$

specifies a long integer.

The **f** conversion specifier applies both to type **float** and to type **double**. There are three additional specifiers that can be used with floating-point numbers. The **e** specifier is equivalent to the type **f** specifier except that the number is output in exponential notation. When the **f** specifier is used, exponential notation will not be used. The **g** conversion specifier is similar to **e** and **f**. When **g** is used, however, the compiler will select either **e** or **f**, whichever keeps the length of the output as short as possible. If the floating-point number has no fractional part (e.g., 15.0), then the **f** and **g** formats will output the number without a decimal point, provided the conversion specification does not call for it.

The **c** and **s** conversion specifiers are used to output character and string data, respectively. We shall consider an example of the use of data of type **char** later in this section. String variables will be discussed later in this chapter.

Table 3–3 summarizes the information on conversion specifiers. Two adjacent % signs are not interpreted as a conversion specifier. They simply represent a percent sign and are used when the percent sign is to be output as text.

Figure 3–2 is an example of the use of the **c** conversion specifier. This program is a modification of the program in Figure 3–1 where we have rewritten the last statement so that it produces formatted output. Note that the text "character" will be output followed by the entered character; this in turn will be followed by several blanks, and then the text "ASCII" and the ASCII code for the entered character. The same variable **ch** is output for both the value

TABLE 3–3 ■ Conversion Specifiers

Specifier	Type	Description
c	char	character output
d	int	decimal output
e	float	exponential output
	double	exponential output
f	float	decimal output
	double	decimal output
g	float	shortest form
	double	shortest form
h	short	must precede d, o, u, or x
l	long	must precede d, o, u, or x
o	int	octal output
s	string	string output
u	unsigned	decimal output
x	int	hexadecimal output
-		left adjust

of the character and for its ASCII code. This can be done because the first output of the value of **ch** is performed with a **%c** conversion specifier, while the second output of that value is performed with a **%hd** conversion specifier. Thus, **ch** is output both as a **char** and as a **short int**.

In conventional C, formatted output is performed with **printf**. This does not make use of streams. The general syntax of the **printf** statement is the same as that for form except that the word **printf** replaces **form**, and stream notation is not used. For instance, in standard C, the output statement of Figure 3–2 would be written as

$$\text{printf("\textbackslash ncharacter \%c   ASCII \%hd",ch,ch);}\qquad \textbf{3–16}$$

When working with C++, you should use the stream forms. We simply present **printf** to provide a reference to conventional C programs. Conventional

FIGURE 3–2 ■ A modification of Figure 3–1 that uses formatted output.

```
/* a program that outputs the ASCII code for a character */
#include <stream.h>
main()
{
    char ch;
    cout << "\nEnter character\n";
    cin >> ch;
    cout << form("\n character %c    ASCII %hd",ch,ch);
}
```

C uses forms such as **scanf** and **getchar** for input. Although they may work, these forms should be avoided when writing C++ programs. Input should be obtained with **cin** and >>.

3–3 ■ A FIRST DISCUSSION OF SCOPE AND LIFETIME—BLOCKS

In all the programs that we have considered thus far, all the variables could be used anywhere in that program following their declaration. However, when more complex programs are considered, we shall see that, in general, variables exist over only certain parts of a program and they exist only for a certain range of time. This is referred to as the *scope* and *lifetime* of the variables, respectively. In this section we shall introduce these ideas. As we progress through the book, scope and lifetime will be considered in greater detail.

Block—Compound Statement

A *block* or a *compound statement* is any group of C++ statements enclosed in curly braces. Note that a block may be empty; that is, it may contain no statements. A variable or constant that is declared within a block is valid only within that block. If a block lies within another block, then a variable that is declared in the outer block is valid within the inner block. However, a variable that is declared in the inner block is not valid in the outer block. The following terminology is used to express these ideas. The scope of a variable or constant is over in the block within which that variable is defined. Additionally, a variable's scope extends over any block enclosed within the block in which the variable is defined. There is one limitation that must be imposed. The scope of a variable does not begin until the variable is declared. The program in Figure 3–3 illustrates some of these ideas.

The program in Figure 3–3 has three blocks. The outer block contains the middle one, and that middle block contains an inner one. The variables **a** and **b** are declared to be of type **int** at the start of the outer block. Thus, the scope of these variables extends over the entire program (all three blocks). Note that **a** is assigned the value 7 and **b** is assigned the value 14 (**2 * a**). The next brace then signifies the start of the middle block. The variable **c** is declared at the start of this block. Thus, its scope extends over the entire middle block, including the inner block. However, its scope does not extend over the outer block. It would be an error to use the variable **c** in the outer block.

The third statement of the middle block is

$$\text{int d} \;=\; \text{c} + 1; \qquad\qquad \textbf{3–17}$$

The variable **d** is declared here and then assigned the value **c** + 1. Note that this statement consists of both a declaration and an executable statement. The scope of the variable **d** extends over the middle block from the point of its declaration to the end of the block, therefore over the inner block as well.

FIGURE 3–3 ■ A program that illustrates scope and shadowing.

```
/* an illustration of scope */
#include <stream.h>
main()
{   // start of outer block
    int a,b;
    a = 7;
    b = 2 * a;
    {   // start of middle block
        int c;
        c = a + 3;
        int d = c + 1; // d cannot be used before this line
        b = b + c;
        {   // start of inner block
            int a,e;
            a = 22;
            e = 3 * a;
            cout << "\ninner a = "  << a;
        }   // end of inner block
    }   // end of middle block
    int g = 29;   // g cannot be used before this line
    cout << "\nouter a = " << a;
    cout << "\nb = "   << b;
}   // end of outer block
```

It would be an error to have a statement containing the variable **d** in the middle block before Statement 3–17.

Note the statement

$$b = b + c; \qquad\qquad 3\text{–}18$$

in the middle block. This illustrates that the scope of **b**, which is declared in the outer block, extends over the middle block.

The brace following 3–18 is the beginning of the inner block. Note that two variables **a** and **e** are declared at the start of this (inner) block. The scope of these variables extends only over this block. In particular, their scope does not extend over the middle and outer blocks. Note that the variables **a** and **b** declared in the outer block extend over all three blocks, and the scope of the variables **c** and **d** extend over the middle and inner blocks.

The variable **a** declared in the inner block requires further consideration. The scope of **a** declared in the outer block extends over the inner block. However, there is another variable called **a** declared in the inner block. These are two *totally distinct variables that happen to have the same name.* When a variable is referenced (i.e., used in a statement) within a block, the compiler searches the declarations of that block that precede the statement. If the variable is declared in the current block, prior to the statement, then the compiler uses that variable. If the variable is not found in that block, then the compiler searches the next outer block and proceeds in this way until a variable with the specified name is found. Thus, any **a** that is referenced in the inner block will be the **a** that is declared there. There is no way that the **a** declared in the outer block can be used in the inner block. The **a** in the outer block is said to be *shadowed* by the **a** in the inner block. Shadowing occurs when a variable that is declared in an inner block has the same name as a variable that is declared in a block that contains the inner block. Note that **a** is assigned the value 7 in the outer block and **a** is assigned the value 22 in the inner block. When **a** is output from the inner block, 22 is output; when **a** is output from the outer block, 7 is output, even though the output statement of the outer block follows the execution of the inner block. Remember that the two **a** variables are different, even though their names are the same.

These ideas can be clarified by considering how the compiler keeps track of variables. The compiler sets up tables, called *symbol tables*, that contain the variable names and the corresponding memory locations used to store the variables. When a variable is encountered in a statement, the compiler goes to the symbol table to determine the memory locations for that variable. These memory locations are used in the machine language program that is ultimately generated. When a variable is referenced, the compiler scans the table for the block in question and attempts to find an entry for that variable. If the entry is present, no further search is made. If an entry cannot be found for the variable in question, then the table for the next outer block is searched. Once the variable name is found in the symbol table, the search stops. If the variable name is not found, then the symbol table for the next outer block is searched, and so on. Different entries in the symbol tables have different addresses. Thus, different entries represent different variables, even if their names happen to be the same.

Consider the statement

$$b = b + c; \hspace{3cm} \textbf{3–19}$$

that is in the middle block. The variable **b** is declared in the outer block and is not declared in the middle block. Thus, Statement 3–19 refers to the **b** declared in the outer block, and changes the value of **b** in the outer block. In fact, there is only one variable **b** in the entire program.

Note the variable **g** that is defined in the outer block after the closing brace of the middle block. The scope of this variable does not extend over either the middle or inner blocks, because it is declared after these blocks in the program. Conceptually, consider that no entry is made in the symbol table until the declaration for the variable is encountered. For instance, the entry for variable **g** is not made until after the execution of the middle and inner blocks. (The actual details of compiler operation may be different from this, but the action is the same.)

The scope of a variable has to do with its position in the source code of the program. In addition to scope, a variable may exist only during certain times when the program is executing. This is called the *lifetime* of the variable. For example, suppose that your program calls a library function. Assume that the function was written in C++ and contained variable declarations. In general, the scope of those variables is only over the function; that is, they cannot be used by the program that called the function. In addition, the variables exist only during the time the function is executing.

For instance, suppose that a program calls the function **sqrt** more than once in the program. The variables used by the **sqrt** function exist only when the function is executing. That is, they come into existence when the function is called; they cease to exist when the function stops executing. The second time the function is called, the variables come into existence again. After execution of the function, its variables cease to exist. When a variable ceases to exist, the system can use its memory locations for other purposes. It may be that different locations are used to store the variables for **sqrt** each time it is called. For instance, if another library function is called, its variables could be stored in the memory locations previously used for the variables of **sqrt**. If that library function subsequently called **sqrt**, then the memory locations used for **sqrt**'s variables would be different than those that were used previously. We have oversimplified here. When we discuss user-defined functions, we shall see that there are two kinds of variables. The variables that cease to exist when the function in which they are declared stops executing are called *automatic variables*. On the other hand, there are variables that exist as long as the program runs, even after the function in which they are defined stops executing. Such variables are called *static variables*. When we discuss user-defined functions, we shall consider automatic and static variables in greater detail.

3–4 ■ POINTERS

When a variable is declared, the compiler reserves memory locations for that variable. In all of the programs that we have considered, and in most programs for that matter, the programmer is not concerned with the addresses of these locations and simply references each variable by its name. In particular, the programmer is not concerned as to where in memory specific addresses lie. On the other hand, some applications, such as those relating to operating systems, require that the programmer address specific locations. Many programming languages do not have this facility and, when such programming languages are used, programmers must resort to assembly language programming. Although assembly language programming can be very useful, it is much more tedious than programming in a higher level language. C++ has features that allow the programmer to deal with specific memory addresses. These features extend the versatility of C++ in other areas.

When a program is compiled, the compiler reserves memory locations for each variable. In general, each word of memory has a numerical address. Each variable's value is stored in one or more consecutive words. For example, in a typical small computer, values of type **char** are stored in one word, values of type **int** are stored in two consecutive words, and values of type **float** are stored in four consecutive words. Appropriate space is reserved to store the data for each declared variable. The address of the first word that stores the value of the variable is called the address of the variable. This address is called a *pointer* to the variable. The compiler substitutes the address for the variable's name when the program is compiled.

There are several ways of referencing a pointer, i. e., the address of a variable. One method involves the ***** operator; it is called the *indirection operator*. Note that the ***** symbol is also used to represent the multiplication operator. These are different operators, and the compiler will recognize which is being used by the context of the statement. The indirection operator is used immediately in front of the name of a variable. In order to designate a variable as a pointer, the indirection operator is placed before the variable's name in a declaration. For instance,

$$\text{int *item,box;} \qquad \text{3–20a}$$
$$\text{float *dist;} \qquad \text{3–20b}$$

Here **item** has been declared to be a pointer to an integer variable, while **box** is simply an integer variable. Similarly, **dist** has been declared to be a pointer to a variable of type **float**. Note that there is no space between the indirection operator and the variable name. The compiler has reserved memory locations for **box**, **item**, and **dist**. However, the memory locations reserved for **item** and **dist** will store the addresses of memory locations. In particular, integer and floating-point data is to be stored in the memory locations whose *addresses* are stored in **item** and **dist**, respectively. The values of these pointers must be initialized if useful data storage is to be accomplished. There are several ways to accomplish this. One is to use the **&** operator, which is called the *address-of operator*. When the address-of operator precedes a variable's name, the result of the operation is the address of that variable. For instance, evaluation of

$$\text{item = \&box;} \qquad \text{3–21}$$

assigns the address of **box** to **item**. The value stored in the memory location pointed at by **item** can be accessed with the indirection operator. For instance, evaluation of

$$\text{*item = 3;} \qquad \text{3–22}$$

stores the integer 3 in the set of memory location(s) pointed at by **item**. Of course, the storage is in the usual integer form. You can assign a numerical value to a pointer. For instance, a statement such as

$$\text{item = 31000;} \qquad \text{3–23}$$

could be executed. In this case, memory location 31000 would store the integer pointed at by item. Note that if two memory locations are used to store an integer, then consecutive memory locations, i.e., 31000 and 31001, are used.

If your program assigns specific numerical locations, then you must be aware of all the details of your operating system. For instance, if inappropriate locations were chosen, you might overwrite memory locations that are used to store the operating system. This could cause all kinds of dire consequences. For instance, the system might "crash," and data would be lost. Of course, if your purpose is to write, or rewrite, an operating system, then such addressing must be used. We have designated an address as an unsigned integer, and in many computer systems this is the case. However, other addressing schemes are used. Consult your computer manual to determine the addressing scheme used by your system.

Consider the statement

$$*\text{dist} = 3.0; \qquad \qquad 3\text{--}24$$

Although this statement appears similar to 3–22, their execution will result in somewhat different operations. Assume that an address has been established and assigned to **dist**. In addition, let us assume that a variable of type **int** is stored in two memory locations, while a variable of type **float** is stored in four memory locations. Thus, when 3–22 is executed, two memory locations are pointed to; when 3–24 is executed, four memory locations are pointed to.

Figure 3–4 is a simple illustration of a program that uses pointers. Two integers are declared; **a** is an integer variable and **b** is a pointer to an integer variable. When the program is run, the value of **a** is entered by the user from the keyboard. Next, **b** is assigned the value of the address of **a**. Thus, **b** now points at **a**. When the statement

$$*\text{b} = 22; \qquad \qquad 3\text{--}25$$

is executed, the value 22 is stored in the set of memory location(s) pointed at by **b**. Because these memory locations store the address of **a**, the value assigned to **a** is changed when 3–25 is executed. In fact ***b** and **a** can be used interchangeably in the program. Note that the value of **b** must be established, i.e., initialized, before data is stored in the memory location to which it points.

FIGURE 3–4 ■ An illustration of addresses and pointers.

```
#include <stream.h>
/* an illustration of pointers */
main()
{
    int a,*b;
    cout << "\nenter a\n";
    cin >> a;
    b = &a;
    cout << "\ncontents of b = " << *b;
    *b = 22;   // must have address of b established before assignment
    cout << "\na = " << a;
}
```

If this is not done, the consequences are unpredictable. For instance, suppose that the statement

$$b = \&a;$$

did not precede 3–25. In that case, some value would be assigned to **b**, but it could be anything because **b** had not been initialized specifically by the program. Thus, when 3–25 was executed, the value 22 would be stored in unknown memory locations, i.e., an unknown address. This value (22) could overwrite the operating system, other data in the program, or the code of the program itself. Any of these actions would result in improper operation. Of course, if luck prevailed, the initial value of **b** would be a suitable unused memory location. However, you should *never* count on such luck.

C++ provides an operator, **new**, that picks allowable memory locations in which to store variables. In addition, these locations will be reserved so that they will not be used by the compiler for other storage. The operatand is the name of a type. It follows the keyword **new** in the statement and specifies the amount of storage. For instance, consider the following program segment.

int *b;	**3–26a**
b = new int[1];	**3–26b**

Statement 3–26a declares that **b** is a pointer to a variable of type **int**. In 3–26b, the **new** operator reserves enough space for a single integer. The pointer to that space is assigned to **b**. Suppose that two consecutive memory locations are used to store type **int**; then the address of the first memory location will be assigned to **b**. In addition, enough consecutive memory locations to store an integer are reserved and will not be used by the compiler for other data storage. Because space is reserved for a single integer, the [1] could be omitted from 3–26b. It is included in the example for completeness. If space for three integers were to be reserved, then the bracketed number would be included. For instance,

$$b = new\ int[3]; \qquad \textbf{3–27}$$

The operator **new** replaces functions such as **malloc** that are used in conventional C. Because **new** is an operator, and is part of the C++ language, it is more easily used than **malloc**.

After program segment 3–26 is executed, the variable **b** stores an address; the memory location pointed at by that address stores the data assigned to ***b**. Whenever a pointer is used, two sets of memory locations are involved. One stores the pointer and the other (i.e., the one pointed at) stores the data.

Figure 3–5 illustrates the use of **new**. This program is a modification of the program in Figure 3–4. Now the address that stores the value represented by ***b** is obtained using **new**. This address is assigned to **b**. Notice that, in this program, there is no connection between the value assigned to **a** and the value assigned to ***b**.

FIGURE 3–5 ■ An illustration of the use of **new**.

```
#include <stream.h>
/* another illustration of pointers */
main()
{
    int a,*b;
    cout << "\nenter a\n";
    cin >> a;
    b = new int[1];
    *b = 22;  // must have address of b established before assignment
    cout << "\ncontents of b = " << *b;
    cout << "\na = " << a;
}
```

The allocation of memory space during compilation is termed *static memory allocation*. Such memory is reserved for the declared variables and cannot be reassigned. On the other hand, **new** allocates storage space during the execution of the program; this is called *dynamic memory allocation*. Memory that is allocated dynamically can be freed and reused later in the program. The operator **delete** is used to free memory that has been allocated by **new**. The operand of **delete** is the *pointer* whose memory allocation is being deleted; for instance,

$$\text{delete b;} \hspace{4cm} \textbf{3–28}$$

If space for more than one integer was reserved, then the bracketed number should *precede* the pointer name; for instance,

$$\text{delete [3] b;} \hspace{4cm} \textbf{3–29}$$

Pointers are often used with strings. Remember that a string is a collection of characters. Figure 3–6 is a simple illustration of such utilization. Note that two character pointers are declared, and memory is allocated for each of these. Eighty-one bytes are allocated to **a**, and 95 bytes are allocated to **b**. We assume that a **char** is stored in one byte. The person running the program is then prompted to enter a word. Note the statement

$$\text{cin} >> \text{a;} \hspace{4cm} \textbf{3–30}$$

Strings are referenced by pointers. Such a pointer points to the first character of the string. This contrasts with the technique used to reference variables of type **int**, **float**, and so on. When 3–30 is executed, operation pauses until the person running the program enters a word and presses RETURN. A similar expression is then executed, and the next word is assigned to **b**. When the last expression is executed, the two words are output with a space between them.

FIGURE 3–6 ■ An illustration of the use of pointers with strings.

```
#include <stream.h>
/* an illustration of pointers and strings */
main()
{
    char *a,*b;
    a = new char[81];
    b = new char[95];
    cout << "\nenter first word\n";
    cin >> a;
    cout << "\nenter second word\n";
    cin >> b;
    cout << "\n" << a << " " << b;
}
```

When data is input from the terminal, a blank space called a *whitespace* often serves to delimit one piece of data from the next. The entered data is stored in a buffer called the *input buffer*. If more data than currently called for is entered, it remains in the input buffer until the program requests additional input. Suppose that there are three separate **cin** statements; their data could have been entered on three separate lines. That is, each item of data is separated, or delimited, by a RETURN. On the other hand, the three items could have been entered on a single line delimited by whitespaces. In either case, the three items of data would be stored in the input buffer. Each of these items would be supplied in turn to the **cin** statements. Thus, when the second and third **cin** statements were executed, operation would not pause because data already in the input buffer would be supplied to the program. Because whitespace (i.e., blank space[s]) serves as a delimiter, only single word strings can be entered from the keyboard. (Note that this is system dependent; check your system to determine how it functions.)

A string can consist of many words. For instance, the following would be a valid string assignment statement for the program in Figure 3–6.

$$a = \text{"The quick brown fox jumped"}; \qquad \textbf{3–31}$$

The string length is limited to 80 characters (see Figure 3–6). Note that shorter strings can be entered. The system keeps track of the actual length of a string by terminating each string with a *null character*. This is usually ASCII 0. Note that the whitespaces in 3–31 do not serve as delimiters because the string is not passed through the input buffer.

Pointer Arithmetic

A pointer points at a memory location. That pointer can be incremented or decremented so that it points at the next memory location. The term "next" has a special meaning in this case. Let us assume that we are working with a computer that stores type **char** in one word, type **int** in two words, and type **float** in four words. Consider that **ch**, **i**, and **f** have been declared as pointers to type **char**, **int**, and **float** respectively. Suppose that **ch** is assigned 10000. That is, it points at address 10000 in memory. Now suppose that

$$ch++; \hspace{5cm} 3\text{-}32$$

is executed. The value assigned to **ch** will now be 10001, as might be expected. Now consider that **i** points at memory location 20000. If

$$i++; \hspace{5cm} 3\text{-}33$$

is evaluated, **i** will be assigned the value 20002. Note that it has been incremented by 2. Let us consider the reason for this. Because integers are stored in two memory locations, two memory locations would be used to store the value assigned to ***i**. When a pointer is incremented, it points at the next *available* memory location that can store a variable of the type pointed at. In the case of integers, for our example, the next available memory location is two more than the original location. Thus, when 3–33 is evaluated, the integer pointer is incremented by 2. In a similar way, if **f** is assigned the value 30000, evaluation of

$$f++; \hspace{5cm} 3\text{-}34$$

will result in **f** being assigned the value 30004.

On the other hand, the value pointed at can be incremented as well. For instance, suppose ***i** is assigned 35. If

$$(*i)++; \hspace{5cm} 3\text{-}35$$

is executed, ***i** will then be assigned 36. Note that 3–35 does not increment a pointer; it simply increments a variable. Thus, the value assigned to the variable is simply incremented by 1.

We have illustrated pointer arithmetic using **++** and **−−**. These are the most portable forms of pointer arithmetic. However other forms can be used. Let us assume that addresses are represented by unsigned integers. Then the following is equivalent to 3–33.

$$i = i + 1; \hspace{5cm} 3\text{-}36$$

Statement 3–33 is equivalent to 3–36, but 3–33 will work on any system, whereas 3–36 will work only on those systems where the address, or an increment in the address, can be represented by an unsigned integer. The C++ compilers for each computer system will contain the details of how much memory is used to store each data type. Thus, if the program is recompiled on a new system, the details of pointer arithmetic will always be correct if the **++** and **−−** operators are used.

Figure 3–7 is an example of a program that uses pointer arithmetic. In it, **new** allocates space for three integers. This will consist of a group of consecutive memory locations. After the **new** statement is executed, **b** points at the bottom of this group, i. e., the lowest numerical address. Thus, when

$$*b \; = \; 22; \hspace{4cm} \textbf{3–37}$$

is executed, 22 will be stored in the first set of memory locations. Next,

$$b++; \hspace{4cm} \textbf{3–38}$$

is executed, and the pointer is incremented. Thus, when the next statement,

$$*b \; = \; 976; \hspace{4cm} \textbf{3–39}$$

is executed, 976 is stored in the next set of memory locations. In a similar way, 2345 is stored in the third set of memory locations. The data is output when

$$\text{cout} \; << \; *b \; << \; " \; " \; << \; *(--b) \; << \; " \; " \; << \; *(--b); \hspace{1cm} \textbf{3–40}$$

is executed. The output is

$$2345 \; 976 \; 22$$

Note that when $*(--b)$ is executed, **b** is decremented before its value is referenced. This is because the decrement operator precedes the **b**. If the decrement operator followed the **b**, then the value of **b** would be used before **b** was decremented. Also note that $*(--b)$ decrements the pointer while $--(*b)$ decrements the value pointed at.

FIGURE 3–7 ■ An illustration of pointer arithmetic.

```
#include <stream.h>
/* an illustration of pointer arithmetic */
main()
{
      int *b;
      b = new int[3];
      *b = 22;
      b++;
      *b = 976;
      b++;
      *b = 2345;
      cout << *b;
      cout << "    " << *(--b);
      cout << "    " << *(--b);
}
```

3–5 ■ ENUMERATED CONSTANTS— ELEMENTARY USER-DEFINED TYPES

We have discussed the use of the keyword **const** to define constants of various types. The C++ keyword **enum** is convenient to use when several constants of type **int** are to be specified. Notice that this **enum** keyword establishes constants of type **int** *only*. The form of the use of **enum** is the word **enum** followed by a list enclosed in curly brackets. The items of the list are separated by commas. For instance, suppose that constants representing the days of the week are to be established. This can be accomplished with the following statement.

enum { SUN=0,MON=1,TUES=2,WED=3,THURS=4,FRI=5,SAT=6} ;   **3–41**

Here we have established the following constants of type **int**: **SUN**, **MON**, **TUES**, **WED**, **THURS**, **FRI**, and **SAT**; their values are **0, 1, 2, 3, 4, 5, 6**, and **7**, respectively. Of course, if the integers to the right of the = were changed, the values of the constants would be changed when the program was compiled.

If the values of the constants are as shown in 3–41, C++ provides a shorter form for the **enum** statement. That is, if the constants are numbered in sequence starting with zero, then each numerical value need not be specified. For instance, the following statement is equivalent to 3–41.

enum { SUN,MON,TUES,WED,THURS,FRI,SAT} ;   **3–42**

In these examples, the constants **SUN**, **MON**, **TUES**, **WED**, **THURS**, **FRI**, and **SAT** are of type **int**. Sometimes, to make the program more readable, it is helpful to define a type name to be synonymous with **int**. This can be done by writing this type name after **enum**. For instance,

enum day { SUN,MON,TUES,WED,THURS,FRI,SAT} ;   **3–43**

Now type **day** is synonymous with type **int**. Note that a synonymous type can be used also with statements of the form of 3–41.

Elementary User-Defined Types

Statements of the type of 3–43 give the appearance of creating a new type. For instance, 3–43 implies that there is a new type called **day** and that **day** has seven possible values. Suppose that a program that manipulated days of the week were written. Each day could simply be represented by an integer, and these integers could be manipulated by the program. However, it would be much clearer to programmers if each of the days were represented by an easily recognizable symbol such as **SUN** or **MON** and were called by a new type name. Thus, we can consider that 3–43 establishes a *user-defined type*, **day**, with values **SUN**, **MON**, **TUES**, **WED**, **THURS**, **FRI**, and **SAT**. Remember that this simply *appears* to be what is occurring; actually, integer constants are being defined.

Figure 3–8 is a simple example of a program with user-defined types. Note that there are two user-defined types, **day** and **time**. Statement 3–43

FIGURE 3–8 ■ An illustration of enumerated integer constants.

```
/* an example of enumerated integer constants */
#include <stream.h>
main()
{
      enum day {SUN,MON,TUES,WED,THURS,FRI,SAT};
      enum time {START=9,END=17};
      float item=9.5;
      day i;
      cout << START << "    " << TUES;
      i = day(item) + WED;
      cout << "\n" << i;
}
```

establishes type **day**. Type **time** has only two elements, **START** and **END**. A variable, **i**, is declared to be of type **day**. Note that this is equivalent to declaring it to be of type **int**. (Remember that the elements of **day** and **time** are actually of type **int**.) Thus, when the first **cout** statement is executed, the numerical values 9 and 2 will be output. The variable item has been declared to be of type **float**; functional notation is used to cast it to type **day** in the next-to-last statement of the program. Note that **i** is output as 12. When **item** is cast to type **day** (that is, type **int**), its fractional part is discarded, resulting in the value 9; **WED** has the value 3. Thus, 12 will be output. We have considered a simple form of a user-defined type here. Much more elaborate ones will be discussed subsequently.

EXERCISES

Check any programs that you write by running them on your computer.

1. *What is the difference between a character and a string?*
2. What are the *ASCII codes*?
3. Write a program that accepts a lowercase character, and outputs the ASCII code for the corresponding uppercase character.
4. Determine the relative size of types **char**, **int**, **short**, **long**, **float**, and **double** for your computer.
5. Write a program that calls for the input of five numbers and then outputs their average in a field 15 characters wide, with two decimal places.
6. Write a program that accepts six integers and then outputs them on separate lines, with their rightmost digits aligned.
7. Repeat Exercise 6, but now align the leftmost digits of the output.
8. Repeat Exercise 3, but output the codes in decimal, octal, and hexadecimal.
9. Comment on the differences among the **e**, **f**, and **g** *conversion specifiers*.

10. Write a simple program that contains a *block* within another block.
11. In the program in Figure 3–3, is there any way to change the value of **a** in the outer block from within the inner block?
12. Indicate the *scope* of all the variables of the program in Figure 3–3.
13. Discuss the meaning of *scope* and *lifetime*.
14. What is meant by a *pointer*?
15. If a program contains the declaration

    float aaa;

    what is the meaning of **&aaa**?
16. Write a program that contains the declaration

    float *zz;

    In the program, a value is to be assigned to ***zz** and then output. Make sure that the proper pointer is established.
17. Write a program that accepts a sentence of exactly five words and then outputs that sentence on the terminal. The sentence should be input on a single line.
18. Modify the program of Figure 3–7 to work with variables of type **float**.
19. Repeat Exercise 18, but now use type **double**.
20. Set up an *enumerated type* called **month**. The values of this type should be the abbreviations of the months of the year, numbered from 1 to 12. Has a new type been established?

CHAPTER 4
Program Control

In all of the programs we have discussed thus far, each executable statement was executed in order. Such a program is said to have a single *branch*. We shall now discuss statements that can be used to write a program with several branches. Not every branch is executed every time the program is run. Which branch is executed depends upon entered and calculated values. In general, programs that incorporate branching are more powerful than those that do not. We shall also discuss procedures that cause control to *loop* back over a set of statements so that they can be repeated more than once.

Although programs that incorporate branching and looping are more powerful than those that do not, they are more prone to logical errors. We shall also discuss techniques of *structured programming* that tend to reduce the occurrence of such errors and make them easier to debug when they do occur.

4–1 ■ LOGICAL OPERATORS

We shall now consider a new group of operators. These operators perform *logical operations* that return either *true* or *false*. For example, we can use logical operators to determine if two variables are assigned equal values. In C++, false is usually represented by a 0, while true is represented by a 1. These are values of type **int**. Often, these are generalized so that false is represented by a 0, while true is represented by *any* non-zero integer. Although this generalization is not standard, it is widely used. For purposes of discussion, in this section, we consider that 0 represents false and 1 represents true.

The operators that cause an expression to return either true or false are called *logical operators*, or *Boolean operators*. There are several classes of logical operators. The first class that we shall consider are the *equality operators*. These are as follows:

$$==\quad \text{Equal}$$
$$!=\quad \text{Not equal}$$

As an example of the use of these operators, consider the following program sequence in which **b**, **c**, **d**, and **e** have been declared to be of type **int**.

$$b = 4; \hspace{4cm} \text{4--1a}$$
$$c = 3; \hspace{4cm} \text{4--1b}$$
$$d = (b \mathrel{!=} c); \hspace{3.3cm} \text{4--1c}$$
$$e = (b == c); \hspace{3.3cm} \text{4--1d}$$

After this sequence is executed, **d** will be assigned the value 1 because **b** is not equal to **c**. On the other hand, **e** will be assigned the value 0 for the same reason. Note that the logical operation of 4–1c returns true when **b** is not equal to **c**, while the logical operation of 4–1d returns true when **b** is equal to **c**.

Actually, the parentheses in 4–1c and 4–1d are not necessary because the logical operators have a higher precedence than the assignment (=) operator. Thus, the logical operations are performed before an assignment and 4–1c and 4–1d can be written as

$$d = b \mathrel{!=} c; \hspace{3.5cm} \text{4--2a}$$
$$e = b == c; \hspace{3.5cm} \text{4--2b}$$

Notice that 4–1c and 4–1d are more readable than 4–2a and 4–2b. Statements that are more readable are less prone to errors. Thus, it is often desirable to include parentheses even when they are not strictly required.

There are other logical operators that are used to make comparisons. These are called *relational operators*. They are defined as follows:

$$>\quad \text{Greater than}$$
$$>=\quad \text{Greater than or equal to}$$
$$<\quad \text{Less than}$$
$$<=\quad \text{Less than or equal to}$$

Consider the statement

$$d = b > c; \hspace{4cm} \text{4--3}$$

The logical expression **b** > **c** will be true if **b** is greater than **c**, and in that case **d** is assigned the value 1. If **b** is equal to or less than **c**, then the logical statement will be false, and **d** is assigned the value 0.

In C++, an assignment statement assumes the value of the assignment. Let us explain this. Consider the statement

$$b = (c = d + e) == f; \hspace{2.5cm} \text{4--4}$$

There is a complete C++ assignment statement, without the terminating semicolon, within the parentheses. When 4–4 is executed, **c** is assigned the value **d + e**. The expression within parentheses is treated as if it were this number. Thus, if **d + e** is equal to **f**, then **b** will be assigned the value 1; if **d + e** is not equal to **f**, then **b** will be assigned the value zero. (Note that the "value of **b**" or "**b**" really means the value assigned to **b**.) In either case, **c** will be assigned the value of **d + e**.

There are two different assignments in 4–4; in one, a value is assigned to **c** and, in the other, a value is assigned to **b**. Such multiple operations can reduce the amount of typing required of the programmer. However, they should be used sparingly. Remember that although C++ provides many shortcuts that allow you to write very terse code, readability should not be sacrificed merely for the sake of convenience.

Figure 4–1 illustrates some simple logical operations. The first three logical operations deal with variables of type **int**. However, they could be any of the numeric types, e.g., **float, double, long,** or **short**. Note that when

$$f \ = \ (g{=}a{+}b) \ >= \ c; \hspace{4cm} \textbf{4–5}$$

is executed, **g** is assigned the value 3, and **f** is assigned the value 1. The next statement is

$$h \ = \ g{==}(d{-}1); \hspace{4.5cm} \textbf{4–6}$$

FIGURE 4–1 ■ (a) An example of some simple logical operations; (b) the output of this program.

```
/* simple logical operations */
#include <stream.h>
main( )
{
    int a=1,b=2,c=1,d=4,e,f,g,h,i;
    char ch1='x',ch2;
    e = a==b;
    f = (g=a+b)>=c;
    h = g==(d-1);
    cout << e << "   " << f << "   " << h;
    ch2 = 'y';
    h = (ch1 != ch2);
    ch2 = 120;
    i = ch1==ch2;
    cout << "\n" << h << "   " << i;
}
```

(a)

```
0  1  1
1  1
```

(b)

When this is executed, the parenthetical expression will be evaluated, yielding 3. Because **g** was assigned the value 3 in the previous statement, the logical operator returns true, and **h** is assigned the value 1.

The remaining logical operations use variables of type **char**. Remember that these actually store integer values. Thus, it is valid to use the relational operators with variables of type **char**. When

$$ch2 = 'y'; \qquad\qquad 4\text{--}7$$

is executed, **ch2** is assigned the value 121, the ASCII code for y. Note that **ch1** is initialized as 120, the ASCII code for x. Hence, when

$$h = (ch1 \; != \; ch2) \qquad\qquad 4\text{--}8$$

is executed, the result of the logical operation will be true, and **h** is assigned the value 1.

In the next statement, **ch2** is assigned the value 120. Thus, it is equal to **ch1**, and the last logical operation returns true.

Logical operations can be made much more versatile through the use of the *logical connectives*:

$$\&\& \qquad \text{AND}$$
$$\| \qquad \text{OR}$$

The logical connectives relate logical operations to each other. Let us define the logical connectives and then explain their use in C++. Suppose that **L1**, **L2**, and **L3** are logical expressions. That is, they are either true or false. Then,

$$\text{L1 AND L2} \qquad\qquad 4\text{--}9$$

will be true if *both* **L1** and **L2** are true. If either, or both, **L1** or **L2** is/are false, then 4–9 will be false. Any number of logical operations can be related by the AND operation. For instance,

$$\text{L1 AND L2 AND L3} \qquad\qquad 4\text{--}10$$

is true only if all of **L1**, **L2**, and **L3** are true. If any, or all, of **L1**, **L2**, and **L3** is/are false, then 4–10 is false.

The OR operation is described by two examples. Consider the logical expression

$$\text{L1 OR L2} \qquad\qquad 4\text{--}11$$

This is true if either, or both, **L1** and **L2** is or are true; it is false only if both **L1** and **L2** are false. The OR operation can relate any number of logical operations. For instance,

$$\text{L1 OR L2 OR L3} \qquad\qquad 4\text{--}12$$

is true if any, or all, of **L1**, **L2**, or **L3** is or are true; it is false only if all of **L1**, **L2**, and **L3** are false.

The symbols listed on page 70 are used in C++ statements in place of the words AND or OR. For instance,

$$b = (a>b)\&\&(c==d)\&\&(d==f) \qquad\qquad 4\text{--}13$$

is assigned the value 1 only if **a>b**, **c==d**, and **d==f** are all true; otherwise, **b** is assigned the value 0. Similarly, consider

$$c = (a>b)\|(c==d)\|(d==f) \qquad\qquad 4\text{--}14$$

The variable **c** is assigned the value 1 if any of the three logical expressions are true; **c** is assigned the value 0 only if all three logical expressions are false.

Logical connectives can be combined in a single expression. For example,

$$d = (a==b)\&\&((c>d)\|(d==f)); \qquad\qquad 4\text{--}15$$

When 4–15 is executed, **d** is assigned the value 1 if **a==b** is true and if either, or both, **c>d** and **d==f** is/are true. If **a==b** is false, or both **c>d** and **d==f** are false, **d** is assigned the value 0. Notice that we have used parentheses to group terms. There is a hierarchy of logical operations; we shall consider it later in this chapter. For the time being, use parentheses to ensure that the statement is evaluated in the desired manner. It is often a good idea to include parentheses if only to make the statements more readable, thus preventing logical errors.

The operator **!** represents NOT. It is a unary operator; i.e., it operates on a single operand. This operator replaces a true with a false, and vice versa. For instance,

$$!(a==b) \qquad\qquad 4\text{--}16$$

is true only if **a** is not equal to **b**.

In 4–4 and 4–5 we demonstrated that a statement could be evaluated as part of a logical statement. This can be extended to AND and OR operations. However, further discussion is necessary. Suppose that we have the logical expression

$$\text{L1 AND L2 AND L3} \qquad\qquad 4\text{--}17$$

If any of **L1**, **L2**, or **L3** is false, the expression is false. When 4–17 is evaluated, **L1**, **L2**, and **L3** are sequentially checked to determine if each of them is true. As soon as a false result is obtained, evaluation should cease, because the result of the entire expression is known (false). Suppose that **L1**, **L2**, or **L3** contain statements that result in assignment (see 4–4 or 4–5). These assignments are called *side effects*, because their execution is not the primary result of the statement. If the expression represented by **L1** contains an assignment, that assignment will always be executed because **L1** will always be evaluated. On the other hand, if **L2** contains an assignment, it may not be executed, because if **L1** is false, **L2** will never be evaluated. Similarly **L3** will not be evaluated unless both **L1** and **L2** are true.

Let us consider side effects with OR operations. Consider the logical expression

$$\text{L1 OR L2 OR L3} \hspace{4cm} 4\text{--}18$$

If any of **L1**, **L2**, or **L3** is true, the entire expression is true. Thus, once any one of **L1**, **L2**, or **L3** is found to be true, no further expressions are evaluated. In general, the complete logical expression is evaluated from left to right; those logical subexpressions contained within it that do not have to be evaluated to obtain the result of the entire expression will *not* be evaluated. Any side effects contained within logical subexpressions that are not evaluated will not be executed. The program in Figure 4–2 illustrates some of these ideas. The first logical expression contains three expressions connected by ANDs. The first of these,

$$(d = 7) == 7;$$

will always be evaluated, and **d** is assigned the value 7. Because the first logical expression is true, the second is evaluated, and **e** is assigned the value

FIGURE 4–2 ■ (a) An illustration of side effects with the AND and OR operations; (b) the output of this program.

```
/* an illustration of logical operations and side effects */
#include <stream.h>
main()
{
    int a=1,b=2,c=3,d=4,e=5,f=6,h;
    cout << form("\nfirst d = %d   e = %d   f = %d",d,e,f);
    h = ((d=7) == 7)&&((e=9) > 11)&&((f=15) < 99);
    cout << form("\nsecond d = %d   e = %d   f = %d",d,e,f);
    h = ((d=15) == 15)||((e=27)==27)||((f=30) > 45);
    cout << form("\nthird d = %d   e = %d   f = %d",d,e,f);
}
```

(a)

```
first d = 4   e = 5   f = 6
second d = 7   e = 9   f = 6
third d = 15  e = 9   f = 6
```

(b)

9. The second logical expression, (9>11), is false and, therefore, there is no further evaluation of the statement. In particular, the value of **f** will remain at 6, its initial value. Note that **h** is assigned the value 0. The total expression is false because the second subexpression is false.

Now consider the second logical statement in Figure 4–2; it consists of OR statements. The first logical expression is evaluated, with **d** being assigned the value 15. This logical expression is true; thus, **h** is assigned the value 1, and no further logical expressions in the statement will be evaluated. For this reason, the values of **e** and **f** will remain at 9 and 6, respectively.

The operations that we have discussed here constitute a simple form of branching, because different statements are executed depending on values calculated elsewhere in the program. However, we shall discuss much more effective branching procedures in the remainder of this chapter. The procedures discussed here should be used only for very simple branching operations because they can lead to programs that are difficult to read and to debug.

Although we have illustrated logical operations using integers, floating-point values can also be used as well. Care should be exercised when floating-point numbers are compared for equality. Floating-point calculations are subject to roundoff error. Thus, two values that should be equal may, in fact, differ by a very small amount even when simple calculations are performed. For instance, suppose that **a** and **b** are supposed to be calculated to be equal values, but after their calculation, the values assigned to **a** and **b** are 3.000000 and 3.000001, respectively. The logical expression **a==b** is false because **a** and **b** are not *exactly* equal. To account for round-off error, **a** and **b** should not be tested to see if they are equal. Instead, they should be tested to determine if their difference is very small. For example, the following statement might be used.

$$c = abs(a - b) < 0.0001; \qquad\qquad \textbf{4–19}$$

Note that the function **abs** is used to ensure that a nonnegative number is compared with 0.0001.

4–2 ■ THE if CONSTRUCTION

We shall now use the logical operators to control program branching in conjunction with the **if** construction. The form of the **if** construction is

$$\text{if(logical expression) statement;} \qquad\qquad \textbf{4–20}$$

The construction consists of the word **if**, followed by a logical expression enclosed in parentheses, followed by an executable C++ statement. If the logical expression is true, the C++ statement is executed; if the logical statement is false, the C++ statement is not executed. For example,

$$if(a>b) \; c \; = \; d+1; \qquad\qquad 4\text{--}21$$

In 4–21, if **a** is greater than **b**, then the statement

$$c \; = \; d \; + \; 1; \qquad\qquad 4\text{--}22$$

will be executed; if **a** is less than or equal to **b**, Statement 4–22 is ignored, and the operation of the program is the same as if Statement 4–21 were not present. The **if** construction would be limited in its use if it could control the execution of only a single statement. However, the statement designated in 4–20 can be a compound statement (block); for example,

$$
\begin{array}{ll}
if((a>b)\|(c==d)) \quad \{ & \qquad 4\text{--}23a \\
\quad c \; = \; d \; + \; 1; & \qquad 4\text{--}23b \\
\quad d++; & \qquad 4\text{--}23c \\
\quad d \; = \; d \; + \; a; & \qquad 4\text{--}23d \\
\} & \qquad 4\text{--}23e
\end{array}
$$

If the logical expression, $(a>b)\|(c==d)$, is true, then the compound Statement 4–23b to 4–23d is executed. If the logical statement is false, then the compound statement is ignored. Because the compound statement is a branch of a program, branching has been achieved using the **if** construction.

Notice that the compound statement in 4–23 is indented. Because the block is clearly indicated by the indentation, the program is made more readable. Such indentation is very helpful to programmers and is ignored by the compiler. We shall consider other examples of indentation as we progress through the book.

A simple program that utilizes the **if** construction is shown in Figure 4–3. Four integers are entered and the largest one is output. Note that the integers are stored in the variables named **first**, **second**, **third**, and **fourth**. When the program is run, **max** is set equal to **first**. (Note that this is an abbreviated way of saying that **max** is assigned the value assigned to **first**.) Now **max** is compared with **second**. If the value assigned to **second** is greater than that assigned to **max**, then **max** will be set equal to **second**; otherwise, no action is taken. Thus, after the first **if** expression is executed, **max** is assigned the larger of the values stored by **first** and **second**. Similarly, after the second **if** statement is executed, **max** will be set equal to the largest value stored by **first**, **second**, or **third**. Thus, after all the **if** statements are evaluated, the value of **max** will be equal to the largest entered integer. This value will be output.

We shall now write a program that obtains the roots of a quadratic equation of the form

$$ax^2 \; + \; bx \; + \; c \; = \; 0 \qquad\qquad 4\text{--}24$$

FIGURE 4–3 ■ An example of the **if** construction.

```
/* program that finds the largest of four entered integers */
#include <stream.h>
main()
{
    int first,second,third,fourth,max;
    cout << "\nEnter four integers\n";
    cin >> first >> second >> third >> fourth;
    max = first;
    if(second > max)max = second;
    if(third > max)max = third;
    if(fourth > max)max = fourth;
    cout << "\nMaximum = "   << max;
}
```

The roots of this equation are given by

$$x_1 = -b + \sqrt{(b^2 - 4ac)}/2a \qquad\qquad \textbf{4–25a}$$

$$x_2 = -b - \sqrt{(b^2 - 4ac)}/2a \qquad\qquad \textbf{4–25b}$$

There are three different conditions. The quantity

$$b^2 - 4ac \qquad\qquad \textbf{4–26}$$

can be zero, positive, or negative. If 4–26 evaluates to zero, then there are two equal roots. It is not necessary to evaluate the square root in this case, because it is zero. If 4–26 is positive, the square root is real; there are two distinct roots of the equation. If 4–26 is negative, then the square root of a negative number must be calculated. The square root of a negative number is called an *imaginary number*. The particular imaginary number, $\sqrt{-1}$, is written as i; for instance,

$$\sqrt{-4} = i\sqrt{4} = i2 \qquad\qquad \textbf{4–27}$$

A program that evaluates the roots of the quadratic equation is shown in Figure 4–4. It contains three branches, one corresponding to each of the three conditions. The variable **tmp** is assigned the value represented by quantity 4–26. The two branches corresponding to **tmp == 0** and **tmp > 0** perform the direct calculation of the roots. When **tmp** is negative, the square root of a negative number must be calculated. It is possible to write such a library function using complex numbers. However, for the purposes of this discussion, assume that the function **sqrt** can be used only with positive numbers. In

FIGURE 4–4 ■ A program that computes the roots of a quadratic equation.

```
/* quadratic root solution */
#include <stream.h>
#include <math.h>
main()
{
    float a,b,c,root1,root2,tmp;
    cout << "\nEquation is a*x*x + b*x + c = 0\n";
    cout << "\nEnter a, b, and c\n";
    cin >> a >> b >> c;
    tmp = b*b - 4.0*a*c;
    if(tmp == 0.0)  {  //equal roots
        root1 = -b/(2.0*a);
        cout << "\nEqual roots are " << root1;
    }  // end if(tmp == 0.0)
    if (tmp > 0.0)  {  //two real roots
        tmp = sqrt(tmp);
        root1 = (-b + tmp)/(2.0*a);
        root2 = (-b -tmp)/(2.0*a);
        cout << "\nRoots are " << root1 << " and " << root2;
    } //end if(tmp > 0.0)
    if(tmp < 0.0)  {  //complex roots
        tmp = -tmp;
        tmp = sqrt(tmp)/(2.0*a);
        cout << "\nRoots are " << -b/(2.0*a) << " + or - i" << tmp;
    }  // end if(tmp < 0.0)
}
```

the third branch of the program, i.e., when **tmp < 0** is **true, tmp** is replaced by −tmp. The value assigned to **tmp** is now positive. Then, **sqrt(tmp)** is evaluated. Although the square root of a positive number is being evaluated by the program, the actual square root is an imaginary number. This is signified by preceding it by the letter i when the value of the square root is output.

Note how the indentation clearly indicates the three branches of the program. In addition, we have included a comment at the end of each compound statement to indicate where it began. For instance, the block that begins with

$$if(tmp == 0.0) \quad \{ \qquad\qquad\qquad \textbf{4–28a}$$

ends with

$$\} \textit{ // end if(tmp == 0.0)} \qquad\qquad\qquad \textbf{4–28b}$$

It may seem as though the comment is not needed in 4–28b because the indentation clearly delineates the block, but in long, complicated programs, comments of this type can be a great help to the programmer. There may be many levels of indentation, and if the programmer forgets an indent, or if the program extends over more than one page, comments indicating the end of blocks can clarify the program and significantly reduce the number of errors.

4–3 ■ THE if-else CONSTRUCTION

The **if** construction can be made more versatile by adding the C++ keyword **else**. The general form of the **if-else** construction is

if(logical expression)statement_a	**4–29a**
else statement_b	**4–29b**

This construction is similar to the **if** construction except that the keyword **else** and **statement_b** are added. If the logical expression is true, **statement_a** is executed, and **statement_b** is ignored. On the other hand, if the logical expression is false, **statement_a** is ignored, and **statement_b** is executed. The two statements, **statement_a** and **statement_b**, can be compound statements (blocks). For example, consider the program segment

if((a==b)&&(c>>d)) {	**4–30a**
c = c + a;	**4–30b**
e = c/a;	**4–30c**
} // end if(a==b)&&(c>>d)) start else	**4–30d**
else {	**4–30e**
c = c−−;	**4–30f**
d = a + b;	**4–30g**
g = a * b;	**4–30h**
} // end if((a==b)&&(c>d)) else	**4–30i**

If the logical expression **(a==b)&&(c>d)** is true, Statements 4–30b and 4–30c will be executed, and Statements 4–30f to 4–30h will be ignored. On the other hand, if the logical expression is false, Statements 4–30b and 4–30c will be ignored, while Statements 4–30f to 4–30h will be executed. Note that indentation and comments are included to clearly delineate the blocks of the **if-else** construction. In particular, note that 4–30d contains a closing brace *and* a comment.

Statement 4–30b causes the value assigned to **c** to change. The variable **c** is part of the logical expression. It may seem as though the conditions of the **if** construction are being changed. However, this is not the case. Because the conditions are tested only at the start of the **if-else** construction, any subsequent changes to the variables involved in those conditions do not affect the result of the test (true or false). For example, the execution of 4–30b will not change the result of the logical expression of 4–30a because that logical expression is evaluated prior to the execution of 4–30b.

The **else** keyword can be followed by another **if** construction. For instance, consider the following:

if(logical_expression_a)statement_a;	4–31a
else	4–31b
if(logical_expression_b)statement_b;	4–31c

If **logical_expression_a** is true, **statement_a** will be executed, and all of 4–31c will be ignored. If **logical_expression_a** is false, **statement_a** will be ignored, but 4–31c will be executed. Thus, if **logical_expression_a** is false and **logical_expression_b** is true, **statement_b** will be executed, while **statement_a** will not. If both **logical_expression_a** and **logical_expression_b** are false, neither **statement_a** nor **statement_b** will be executed. In all cases, execution continues with the next statement in the program.

Several **if-else** constructions can be nested. In such cases, the programmer must know how the compiler relates the **if** and **else** keywords. For instance, consider the following program sequence.

if(logical_expression_a)statement_a;	4–32a
if(logical_expression_b)statement_b;	4–32b
if(logical_expression_c)statement_c;	4–32c
else	4–32d
statement_d;	4–32e

In order to determine which **if** and **else** are associated, use the following rule. A particular **else** is associated with the last encountered **if** statement that itself is not associated with an **else**. Thus, in 4–32, the **if** of 4–32c and the **else** are associated. That is, if **logical_expression_c** is true, **statement_c** will be executed, while **statement_d** will not. On the other hand, if **logical_expression_c** is false, **statement_c** will not be executed, but **statement_d** will be.

In general, in a series of nested **if-else** statements, the following procedure can be used to associate **else** and **if** keywords. Find the innermost **else**; this is associated with the nearest preceding **if** statement. Now take the next **else** statement; it is associated with the closest preceding **if** statement that has not been associated with an **else** statement. Proceeding in this way, each pair of **if** and **else** statements can be associated.

The preceding rule can be overridden through the inclusion of curly braces. It is a good idea to use curly braces to mark blocks of statements to relate associated **if** and **else** rather than to rely on rules; the blocks remove any potential source of confusion. That is, when there are nested **if-else** constructions, it is a good practice to set up blocks that specifically associate the corresponding **if** and **else** expressions. As an example, consider the following program segment.

if(logical_condition_a)statement_a;	4–33a
if(logical_condition_b) {	4–33b

```
            statement_b;                               4–33c
        if(logical_condition_c)                        4–33d
            statement_c;                               4–33e
            else {    // start else of
                //if(logical_condition_c)              4–33f
                statement_d;                           4–33g
            }    // end if(logical_condition_c) else    4–33h
    }   // start else of if(logical_condition_b)        4–33i
    else                                               4–33j
        statement_e;                                   4–33k
```

Statement 4–33a is independent of the rest of the segment. If **logical_condition_b** and **logical_condition_c** are true, then **statement_b** and **statement_c** are executed. If **logical_condition_b** is true and **logical_condition_c** is false, **statement_b** and **statement_d** are executed. If **logical_condition_b** is false, **statement_e** is executed, but neither **statement_c** nor **statement_d** is executed. Blocks can be used to increase the versatility of nested **if-else** constructions. In addition, the presence of the curly braces, indentation, and comments makes the program much more readable for programmers. Note that the curly brace of 4–33f and line 4–33h could be deleted. They are included to demonstrate that unnecessary braces can be added simply to improve the clarity of the program. You should always attempt to write programs that are readable. The time spent entering a small amount of extra text is much more than offset by the debugging time saved.

Figure 4–5 is an example of a program that uses nested **if-else** constructions. This is a modification of the program in Figure 4–4 that calculated the roots of a quadratic equation. The three branches of the program are obtained using a nested **if-else** construction. If

$$tmp == 0.0 \qquad\qquad 4–34$$

is true, the equal root calculations are performed. The remainder of the program consists of the **else** branch that is associated with the first **if** statement. Thus, when 4–34 is true, the remainder of the program is skipped.

If 4–34 is false, then the **else** branch associated with the first **if** statement is executed. The first statement of this branch is an **if** statement that tests if

$$tmp > 0.0 \qquad\qquad 4–35$$

is true. The second **if** statement is also part of an **if-else** construction. If 4–35 is true, the "two real roots" branch is executed. If 4–35 is false, the "complex roots" **else** branch is executed. Thus, this program performs the same calculations as are performed in the program in Figure 4–5. Notice how the indentation and comments make the program readable. To reiterate, you should always make every effort to make your programs clear and readable.

FIGURE 4–5 ■ A modification of Figure 4–4 that uses the **if-else** construction.

```
/* quadratic root solution */
#include <stream.h>
#include <math.h>
main()
{
    float a,b,c,root1,root2,tmp;
    cout << "\nEquation is a*x*x + b*x + c = 0\n";
    cout << "\nEnter a, b, and c\n";
    cin >> a >> b >> c;
    tmp = b*b - 4.0*a*c;
    if(tmp == 0.0)  {  //equal roots
        root1 = -b/(2.0*a);
        cout << "\nEqual roots are " << root1;
    } // end if(tmp == 0.0) start else
    else {
        if (tmp > 0.0)  {  //two real roots
            tmp = sqrt(tmp);
            root1 = (-b + tmp)/(2.0*a);
            root2 = (-b -tmp)/(2.0*a);
            cout << "\nRoots are " << root1 << " and " << root2;
        } //end if(tmp > 0.0) start else
        else    {  //complex roots
            tmp = -tmp;
            tmp = sqrt(tmp)/(2.0*a);
            cout << "\nRoots are " << -b/(2.0*a) << " + or - i" << tmp;
        }  // end end if(tmp > 0.0) else
    }  // end if(tmp == 0.0) else
}
```

4–4 ■ LOOPING

There are occasions when the same sequence of instructions is repeated many times. It would be tedious, and a potential source for typographical errors, to have to retype the sequence over and over again. In addition, because the number of required repetitions may vary depending upon the data that is used, simply repeating the instructions is not practical. C++ provides several instructions that provide the desired *looping*. We shall consider them here.

The first construction that we shall consider uses the keyword **for** and, for that reason, is called a *for loop*. The general form of the **for** loop construction is

$$\text{for(exp1;logical\_exp2;exp3)statement\_a;} \qquad \textbf{4–36}$$

The following occurs when the **for** loop is encountered in the program. First the expression **exp1** is executed. This is done only at the start of the loop; **exp1** is never executed again. Next, **logical_exp2**, which is called the *loop terminating condition*, is tested. If **logical_exp2** is false, **statement_a** is not executed, looping terminates, and the statement in the program following 4–36 is executed. If **logical_exp2** is true, **statement_a** is executed, and then **exp3** is executed. Next, **logical_exp2** is tested again, and the operation continues. Note that **statement_a** can be a compound statement that is executed once for each pass through the loop; **logical_exp2** is tested at the start of each pass through the loop; **exp3** is executed at the end of each pass through the loop.

Let us consider a program segment that illustrates looping. The following computes the sum of the first 10 integers. We assume that **item** and **sum** have been declared as integers.

sum = 0;	**4–37a**
for(item = 1;item<=10;item ++)sum = sum + item;	**4–37b**

First, **sum** is initialized to zero before the loop is entered. At the beginning of the **for** loop, **item** is assigned the value 1. The test,

$$item <= 10 \qquad\qquad \textbf{4–38}$$

is then performed. Because this is true,

$$sum = sum + item; \qquad\qquad \textbf{4–39}$$

is executed, and the value assigned to **sum** is now 1. At this point, the first pass through the loop is complete. Next,

$$item ++ \qquad\qquad \textbf{4–40}$$

is executed; **item** is assigned the value 2. Now control returns to the start of the loop, and test 4–38 is evaluated again. Because **item** is now assigned the value 2, the test again returns true, and the looping continues. Thus, after the next pass through the loop, **sum** will be assigned the value 3, and then **item** will be incremented. Looping will proceed until **item** is incremented to 11, after the tenth pass through the loop. Now when 4–38 is evaluated, the test fails, and looping ceases.

We have assumed that **logical_exp2** (see 4–36) was actually a logical expression. However, it could be an integer arithmetic expression because 0 is considered to be false, and, in most systems, any non-zero integer is considered to be true.

Figure 4–6 is a program that computes factorial **n**, using **for** looping. Factorial **n** is defined as the product of the integers 1 to **n**. That is,

$$n! = 1(2)(3)\ldots(n) \qquad\qquad \textbf{4–41}$$

In the program, the user inputs a value for **n**. The **for** loop consists of the single line

$$for(i = 2;i<=n;i ++) \; fact = fact * long(i); \qquad\qquad \textbf{4–42}$$

FIGURE 4–6 ■ A program that computes factorial **n**.

```
/* illustration of for looping */
#include <stream.h>
main()
{
    int i,n;
    long fact=1;
    cout << "\nProgram computes factorial n, enter n\n";
    cin >> n;
    for(i=2;i<=n;i++) fact = fact * long(i);
    cout << "\nfactorial " << n << " = " << fact;
}
```

The variable **fact** is initialized to 1 before the **for** loop in the program. On each pass through the loop, the value assigned to **fact** is multiplied by successively larger integers. Thus, when looping terminates, the desired factorial will be computed. Factorial **n** increases very rapidly as **n** increases. To allow **fact** to take on large values, we have declared **fact** to be **long**. Because **i** is of type **int**; it is converted to **long** in 4–42.

Another example of looping is shown in Figure 4–7a. This program computes the average of up to 1001 nonnegative numbers. The **for** loop is

for(int i = 0;i<=1000;i ++) {	4–43a
cout << "\nenter number ";	4–43b
cin >> data;	4–43c
if(data < 0.0)break;	4–43d
sum = sum + data;	4–44e
count++;	4–43f
} // end for(int i = 0;i<=1000;i ++)	4–43g

The program introduces the C++ keyword **break**. When **break** is executed, the loop that contains it terminates immediately. For instance, the loop 4–43 will loop 1001 times according to 4–43a. However (see 4–43d), if the user enters a negative number, **break** is executed, and looping terminates.

The variable **i**, which serves to count the number of times the loop has been executed, is declared as part of the **for** statement. It could have also been declared at the start of the program. The **for** statement is part of the block that contains it. Thus, the scope of **i** is from the point of its declaration to the end of the program. If **i** had been declared within the block 4–43b to 4–43f, its scope would have been only over that block.

In the program, **sum** and **count** are both initialized to zero. On each pass through the loop, **count** is incremented by 1, and the input value is added to **sum**. When a negative value is entered, neither of these operations takes place, and, instead, looping terminates. Next, the average is obtained by dividing **sum** by **count**.

FIGURE 4–7 ■ (a) A program that averages nonnegative numbers; (b) A modification of this program that uses an indefinite loop.

```
/* program averages nonnegative numbers */
#include <stream.h>
main( )
{
      int count=0;
      float ave,sum=0.0,data;
      for(int i=0;i<=1000;i++)   {
            cout << "\nenter number ";
            cin >> data;
            if(data < 0.0)break;
            sum = sum + data;
            count++;
      }   // end for(int i=1;i<1000;i++)
      ave = sum/(float)count;
      cout << "\naverage = " << ave;
}
```

(a)

```
/* program averages nonnegative numbers */
#include <stream.h>
main( )
{
      int count=0;
      float ave,sum=0.0,data;
      for( ; ; )   {
            cout << "\nenter number ";
            cin >> data;
            if(data < 0.0)break;
            sum = sum + data;
            count++;
      }   // end for( ; ; )
      ave = sum/(float)count;
      cout << "\naverage = " << ave;
}
```

(b)

Unless the user enters a negative number earlier, the program in Figure 4–7a always terminates after 1001 numbers have been entered. That is, it does not average an arbitrary number of entered numbers. A **for** loop can be made to loop indefinitely if its terminating condition is never met; for instance,

$$\text{for}(i = 1; i < 2; \ ) \qquad\qquad \textbf{4–44}$$

Here **i** is never incremented, and thus it will never become greater than 2; this loop will never terminate. Of course this assumes that the value of **i** is not changed within the body of the loop. A simpler procedure for obtaining a loop that never terminates is to make the test condition a positive number.

For instance,

$$\text{for}(\ ;1;\ ) \hspace{4cm} \textbf{4–45}$$

Another form of never-terminating **for** loop is one that begins with

$$\text{for}(\ ;\ ;\ ) \hspace{4cm} \textbf{4–46}$$

When you write a program with a loop that does not have conditions that cause termination, that program will run indefinitely. If this is not what is required, some form of termination, such as a **break** statement, should be built into the body of the loop. The program in Figure 4–7b is a modification of that in Figure 4–7a. The construction of 4–46 is used here.

The termination of the looping of the program in Figure 4–7b is based on a single logical condition. C++ provides other forms of looping that are directly related to this type of operation. The first that we shall consider is the *while loop*, which makes use of the keyword **while**. The general form of the **while** loop is

$$\text{while(logical\_expr)statement\_a;} \hspace{2.5cm} \textbf{4–47}$$

When the **while** statement is initially encountered, the **logical_expr** is evaluated. If it is false, no further action is taken, and the next statement in the program is executed. If the **logical__** is true, **statement_a**, which can be a compound statement, is executed. After execution is completed, **logical_expr** is evaluated again; if it is true, **statement_a** is executed, and looping continues as discussed. Looping terminates when the test of **logical_expr** results in the value false. Note that when the **while** loop is used, the test for continuation of looping occurs at the beginning of the loop.

In most **while** loops, the execution of **statement_a** will eventually change the result of the evaluation of **logical_expr**. If this is not the case, looping continues indefinitely, unless **statement_a** includes a break statement. (There are other statements that can terminate execution; we shall consider them subsequently.) The program in Figure 4–8 is an example of the use of a **while** loop. This is a modification of the averaging program in Figures 4–7a and 4–7b. The **while** loop is

```
while((cin >> data)&&(data >= 0.0))   {        4–48a
    sum = sum + data;                          4–48b
    count++;                                    4–48c
}   //end while((cin >> data)&&(data >=0.0))   4–48d
```

The looping condition is

$$(\text{cin} >> \text{data})\&\&(\text{data} >= 0.0) \hspace{2.5cm} \textbf{4–49}$$

FIGURE 4–8 ■ An illustration of a **while** loop.

```
/* program averages nonnegative numbers */
#include <stream.h>
main()
{
    int count=0;
    float ave,sum=0.0,data;
    cout << "\nenter numbers; terminate with -1\n";
    while((cin >> data)&&(data >= 0.0))  {
        sum = sum + data;
        count++;
    }  // end while((cin >> data)&&(data >= 0.0))
    ave = sum/(float)count;
    cout << "\naverage = " << ave;
}
```

The data input statement is incorporated into the test; i.e., the input of data is a side effect. It is often convenient to do this. There are two conditions that are tested. The first is the value returned by **cin**; **cin** returns true as long as the input does not fail. Although such tests should be used when reading from disk files, the inclusion of the test for **cin** is usually not necessary when there is a simple input of data from the terminal. (File manipulation will be discussed later in the book.) The test for **cin** is included in 4–49 so that new data can be read and tested as part of the **while** condition. Note that as soon as negative data is input, looping terminates because of the second part of the test 4–49. The remaining details of the program follow those of Figures 4–7a and 4–7b.

The looping condition for the **for** and **while** loops is tested at the beginning of each pass through the loop. C++ also provides a **do-while** construction, where the testing is performed at the end of each pass through the loop. Such a loop is called a *do loop* and uses the keywords *do* and *while*. The form of the **do-while** construction is

do	4–50a
statement_a	4–50b
while(logical_expr);	4–50c

When this construction is encountered, **statement_a**, which may be a compound statement, is executed. Then **logical_expr** is tested. If it is false, looping terminates, and the next statement in the program is executed. If **logical_expr** is true, then **statement_a** is executed again. Next, **logical_expr** is tested to determine if looping is to continue. **Statement_a** will always be executed at least once in the **do-while** construction. This is not the case in the **while** or **for** loops; in those cases, there would be no pass through the loop if the test condition is false when the loop is first encountered. It may seem as though a loop in which a statement would never be executed should never be written in the first place. However, the test condition might depend upon calculated values that, in turn, depend on entered data. Thus, there could be perfectly reasonable programs containing loops which, for certain data, would never be cycled.

The program in Figure 4–9 uses a **do-while** construction to compute the factorial. A **break** expression is used to terminate looping if the entered number is 0 or 1. Note that factorial 0 is defined as 1. The initial values of **fact** and **i** are 1 and 2, respectively. Note that **fact** is multiplied by **i** and then **i** is incremented. When the value of **i** becomes equal to **n + 1**, looping terminates.

The **break** operation can be applied to all types of looping. We shall expand upon this in the next section. When **break** is executed, looping terminates. There are occasions when it is necessary to terminate only the current pass through the loop, but not to terminate the loop completely. This is accomplished with the keyword **continue**. For instance, consider the following program sequence

while(a > b) {	4–51a
c = b + 1;	4–51b
if(c = 10)continue;	4–51c
d = c + a;	4–51d
b++;	4–51e
} // end while(a > b)	4–51f

Assume that **a** is greater than **b**. In that case, the loop cycles. If, on a particular pass through the loop, **c** is equal to 10, Statements 4–51d and 4–51e will *not* be executed. However, looping will continue. On successive passes through the loop, **c** will not equal 10 and, thus, all the statements of the loop will be executed. Looping will terminate completely when **b** becomes equal to or greater than **a**.

FIGURE 4–9 ■ An illustration of a **do-while** loop.

```
/* calculation of factorial */
#include <stream.h>
main()
{
    int i=2,n;
    long fact=1;
    cout << "\nProgram computes factorial n, enter n\n";
    cin >> n;
    do {
        if(n <= 1) break;
        fact = fact * long(i);
        i++;
    } while(i != n+1);
        cout << "\nfactorial " << n << " = " << fact;
}
```

4–5 ■ NESTED LOOPS

There are many programs in which a loop lies within another loop. Such *nested loops* are often very versatile. Each of the looping procedures discussed in the last section involved repeated execution of a statement. This statement often is a block, or a compound statement. If that block itself contains a loop, nested looping results. Note that an inner nested loop will always be *completely* contained within the outer loop that contains it. As an example of nested looping, consider the following construction.

for(i = 1;i<=10;i++) {	4–52a
statement_seq_a	4–52b
while(j<20)statement_b;	4–52c
statement_seq_c	4–52d
} // end for(i = 1;i<=10;i++)	4–52e

Expressions 4–52b and 4–52d represent sequences of zero or more statements; they are not necessarily compound statements. However, Statements 4–52b to 4–52d represent a single compound statement. Statements 4–52 illustrate a **while** loop nested within a **for** loop. There will be 10 passes through the outer **for** loop corresponding to the values **i** = 1, 2, 3, . . ., 10. Suppose that one statement in **statement_seq_a** sets **j** equal to 1 and that a statement in **statement_b** increments **j** by 1. On each pass through the **for** loop, **statement_seq_a** will be executed; next, the **while** loop will be encountered and executed. Each time that this occurs, **j** will be equal to 1 because it is set to that value in **statement_seq_a**. Hence, for this example **statement_b** will be executed 20 times corresponding to each of **j** =1, 2, . . ., 20 because **j** is incremented by 1 by **statement_b** for each pass through the **while** loop. The **while** loop will then terminate, and **statement_seq_c** will be executed. Now **i** will be incremented and tested. If **i** is less than or equal to 10, the loop will cycle again. After all the looping is complete, **statement_seq_a** and **statement_seq_c** will have been executed 10 times, while **statement_b** will have been executed 200 times. Remember that **statement_b** is executed 20 times for each pass through the **for** loop.

As an example of nested looping, we shall write a program that computes the Pythagorean triples. These are integers that could be sides of a right triangle; that is, they satisfy the equation,

$$i^2 + j^2 = k^2 \qquad \text{4–53}$$

The program is illustrated in Figure 4–10. There are two levels of nesting. The user enters the maximum value to be used for both **i** and **j**. The outer loop cycles **i** for values of 1 to **max**. The variable **ii** is assigned the value **i * i**, and the middle loop is executed. In this loop, the value of **j** is cycled from **i** + 1 to **max**. Note that if smaller values of **j** were used, duplicate triples would be found. For instance, (3,4,5) is a Pythagorean triple; so is (4,3,5). However,

FIGURE 4–10 ■ A program that uses nested loops to compute the Pythagorean triples.

```
/* program computes pythagorean triples */
#include <stream.h>
main()
{
    int i,j,k,ii,jj,kk,max;
    cout << "\nenter maximum for i and j\n";
    cin >> max;
    for(i=1;i<=max;i++)  {
        ii = i * i;
        for(j=i+1;j<=max;j++)  {
            jj = ii + j * j;
            kk = 1;
            k = j + 1;
            while(kk>0)  {
                kk = jj - k * k;
                if(kk == 0)  {
                    cout << "\n" << i << "   " << j << "   " << k;
                    break;
                } // end if(kk == 0)
                k++;
            }  // end while(kk>0)
        }  // end for(j=i+1;j<=max;j++)
    }  // end for(i=1;i<=max;i++)
}
```

these are essentially duplicate values. To speed the operation and reduce the amount of output data, duplicate values are not found by this program. The value of

$$jj = ii + j * j; \qquad\qquad 4\text{--}54$$

is then computed. Notice that **jj** corresponds to the left side of 4–53. An initial value of **j + 1** is established for **k**. Note that **k** must be larger than either **i** or **j**. The value of **kk** is assigned the value 1.

The inner loop is a **while** loop. The condition for looping is

$$kk > 0 \qquad\qquad 4\text{--}55$$

The reason that **kk** was assigned the value 1 in the middle loop was to ensure that the inner loop cycles at least once for each pass through the middle loop. The actual value of **kk** is computed in the inner loop. Its value is

$$kk = jj - k * k; \qquad\qquad 4\text{--}56$$

If **kk** is zero, then a Pythagorean triple has been found. If **kk** is greater than zero, it is possible that a larger value of **k** will yield a triple. On the other hand, if **kk** is negative, then larger values of **k** will not yield a triple for the particular values of **i** and **j**. Therefore, if **kk** is less than zero, the condition of the **while** statement fails, and the compound statement of the **while** construction is not executed. Next, **k** is incremented, and the **while** loop cycles again. If **kk** becomes negative, the **while** loop terminates, and the middle loop resumes cycling. Note that the **while** loop is the last "statement" of the middle loop.

If **kk** is zero, the condition of the **if** statement is true, and the compound statement of the **if** construction will be executed. The values of **i**, **j**, and **k** now correspond to a Pythagorean triple, and they are output. Next, the **break** statement is executed. This terminates the operation of the **while** loop. Now, the middle loop cycles again. After all loops have cycled completely, all Pythagorean triples for **i** and **j** less than or equal to **max** will be output.

Consider the operation of the **break** statement. When a **break** statement is executed, the operation of the innermost loop containing that **break** statement immediately ends. Any outer loops are not affected by the execution of the **break** statement. If there are three nested loops, and all of them are to be terminated, then there must be three separate **break** statements, one corresponding to each loop. For instance, the program in Figure 4–11 is a

FIGURE 4–11 ■ A modification of the program of Figure 4–10 that finds a single Pythagorean triple.

```
/* program computes first pythagorean triple in range */
#include <stream.h>
main()
{
    int i,j,k,ii,jj,kk,max,min,find=0;
    cout << "\nenter maximum for i and j\n";
    cin >> max;
    cout << "\nenter minimum for i and j\n";
    cin >> min;
    for(i=min;i<=max;i++)  {
        ii = i * i;
        for(j=i+1;j<=max;j++)  {
            jj = ii + j * j;
            kk = 1;
            k = j + 1;
            while(kk>0)  {
                kk = jj - k * k;
                if(kk == 0)  {
                    cout << "\n" << i << "   " << j << "   " << k;
                    find = 1;
                    break;
                } // end if(kk == 0)
                k++;
            }  // end while(kk>0)
            if(find == 1)break;  // end looping of j loop
        }  // end for(j=i+1;j<=max;j++)
        if(find ==1)break;  // end looping of i loop
    }  // end for(i=1;i<=max;i++)
}
```

modification of the program in Figure 4–10. Now the program terminates after the first Pythagorean triple is found. Note that the minimum, as well as the maximum, values of **i** and **j** are entered by the user. That is, the program searches for a triple where the values of **i** and **j** are greater than or equal to **min** and less than or equal to **max**.

The details of the program are very similar to those of Figure 4–10. Note that the variable **find** is initialized to 0. When a triple is found, its value is output, and **find** is set equal to 1. Next **break** is executed. Thus, the inner loop terminates. The middle loop continues its execution, so that the statement

$$\text{if(find == 1)break;} \qquad\qquad \textbf{4–57}$$

is executed. Because **find** now equals 1, **break** is again executed, and the operation of the middle loop is terminated. Operation of the outer loop continues. Still another statement of the form of 4–57 is immediately executed. Thus, the operation of the outer loop terminates, and the program ends as soon as a single Pythagorean triple is found. Note that three different **break** statements were executed to terminate the operation of the three loops.

4–6 ■ THE switch-case CONSTRUCTION

A C++ construction that makes use of the keywords **switch** and **case** is very convenient to use when a program has many branches. The general form of the **switch-case** construction is

```
switch(expr) {                              4–58a
    case const_expr_a: statement_a          4–58b
    case const_expr_b: statement_b          4–58c
    case const_expr_c: statement_c          4–58d
            .
            .
            .
    default: statement_def                  4–58e
}                                           4–58f
```

In this construction, the words **switch**, **case**, and **default** and the colon are entered exactly as written; **expr** represents an expression whose value can be computed, and **statement_a, statement_b, . . . , statement_def** are executable statements, which could be blocks. The **const_expr_a, const_expr_b, . . .** are constant expressions, i.e., expressions made up of constants. The **expr** and all the **const_expr**'s must be of the same type.

The operation of the **switch-case** construction is as follows: The expression **expr** is evaluated. If it is the same as **const_expr_a**, then

statement_a, **statement_b**, **statement_c**, ..., and **statement_def** will be executed. In this case, **expr** is said to *match* **const_expr_a**. If **expr** matches **const_expr_b**, then **statement_b**, **statement_c**, ..., and **statement_def** will be executed. Similarly, if **expr** matches **const_expr_c**, **statement_c**, ..., and **statement_def** will be executed. If **expr** does not match any of the **const_expr**'s, then only **statement_def** will be executed. In general, all the statements of the **switch-case** expression starting with the first match will be executed. If there is no match, and the default statement and **default:** are present, then **statement_def** is executed. If there is no match and no default provision is made, no action will be taken. After the execution of the **switch-case** construction is complete, the next statement in the program is executed. No two **const_expr**'s may have the same value.

If a **break** statement is executed, the **switch-case** operation terminates, and the statement following the **switch-case** construction in the program is executed. In typical **switch-case** constructions, each of the statements **statement_a**, **statement_b**, ..., **statement_def** are compound statements whose last statement is **break**. In this case, if **expr** matches **constant_expr_a**, then only **statement_a** will be executed. Similarly, if **expr** matches **constant_expr_b**, then only **statement_b** will be executed, and so forth. That is, only the block of statements corresponding to a specific **const_expr** is executed because the **break** statement transfers control to the next statement following the **switch-case** construction. This is analogous to **break** transferring control out of a loop.

A program illustrating the **switch-case** construction is shown in Figure 4–12. Note that there are four choices specified: 1, 2, 3, and 5. If 1 is entered by the user of the program, the sequence of statements,

b = 7;	4–59a
cout << "\nchoice 1; b = " << b;	4–59b
break;	4–59c

is executed. After the **break** statement is executed, control exits the **switch-case** construction.

If the user enters 2, the operation is somewhat different. In this case, the sequence of statements

b = 9;	4–60a
cout << "\nchoice = 2; b = " << b;	4–60b
b = 15;	4–60c
cout << "\nchoice = 3; b = " << b;	4–60d
break;	4–60e

will be executed. Because there is no **break** before the start of the **case** 3 statements, operation continues, and 4–60c to 4–60e are executed. When 4–60e is executed, operation of the **switch-case** construction ends. If the user

FIGURE 4–12 ■ An example of the **switch-case** construction.

```
/* an example of the switch-case construction */
#include <stream.h>
main()
{
        int choice,b;
        cout << "\nEnter choice 1, 2, 3, or 5\n";
        cin >> choice;
        switch(choice)    {
            case 1:
                b = 7;
                cout << "\nchoice 1; b = "  << b;
                break;
            case 5:
                b = 20;
                cout << "\nchoice 5; b = " << b;
                break;
            case 2:
                b = 9;
                cout << "\nchoice 2; b = "  << b;
                // note that break statement is not present
            case 3:
                b = 15;
                cout << "\nchoice 3; b = " << b;
                break;
            default:
                cout << "\nwrong entry";
                break;
        }  // end switch-case
}
```

enters 3, Statements 4–60c to 4–60d are executed. Note that it is not necessary to list the various **case** options in numerical order.

The expression **expr** of 4–58a can be any expression of the proper type. For instance, the first line of the **switch-case** construction of the program in Figure 4–12 could be

$$\text{switch(choice + a)} \ \{ \qquad\qquad 4\text{–}61$$

where **a** is an integer variable (or constant) whose value had been assigned previously in the program.

The constant expressions can be expressions. However, they must be constants. For instance, the following is valid

$$\text{case } 5+c: \qquad\qquad 4\text{–}62$$

only if **c** has been declared to be a constant.

The **case** constant expressions need not be integers. Figure 4–13 is a modification of Figure 4–12 where characters are used to choose a particular

FIGURE 4–13 ■ A modification of the program of Figure 4–12 that uses a character for the **case** constant expression.

```
/* an example of the switch-case construction */
#include <stream.h>
main()
{
    int b;
    char choice;
    cout << "\nEnter choice a, b, c, or e\n";
    cin >> choice;
    switch(choice)    {
        case 'a':
            b = 7;
            cout << "\nchoice a; b = "  << b;
            break;
        case 'e':
            b = 20;
            cout << "\nchoice e; b = " << b;
            break;
        case 'b':
            b = 9;
            cout << "\nchoice b; b = "  << b;
            // note that break statement is not present
        case 'c':
            b = 15;
            cout << "\nchoice c; b = " << b;
            break;
        default:
            cout << "\nwrong entry";
            break;
    }   // end switch-case
}
```

branch of the **case** construction. In this case, the variable choice is declared to be of type **char**, and the constant expressions are written as character constants. Note that these are enclosed in single quotes.

Enumerated types can be used as the constant expressions in the **switch-case** construction. Remember that these are actually synonyms for integers.

4–7 ■ BITWISE OPERATIONS

C++ provides operators that manipulate the individual bits of the binary representation of integers. These operators allow C++ to perform operations that might ordinarily be done in assembly languages. If you are not familiar with, or do not care about, such operations, this section can be skipped. They will not be required for the rest of the book.

In this section we consider that integers are represented in binary form. We also assume that the reader is familiar with AND, OR, and XOR operations as performed on the individual bits of binary integers; they are discussed only briefly. Binary numbers consist of sequences of 0s and 1s. When a bitwise AND operation is performed on the binary representations of two numbers, a third binary number is generated. Each digit of the result is formed by performing an AND operation on the corresponding bits of the original numbers. The AND operation is such that if both bits are 1, the result is 1; if either, or both, of the bits of the original numbers is 0, the result is 0. When a bitwise OR is performed, if either or both of the bits of the original numbers is 1, then the result is 1; if both bits are 0, the result is 0. The XOR operation is such that if both bits of the original numbers are 1, or both bits are 0, the result is 0; if one bit is 1 and the other is 0, then the result is 1.

The C++ symbol for bitwise AND is **&**. For instance, consider the following statement.

$$c = a \mathrel{\&} b; \hspace{4cm} \textbf{4–63}$$

where we assume that **a**, **b**, and **c** are of type **int** and that values have been assigned to **a** and **b**. When (4–63) is executed, **c** will be assigned the number that results when the AND operation is applied to corresponding bits of **a** and **b**. Note that although numbers are stored in binary form, they are usually input and output in decimal form. For instance, the values entered for **a** and **b** could have been 34 and 56.

The C++ symbols for OR and XOR are | and ∧, respectively. The form of their use is the same as that described previously for **&**.

Two other operations commonly performed on binary numbers are shifting bits to the right or left. For instance, if the binary number

$$1011 \hspace{5cm} \textbf{4–64}$$

is shifted three bits to the left, the resultant number is

$$1011000 \hspace{4.5cm} \textbf{4–65}$$

Note that a three-bit left shift is equivalent to multiplying the number by 8_{10}. When a number is left shifted, it is padded on the right with zeros. When a number is right shifted, its rightmost bits are lost. For instance, if the number 1011 is right shifted three bits, the number 1 results.

In C++ the operators for left shift and right shift are ≪ and ≫, respectively. Note that these symbols are also used for stream output and input. The C++ compiler will recognize the appropriate operator by the context. The form of the use of the shift operators is

$$c = a \gg n; \hspace{4cm} \textbf{4–66}$$
$$d = a \ll n; \hspace{4cm} \textbf{4–67}$$

When these are executed, **c** is assigned the number formed when **a** is right shifted by **n** bits. Similarly, **d** is assigned the value of the number formed when **a** is left shifted by **n** bits.

Another operation often performed on a binary number is taking its *one's complement*. This involves replacing each 1 in the binary number with a 0 and each 0 with a 1. The C++ one's complement operator is ~. For instance, when

$$c = {\sim}a;\hspace{6cm}\textbf{4-68}$$

is executed, **c** is assigned the one's complement of **a**.

The program in Figure 4–14a illustrates bitwise operations. Notice that the user enters two decimal numbers. The various operations that we have discussed are performed, and the results are output. Formatted output is used so that the output can be in hexadecimal form. A typical input and output for this program is shown in Figure 4–14b.

FIGURE 4–14 ■ (a) A program that performs some bitwise operations; (b) the output for a simple run of the program.

```
/* bitwise manipulations */
#include <stream.h>
main( )
{
    int a,b,c;
    cout << "\nenter a and b\n";
    cin >> a >> b;
    c = a & b;
    cout << form("\na = %x   b = %x\na AND b = %x",a,b,c);
    c = a | b;
    cout << form("\na OR b = %x",c);
    c = a ^ b;
    cout << form("\na XOR b = %x",c);
    c = a >> 3;
    cout << form("\na right shifted by 3 = %x",c);
    c = a << 3;
    cout << form("\na left shifted by 3 = %x",c);
    c = ~a;
    cout << form("\none's complement of a = %x",c);
}
```

(a)

```
enter a and b
234
567


a = ea   b = 237
a AND b = 22
a OR b = 2ff
a XOR b = 2dd
a right shifted by 3 = 1d
a left shifted by 3 = 750
one's complement of a = ff15
```

(b)

When any of the operations discussed in this section are performed on a variable, and the result is assigned to the same variable, C++ provides a shorthand notation for the operation. The first and second statements in each of the following pairs of operations are equivalent:

$$
\begin{array}{ll}
\text{a \&= b;} & \text{4–69a} \\
\text{a = a \& b;} & \text{4–69b}
\end{array}
$$

$$
\begin{array}{ll}
\text{a |= b;} & \text{4–70a} \\
\text{a = a | b;} & \text{4–70b}
\end{array}
$$

$$
\begin{array}{ll}
\text{a ^= b} & \text{4–71a} \\
\text{a = a ^ b;} & \text{4–71b}
\end{array}
$$

$$
\begin{array}{ll}
\text{a >>= n;} & \text{4–72a} \\
\text{a = a >> n;} & \text{4–72b}
\end{array}
$$

$$
\begin{array}{ll}
\text{a <<= n;} & \text{4–73a} \\
\text{a = a << n;} & \text{4–73b}
\end{array}
$$

These are analogous to the operations performed with addition, subtraction, multiplication, and division.

4–8 ■ HIERARCHY—SOME ADDITIONAL TOPICS

There are times when a variable is to be assigned one of two values depending upon some logical condition. This *conditional assignment* can be achieved with the **if-else** construction. However, C++ includes special operators that reduce the amount of writing required. The conditional assignment makes use of the **?** and **:** operators. The form of their use is

$$
\text{var = logical\_expr ? expr1 : expr2;} \qquad \textbf{4–74}
$$

The **=**, **?**, and **:** are written exactly as shown. If **logical_expr** is true, then **expr1** is evaluated, and the result is assigned to **var**. If **logical_expr** is false, **expr2** is evaluated, and the result is assigned to **var**. Note that both **logical_expr** and one of *either* **expr1** *or* **expr2** are always evaluated. In particular, both **expr1** and **expr2** will never be evaluated. This is of importance if there are side effects to either, or both, of **expr1** and **expr2**. Note that **logical_expr** may be an integer expression because in most systems, 0 represents false, while any other number represents true. Conditional assignment is also known as the *arithmetic if*.

Figure 4–15 contains a simple program that utilizes conditional assignment. The user enters two integers and a character. If the character is +, then **ans** is assigned the sum of the two entered numbers. On the other hand, if the character is not +, then the two numbers are multiplied.

FIGURE 4–15 ■ An illustration of conditional assignment.

```
/* an illustration of conditional assignment */
#include <stream.h>
main()
{
    char ch;
    int ans,i1,i2;
    cout << "\nEnter two integers\n";
    cin >> i1 >> i2;
    cout << "\nEnter + to add any other character to multiply\n";
    cin >> ch;
    ans = (ch == '+') ? i1 + i2 : i1 * i2;
    cout << "\nAnswer = " << ans;
}
```

Hierarchy

In Section 3–4 we discussed the hierarchy of arithmetic operators. Since then, we have introduced many additional operators and they have a hierarchy as well. Table 4–1 lists the hierarchies of all of the operators that we have considered. The operators in the table are arranged in 14 groups. Operators in the same group have the same hierarchy; the first grouping has the highest hierarchy, and so on. The rules of hierarchy can be modified by the use of parentheses. This follows the discussions in Section 3–4. Indeed, even if they do not affect the operation of the program, parentheses should be included if they make the statement more readable. Parentheses should always be used for clarity when two operators are adjacent, even if they are not required by the C++ compiler.

Sometimes a statement involving several contiguous operators may appear to be ambiguous. For instance, consider the expression

$$c = i*++i; \qquad\qquad \textbf{4–75}$$

Suppose that, prior to the execution of 4–75, **i** was assigned the value 7. When Expression 4–75 is evaluated, the value stored in memory for **i** is read and used in the calculation. Because the same variable appears twice in the statement, its value is read twice from memory. The following question then arises: is the value of the **i** to the left read before the value of the **i** to the right is read and incremented? If the answer to this question is yes, then **c** is assigned the value 7*8 = 56. On the other hand, if the **i** on the right is read and incremented before the **i** to the left is read from memory, **c** is assigned the value 8*8 = 64. The compiler, however, is not confused. It uses the following rules. All operators except the unary operators and the assignment operators are *left associative*. The unary and assignment operators are *right associative*. Left associativity means that an expression is scanned from left to right at each hierarchy level to determine the values of the variables. Thus, for 4–75,

TABLE 4–1 ■ Hierarchy of Operators Considered Thus Far

sizeof	

++	increment
−−	decrement
−	unary
+	unary
&	address of
*	dereference
new	allocate space
delete	deallocate space
~	complement
!	not
( )	cast

*	multiply
/	divide
%	remainder

+	addition
−	subtraction

<<	shift left
>>	shift right

<=	less than or equal to
<	less than
>=	greater than or equal to
>	greater than

the **i** to the left is replaced by 7 in the calculation, while the **i** to the right is replaced by 8.

As a practical matter, Statement 4–75 is *extremely poor form*. Such compact statements can lead to subtle, hard-to-find bugs and should never be used. It would be far better form to define an additional variable and rewrite 4–75 as the sequence

$$tmp = i;$$ 4–76a
$$c = tmp * (++i)$$ 4–76b

It would be even clearer to write

$$tmp = i;$$ 4–77a
$$i++;$$ 4–77b
$$c = tmp * i;$$ 4–77c

TABLE 4–1 ■ **(continued)**

==	equal
!=	not equal
&	bitwise AND
^	bitwise XOR
|	bitwise OR
&&	logical AND
||	logical OR
? :	conditional assignment
==	assignment
+=	add and assign
−=	subtract and assign
*=	multiply and assign
/=	divide and assign
%=	remainder and assign
<<=	shift left and assign
>>=	shift right and assign
&=	bitwise AND and assign
|=	bitwise OR and assign
^=	bitwise XOR and assign
,	comma, used as separator

Remember that shortcut operations should not be used if they reduce the readability of your program.

4–9 ■ THE goto CONSTRUCTION

We shall now discuss the **goto** statement, which can be used to transfer control to any point in a program of the type that we have considered. (The **goto** statement cannot be used to transfer control from one program to a library function or function that you write yourself. Such functions will be discussed in the next chapter.) The **goto** construction consists of the keyword **goto** and a *label*. Although the **goto** construction is very powerful, its misuse results in programs that are extremely difficult to debug. Modern procedures often stress *gotoless programming*. In general, you should avoid the use of the **goto** construction in almost every circumstance. We include a discussion of it here for completeness. Additionally, there are some rare occasions when the **goto** construction is helpful and, in fact, should be used.

The form of the use of **goto** is

$$goto\ foo; \hspace{6cm} \textbf{4-78}$$

The identifier **foo** is a label. The rules for choosing a label name are the same as those for choosing a variable name. A variable and a label, however, should not have the same name. Although there can be several labels in a program, no two labels can have the same name. When 4–78 is executed, control jumps to the executable statement following the label. The label name in the program is followed by a colon. For instance, consider the program sequence

a = 3;	**4–79a**
foo:	**4–79b**
a++;	**4–79c**
b = a + 2;	**4–79d**
if(a < 7)goto foo;	**4–79e**
c = d + 2;	**4–79f**

The first time this sequence is executed, the label **foo:** will be ignored. The first time 4–79e is executed, **a** is less than 7, and the **goto** statement is executed. Now, control will jump to the statement following the label. Thus, 4–79c, 4–79d and 4–79e will be executed a second time. At this point, **a** is still less than 7, and the procedure will be repeated. When **a** becomes greater than or equal to 7, the **goto** statement will not be executed, and 4–79f will be executed for the first time.

The label can precede or follow the **goto** statement in the program. A single program can have any number of **goto** statements. More than one **goto** statement can reference the same label, but no two labels may have the same name in a single program. It is possible to write programs with **goto** statements where the control loops back over itself like a pretzel. It is easy to become confused about the logic of such programs, and very nasty bugs can develop. *Avoid the use of **goto** constructions.*

The **goto** construction can be used if it is very straightforward *and if it would be very tedious* to use another construction. For instance, a **goto** statement can terminate looping by transferring control outside the loop. If there is only a single loop, then the **goto** should not be used; the **break** statement should be used instead. Suppose, however, that there are many levels of nested looping. A separate **break** statement would be required for each level of nesting while a single **goto** statement would suffice to terminate all looping. The program in Figure 4–11 used three **break** statements to terminate looping. In Figure 4–16 we have rewritten that program using a single **goto** statement to terminate all looping. Note that once a single Pythagorean triple is found

$$goto\ ender; \hspace{6cm} \textbf{4-80}$$

FIGURE 4–16 ■ An illustration of the **goto** construction. Remember that the use of **goto** should be avoided.

```
/* program uses goto */
/* ****** remember goto construction should be avoided ****** */
#include <stream.h>
main()
{
    int i,j,k,ii,jj,kk,max,min;
    cout << "\nenter maximum for i and j\n";
    cin >> max;
    cout << "\nenter minimum for i and j\n";
    cin >> min;
    for(i=min;i<=max;i++)  {
        ii = i * i;
        for(j=i+1;j<=max;j++)  {
            jj = ii + j * j;
            kk = 1;
            k = j + 1;
            while(kk>0)  {
                kk = jj - k * k;
                if(kk == 0)  {
                    cout << "\n" << i << "    " << j << "    " << k;
                    goto ender;  // terminate three loops
                } // end if(kk == 0)
                k++;
            }  // end while(kk>0)
        }  // end for(j=i+1;j<=max;j++)
    }  // end for(i=1;i<=max;i++)
    ender:  // label
    ;   // null statement
}
```

is executed and, because the label **ender:** lies just outside the end of all three loops, looping terminates.

The statement following a label must be an executable statement. Logically, no executable statement need follow **ender:** in the program in Figure 4–16. The C++ syntax, however, requires it. Although a dummy statement such as **i = 3;** could be added following the label, C++ allows *null statements*. These are executable statements that have no text and do nothing. In Figure 4–16 the statement

;   **4–81**

that precedes the closing brace is a null statement that satisfies the requirement that an executable statement follow a label.

We conclude this section by reiterating: do not use the **goto** construction unless it is a very straightforward operation, and if the use of some other construction would require very many additional statements to be written. The use of **goto** has been widely studied. It is found that eliminating **goto** constructions from programs substantially reduces the numbers of errors that occur and makes those errors that do occur easier to correct.

4-10 ■ A BASIC DISCUSSION OF STRUCTURED PROGRAMMING

When you start to write a program, it is not a good idea to sit down at the keyboard and start entering C++ statements, or statements in any other programming language for that matter. Instead, you should develop the logic of the program. This logic is called an *algorithm*. Because the algorithm consists only of the logic, without the specific programming details, you do not have to concern yourself with the specifics of the programming language. Once the algorithm is written, the programming details can be added.

Let us illustrate these ideas by writing the algorithm for the Pythagorean triple program in Figure 4–10.

```
enter maximum value n
loop for values of i from 1 to n
    calculate ii = i * i
    loop for values of j from i + 1 to n
        calculate jj = ii + j * j
        initialize k = j + 1
        initialize kk
        loop while kk >= 0                              4–82
            kk = jj − k * k
            if kk == 0
                print i, j, and k then exit inner loop
            increment k
        end inner (k) loop
    end middle (j) loop
end outer (i) loop
```

Note that 4–82 expresses the ideas of the program in Figure 4–10. However, 4–82 contains none of the details required by C++. Indeed, this algorithm could be used to write a Pythagorean triple program in many of the different programming languages. Remember that the algorithm contains only the logic of the program, not its details. When you write complicated programs, you should establish the algorithm before you get involved with the details of programming.

A program is set up to perform a task. When the task is complex, many different algorithms, each of which achieves the same results, can be written. A different program can be written for each algorithm. It has been found that the number of logical bugs that occur is related to the form of the program. Structured programs have far fewer bugs than do those programs that are not structured; those bugs that do occur in structured programs are easier to find than are bugs in nonstructured programs. One of the prime rules of structured programming is to avoid **goto** statements. In fact, some people call structured programs **goto**less programs.

Programs should be written so that they are easy to read and understand. The variable names should be chosen so that they are self-explanatory. For instance, choose the name **velocity** rather than **v**. Comments should be distributed throughout a program so that the ideas of the operations are explained. Such programs are said to be *self-documentating*. Writing self-documentating programs will not only help other people who read your programs, but will also help you when you come back to your programs after putting them aside for a time. Of course, each individual statement should be written to be readable. Remember that shorthand notation that reduces the understandability of the program should be avoided.

If programs are to be run by others, especially those who are not experienced, there should be written documentation that explains what the program does and how the program is to be run. The documentation should be clearly written and contain numerous examples. Primarily, of course, the program itself should be self-explanatory. The person running the program should be guided through the steps that he or she must perform by appropriate prompts. Documentation should also clearly indicate any of the peripheral equipment that is necessary. For instance, printers or modems might be required. All specifications for these devices should be given so that the person running the program does not have to resort to a trial and error procedure to make the program work.

When programs are written and documented properly, they contain few logical bugs. Those that do occur are relatively easy to find; the program is easily run by users. Such programs will be successful and widely used.

EXERCISES

Check any programs that you write by running them on your computer.

1. Write a program that accepts two integers and outputs a 0 if the first number is greater than the second number; otherwise, a non-zero number is output.
2. Write a program that accepts three integers and outputs a number other than 0 if the first input integer is equal to the second and greater than the third number; a 0 should be output otherwise.
3. Write a program that accepts three integers and outputs a number other than 0 if the first input integer is equal to the second or greater than the third.
4. What is meant by a *side effect*?
5. Write a program that accepts four input characters and outputs the one that is alphabetically first.
6. Repeat Exercise 5, but now output the character that is alphabetically last.
7. Write a program that is used to compute a student's letter grade. Three numerical grades are to be entered and their average computed. If the average is greater than 90, the assigned grade is A; if the average is less

than 90 and greater than or equal to 80, the grade is B; if the average is less than 80 and greater than or equal to 70, the grade is C; if the average is less than 70 and greater than or equal to 60, the grade is D; if the average is less than 60, the grade is F. Do not use looping in the program.

8. Repeat Exercise 7, but now use a **for** loop to compute the average.

9. Repeat Exercise 8, but now have the number of test grades entered by the person running the program.

10. Repeat Exercise 8 with an arbitrary number of tests. The program is to prompt for an additional grade until a negative number is entered for a grade.

11. Repeat Exercise 10, but now use a **while** loop.

12. Modify the program of Exercise 10 so that grades can be entered for an arbitrary number of students. The person running the program is to be asked if he or she wants to run the program again. If the answer is not Y or y, the program is to terminate; otherwise, it should repeat. Use nested **for** loops that cycle indefinitely.

13. Repeat Exercise 12, but now use **while** loops.

14. Repeat Exercise 12, but now use **do** loops.

15. Write a program that computes the function

$$f = 2.0x + 3.0xy + y^2$$

for the following values of **x** and **y**:

$$x = 0.0, 0.1, 0.2, \ldots, 2.0$$
$$y = 1.0, 1.1, 1.2, \ldots, 4.0$$

16. Modify the program in Figure 4–10 so that values of **n** greater than 200 can be used.

17. Write a program that accepts two numbers. The user is then presented with a menu of options that specifies:

> 1 add the numbers
> 2 subtract the numbers
> 3 multiply the numbers
> 4 divide the numbers

In response, the person running the program enters 1, 2, 3, or 4, and the sum, difference, product, or quotient is output. If a number other than 1, 2, 3, or 4 is entered, the phrase "wrong input" is to be output and the program should terminate. The program is to terminate after any output. Use the **switch-case** construction.

18. Repeat Exercise 17. Now if a number other than 1, 2, 3, or 4 is entered in response to the menu, the user is to be prompted for an appropriate response. Hint: Include the **switch-case** construction within a loop.

19. Write a program that accepts an integer. The output is to be another integer whose binary representation is the same as that of the entered integer except that all bits except the first, third, and fifth are replaced by 0s.

20. Use *conditional assignment* to output the greater of two entered integers.

21. Repeat Exercise 10; now use a combination of **if** and **goto** statements to implement the looping.

22. Why is it poor form to use **goto**'s in most programs?

23. Describe the procedures used to write a *self-documenting program*.

CHAPTER 5
Functions

Very often, the same calculations are repeated several times in a single program. It would be a waste of time, and an additional opportunity for typographical errors, if the C++ statements had to be repeated at each point in the program where those calculations were made. In addition, the same calculations might be repeated in many different programs. It would be desirable to write the C++ instructions needed to carry out the desired operations only once, and then use those instructions in many programs. C++ provides the programmer with the ability to write *functions* for this purpose. We have already encountered library functions that are provided with C++ systems. In this chapter we shall discuss procedures that allow programmers to write their own functions.

Functions are also used to break long complex programs into short modules. Such short modules are more easily written and debugged than is a single, long program. In addition, the use of functions allows a long programming task to be divided among several programmers, each of whom writes one or more functions. Ultimately, the functions are combined into a single program.

5–1 ■ FUNCTIONS

In this section we consider some of the basic ideas involved in writing functions. When a program uses a function, that program is said to *call* the function. One program can call a function, and that function can, in turn, call other functions. The first program is called the *main* program. That is why we have started each C++ program with **main**(). In the discussions of this section we assume that the main program is calling a function.

The calling program can provide the function with values; such values are said to be *passed* to the function. These values are often the values assigned to variables. However, other values, such as the address of a variable or a string, can also be passed to functions. In many circumstances, the function calculates a value and sends it back to the calling program; such values are said to be *returned* to the main program.

The first line of a function includes the type of the value returned by the function, followed by the name of the function, followed by a list of variable names and their types enclosed in parentheses and separated by commas. The list is called a *formal parameter list*. (Actually, the formal parameter list can contain items other than variable names; this is discussed in the next section.) The first line of a function that averages three numbers might be

float average_three(float test1,float test2,float test3)   5–1

When a function *returns* or provides a value to the calling program, the type of that value must be declared. This is done by preceding the name of the function by the name of the type. In example 5–1, **average_three** returns a number of type **float**. Thus, the name of the function is preceded by **float** in 5–1.

The formal parameter list of 5–1 includes the names of three variables: **test1**, **test2**, and **test3**. This signifies that the function is to be passed three values, and that these values will be stored in three variables called **test1**, **test2**, and **test3**. The type of each of these variables is specified in the formal parameter list: i.e., each variable name is preceded by its type. In this case, each variable is of type **float**; therefore the word **float** precedes each variable in the formal parameter list. The formal parameter list has declared three variables that can be used throughout the function, on either side of an assignment.

Figure 5–1 illustrates the use of the **average_three** function. There are two parts to this figure: the main program and the function. We shall start by considering the function and then discuss the main program. The function is illustrated in Figure 5–1b. The function name, or *function definition*, is the same as 5–1. That is, the function is called **average_three**; it returns a value of type **float**; there are three variables in the formal parameter list, which are all of type **float**.

An opening brace follows the function definition. From this point on, the function looks very much like a program. We shall discuss the differences as we proceed. When the function is called by the main program, values are supplied for **test1**, **test2**, and **test3**. These variables are assigned the supplied values.

The average is computed by adding the values assigned to **test1**, **test2**, and **test3** and dividing the resulting sum by 3.0. In a main program, this value would be output. However, for the function we are writing, the value is to be returned to the main program. The keyword **return** is used for this purpose. When **return** is executed, the operation of the function ceases, and control returns to the main program. If a variable or constant follows the word **return**, the current value of that variable or constant is returned to the

FIGURE 5-1 ■ A simple illustration of the use of a function. (a) The main program; (b) the function.

```
/* main program */
#include <stream.h>
main()
{
    extern float average_three(float,float,float);
    float g1,g2,g3,ave;
    cout << "\nenter three grades\n";
    cin >> g1 >> g2 >> g3;
    ave = average_three(g1,g2,g3);
    cout << "\naverage = " << ave;
}
```

(a)

```
/* function called by main program */
float average_three(float test1,float test2,float test3)
{
    float average;
    average = (test1 + test2 + test3)/3.0;
    return average;
}
```

(b)

main program. In Figure 5-1, the value of **average** is returned to the main program.

Now consider the main program of Figure 5-1a. Every function used in a program must be declared in that program. The type of the value returned by the function is declared by preceding the function name with that type. The type(s) of the values passed to the function must be declared as well. These values are termed the *arguments* of the function. In this case, all the arguments are of type **float**. Thus, the declaration of the function in the main program is

$$\text{extern float average\_three(float,float,float);} \qquad 5\text{-}2$$

Note the keyword **extern**; this signifies that the function may be in a different place from the main program. Actually, functions and main programs are stored in disk files. Sometimes both the main program and the function are stored in the same file; in this case, the word **extern** could be omitted from 5-2. Often, however, functions and main programs are written at different times, and are stored in different files. In such cases, the word **extern** is required. It is included in 5-2 for generality.

The values of the three grades to be averaged are entered and stored in **g1**, **g2**, and **g3**. The function **average_three** is called using the statement

$$\text{ave} = \text{average\_three(g1,g2,g3);} \qquad 5\text{-}3$$

The function is called simply by writing its name. The returned value will replace the function in the assignment. Thus, after 5–3 is executed, **ave** will be assigned the desired average. The arguments **g1**, **g2**, and **g3** represent the values assigned to the variables. Note that the function is passed the actual *values* assigned to the variables, not their addresses, so the function cannot change the values assigned to **g1**, **g2**, or **g3** in the main program. We shall see how to accomplish this in the next section.

The variables of the function are different from those of the main program. This would be true even if they had the same names. The scope of the variables declared in the main program does not cover the function, and the scope of the variables declared in the function does not cover the main program. When the program is compiled, space is reserved for the variables of the main program, and there is a block of space that can be used by functions, but no space is reserved for the particular variables of the functions called by the program. Memory locations used by the variables of a function are reserved when the function is *called*. After the execution of the function is complete, this memory space is released, and it can be used by other functions. We have not considered all the details of variables here. We shall consider this subject in greater detail subsequently.

The fact that the variables in functions are different from those in the main program is of great importance. When a programmer writes a function, he or she probably does not know the names of the variables in the programs that will call the function. Because functions may be used by many different programs, the programmer probably does not even know which program will call the function. If the names of the variables of the function could conflict with those in the main program, it would be impractical to write functions. Fortunately, this is not the case, and variables in functions can be completely isolated from those in the calling programs.

We have indicated that the type of the function must be declared both in its first line and in the calling program. If the function returns type **int**, this declaration is not necessary because type **int** is the default. For instance, if the function **average_three** of Figure 5–1 returned a value of type **int**, the word **float** could be replaced by **int** following the word **extern** in the main program, and the word **float** could be replaced by **int** in the first line of the function. Alternatively, because **int** is the default, the type declaration could be omitted in both places. However, it is better programming practice to include it because it clarifies the program for readers.

It is possible to write functions that accept no arguments. It is also possible to write functions that return no values. As an example, the program in Figure 5–2 contains a function that averages an arbitrary number of non-zero grades and outputs the results. The function takes care of both the input and output of the data. The main program's only purpose is to call the function.

Because the compiler expects to know the type of the function's returned value, a special type is established to indicate that no value is returned; it is called **void**. Note the declaration in the main program

FIGURE 5–2 ■ An example of a function that returns no value and is passed no argument. (a) The main program; (b) the function.

```
/* main program */
#include <stream.h>
main()
{
    extern void average();
    average();
}
```

(a)

```
/* function called by main program */
void average()
{
    float sum=0.0,ave,tmp;
    int count=0;
    cout << "\nenter grades, terminate with negative number\n";
    while((cin >> tmp) &&(tmp >= 0.0))    {
        sum = sum + tmp;
        count++;
    }  // end while((cin >> tmp) && (tmp >= 0.0))
    ave = sum/(float)count;
    cout << "\naverage = " << ave;
    return;
}
```

(b)

extern void average();   5–4

The word **void** indicates that the function returns no value. The empty parentheses indicate that no arguments are passed to the function. Note that the parentheses *must* be included, even if they are empty. They signify that average is a function, rather than a variable.

The first line of the function is

void average()   5–5

This declares that the function does not return a value. The empty parentheses indicate that the formal parameter list is empty; thus, no arguments are passed to the function.

In the discussion of this section, all the arguments to the functions were actual values; that is, data was supplied to the function. This is called *pass by value*. Although each argument to a function was a variable, the function was passed only the value currently assigned to that variable. The function, therefore, could not modify the value of a variable in the main program even though that variable appears as an argument to the function. For instance, in the main program of Figure 5–1a, the function is called with **g1**, **g2**, and **g3** as arguments. The function, however, knows nothing about these variables or where they are stored in memory; all the function knows is the current numeric value assigned to each variable that is passed to it when the main program calls the function. Thus, the function cannot alter the values assigned to these variables in the main program. In the next section we shall consider passing a variable's *address* to a function. When this is done, the function can actually modify the value assigned to a variable in the calling program.

5–2 ■ ARGUMENT PASSING: PASS BY VALUE; PASS BY REFERENCE

In the last section we discussed pass by value, where the arguments to the function were values assigned to variables. In fact, constants could be passed in this manner as well. For instance, this is a valid call to the function **average_three** of Figure 5–1.

$$average\_three(x,95.0,y); \hspace{3cm} \textbf{5–6}$$

where **x** is a variable of type **float**, **y** is a constant of type **float**, and the second argument is a numerical constant.

As noted in the last section, when values are passed by value, the function has no knowledge of the address of any of its arguments and therefore cannot change the value of any variable in the main program. This is often desirable. Sometimes, however, it would be desirable for a function to be able to change values in the main program. For example, although a function can return only a single value, there are occasions when several values calculated by a function are required by the calling program. If the function could change values in the calling program, then, in effect, more than one calculated value could be returned to the main program.

C++ provides several means whereby the addresses of variables in the calling program can be provided to a function. With this information available, the function can change the value assigned to these variables in the calling program. When a variable's address is provided to a function, the arguments are said to be *passed by reference*. We shall illustrate one procedure that enables pass by reference. Suppose that a function is to be passed two numbers, one of type **int** and one of type **float**. The function is to square the integer, cube the floating-point number, return the sum of the passed numbers to the calling program, and also return the resulting square and cube to the calling program. The function is called **square_cube_sum**. Its first line is

$$float\ square\_cube\_sum(int\&\ x,float\&\ y); \hspace{2cm} \textbf{5–7}$$

This line indicates that the function returns a value of type **float**, and that its arguments are the addresses of a variable of type **int** and a variable of type **float**. No memory space is reserved for the variables **x** and **y** when the function is called. Instead, when the addresses are passed to the function, their memory locations are used by the variables **x** and **y** of the function. Because of this, the variable **x** within the function is actually the same as the corresponding variable in the calling program. A similar statement can be made for **y**. The variables in the calling program do not necessarily have to be called **x** and **y**. No matter what their names, the variables in question are designated by the addresses supplied to the function.

The function declaration in the main program is

$$\text{extern float square\_cube\_sum(int\&,float\&)} \qquad \textbf{5--8}$$

The declarations **int&** and **float&** indicate to the compiler that the addresses of the variables, rather than their values, are to be provided to the function.

The program in Figure 5–3 contains a main program that calls the function **square_cube_sum**, and the function itself. The person running the main program enters the values of **w** and **y**. The function is called using the statement

$$\text{ans = square\_cube\_sum(w,y);} \qquad \textbf{5--9}$$

Note that the variables themselves are used as arguments. Because of the declaration 5–8, the compiler writes the program so that the addresses, rather than the values assigned to the variables, are passed to the function. Note that the programmer does not have to keep track of these details.

FIGURE 5–3 ■ An illustration of pass by reference.

```
/* an illustration of pass by reference */
#include <stream.h>
main()
{
    extern float square_cube_sum(int&,float&);
    int w;
    float y,ans;
    cout << "\n enter w and y\n";
    cin >> w >> y;
    ans = square_cube_sum(w,y);
    cout << "\n w square = " << w << "    y cube = " << y;
    cout << "\nanswer = "  << ans;
}


float square_cube_sum(int& x,float& y)
{
    float result;
    x = x * x;
    y = y * y * y;
    result = float(x) + y;
    return result;
}
```

Now consider the function. The data passed to the function is considered to be addresses because of the form of the first line of the function. Note that, within the function, **x** and **y** are used just as ordinary variables would be. When a value is assigned to **x** in the function, that value is stored in the memory locations that "belong" to **w** in the main program. Thus, when the value assigned to **x** is changed in the function, the value assigned to **w** is changed in the main program. It does not matter what the variables are called. Note that the names of **w** and **x** are different. However, the second variable passed to the function is called **y** in both the function and in the main program. Remember that the names in the function and the names in the main program are independent. After the function has completed execution, the values assigned to **w** and **y** in the main program will be replaced by their square and cube, respectively. The single value returned by the function, which is the sum of the square of the original value of **w** and the cube of the original value of **y**, is to be assigned to **ans**.

Not all the arguments of a function have to be passed in the same manner. For instance, consider the following first line of a function called **test**.

$$\text{int test(int i,int\& j,float k,float\& w);} \qquad \textbf{5-10}$$

Here **i** and **k** are passed by value, while **j** and **w** are passed by reference. A declaration in the main program corresponding to 5–10 is

$$\text{extern int test(int,int\&,float,float\&);} \qquad \textbf{5-11}$$

Sometimes, although it is convenient to pass by reference, it is undesirable for the function to change the value of the variable in the main program. Of course, this can be accomplished by not using the variable in question to the left of an assignment within the function. However, if the variable was inadvertently used to the left of an assignment inside the function, a hard-to-locate bug could develop. It is possible, however, to declare one or more terms in the formal parameter list to be constants. As such, these cannot be changed by the function. For instance, consider the first line of a function:

$$\text{int abc(int x, const int\& y);} \qquad \textbf{5-12}$$

Here **x** is passed by value and **y** is passed by reference. However, **y** is declared to be a constant within the function and the value assigned to **y** cannot be changed within the function. The declaration in the main program corresponding to 5–12 is

$$\text{extern int abc(int, const int\&)} \qquad \textbf{5-13}$$

The form of the pass by reference can be modified. For instance, we can write a function declaration such as

$$\text{int test(int i,int \&j,float k,float \&w)} \qquad \textbf{5-14}$$

This is equivalent to 5–10. In 5–14, however, the ampersand (**&**) is associated with the variable name rather than with the type. To the compiler, however, it conveys the same information. That is, it signifies that the address of the variable is to be passed to the function.

There is another form that can be used with pass by reference. It is not as convenient as the type that we have discussed; however, unlike the form that we have just discussed, it is a form that can be used with standard C. Thus, you may have occasion to see this form. The form is illustrated in Figure 5–4. The form of the function declaration is

$$\text{float square\_cube\_sum(int* x,float* y);} \qquad \textbf{5–15a}$$

Alternatively, this may be written as

$$\text{float square\_cube\_sum(int *x,float *y);} \qquad \textbf{5–15b}$$

Here **x** is declared to be a pointer to an integer variable, and **y** is declared to be a pointer to a floating-point variable. The declaration of the function in the main program is analogous to 5–15. In this case, the address of each variable must be passed explicitly to the function. For instance, the statement in the main program that calls the function is

$$\text{ans = square\_cube\_sum(\&w,\&y);} \qquad \textbf{5–16}$$

FIGURE 5–4 ■ Another form of pass by reference.

```
/* an illustration of pass by reference */
#include <stream.h>
main()
{
    extern float square_cube_sum(int*,float*);
    int w;
    float y,ans;
    cout << "\n enter w and y\n";
    cin >> w >> y;
    ans = square_cube_sum(&w,&y);
    cout << "\n w square = " << w << "    y cube = " << y;
    cout << "\nanswer = "  << ans;
}



float square_cube_sum(int* x,float* y)
{
    float result;
    *x = *x * *x;
    *y = *y * *y * *y;
    result = (float)*x + *y;
    return result;
}
```

Because the addresses are passed explicitly, the de-referencing operator, *****, must be used to refer to the data assigned to the variable in the function. For instance, the statement that is used to square the value assigned to **x** in the function is

$$*x = *x * *x;$$
5–17

Because the **x** passed to the function refers to the address of a variable, the value associated with that address is referred to as ***x**; this follows the discussion in Section 3–4.

The program in Figure 5–3 is far easier to read and is less prone to errors than is the program in Figure 5–4. In the program in Figure 5–3, each variable is referenced by its name in both the main program and in the function. In the program in Figure 5–4, on the other hand, the **&** and ***** operators must be used. Thus, the form of Figure 5–3 is preferable to use with pass by reference. In this form, the compiler keeps track of the details of the addressing and the programmer is free to concentrate on the logic of the programming.

5–3 ■ VARIABLES

When a variable is declared in a main program, that variable is assigned memory space by the compiler. In effect, the variable represents those memory locations. That variable exists during the time that the program is executing. For the functions that we have considered thus far, memory locations are reserved for the variables of the function at the time the function is executed. After the execution of the function is complete, this memory is released and can be used to store the variables of other functions. It is possible to declare variables in a function that remain in existence after control returns to the main program. If the function is called again, these variables, and the values last assigned to them, are still in existence and can be used by the function.

Automatic Variables

The type of variables we have dealt with thus far are called *automatic variables*, and they can be designated by the keyword **auto**. In general, however, automatic variables are the default for functions, and therefore, it is not necessary to use the keyword **auto**. However, the following would be a specific designation that variables are automatic.

auto int i,j,k;   5–18

Remember that automatic variables are the default for functions. Storage space for these variables is reserved when the function is called and is released when the execution of the function is completed. The *lifetime* or *extent* of an automatic variable covers only the time during which the function is executing. For instance, consider the program in Figure 5–1. The variables **test1**, **test2**, **test3**, and **average** come into being, i.e., have memory space reserved for them, when the function **average_three** is called. They cease to exist when the function returns control to the main program. Suppose that the main program calls **average_three** several times. The variables of the function would come into existence, and then cease to exist, once for each time that the function is called. The variables may be stored in different memory locations each time that the function is called.

There is a particular block of memory used for storing the automatic variables of functions. When a function is called, space for its automatic variables is reserved in this block of memory. When the function returns control to the calling program, this space is released and can be used by another function. This conserves memory. If this were not done, memory would have to be reserved for every variable of every function that could be called during the running of the program; much more memory would be required in this case.

Static Variables

Sometimes it is desirable for some of a function's variables to remain in existence after the function returns control to the calling program. For instance, suppose that a function is called several times by the main program and that the function performs calculations based on a value that was calculated the last time that the function was called. If this value were stored in an automatic variable, it would have to be calculated each time the function was called. However, C++ provides a class of variables, called *static variables*, that remain in existence after the function that defines them returns control to the calling program. The compiler usually reserves space for static variables of functions just as it does for the variables of the main program. Thus, the values of a function's static variables are preserved.

An example of the use of static variables is shown in Figure 5–5, which is a modification of the program in Figure 5–1. In the program in Figure 5–1, the function returned the average of three grades. In the program in Figure 5–5, the program still returns the average of three grades. However, an endless loop has been added to the main program. The user is asked if an additional set of grades is to be averaged. If the answer is **Y** or **y**, operation of the loop repeats. In addition to the average of the three grades, the program outputs a running average of all grades.

The function has two static variables; their declarations are

static int total_count = 0;	5–19a
static float total_sum = 0.0;	5–19b

Variables are declared to be static by preceding their declaration with the keyword **static**. Note that the two variables are initialized to zero. The first time that the function is called, the initial values of the variables **total_count**

FIGURE 5–5 ■ An illustration of the use of static variables. (a) The main program; (b) the function that uses the static variables.

```
/* an illustration of static variables */
#include <stream.h>
main()
{
    extern float average_three(float,float,float);
    float g1,g2,g3,ave;
    char ch;
    for( ; ; )    {
        cout << "\nenter three grades\n";
        cin >> g1 >> g2 >> g3;
        ave = average_three(g1,g2,g3);
        cout << "\naverage = " << ave;
        cout << "\nDo you want to average another set of grades Y or N?\n";
        cin >> ch;
        if((ch != 'y')&&(ch != 'Y'))break;
    } // end for( ; ; )
}
```

(a)

```
/* function called by main program */
float average_three(float test1,float test2,float test3)
{
    float average,running_average,sum;
    static int total_count=0;
    static float total_sum=0.0;
    sum = test1 + test2 + test3;
    average = sum/3.0;
    total_count = total_count + 3;
    total_sum = total_sum + sum;
    running_average = total_sum/total_count;
    cout << "\nrunning_average = " << running_average;
    return average;
}
```

(b)

and **total_sum** are zero. On succeeding calls to the function, the values assigned to the static variables are those values that were assigned at the time of the last exit from the function.

Actually, the initialization of the static variables to zero is unnecessary. In contrast to automatic variables, which are not initialized by most compilers, static variables are *always* initialized. The default value for the initialization is zero. Thus, if no initial value is specified for a static variable, it is initialized to zero.

In the function in Figure 5–5b, **total_count** is incremented by 3 each time the function is called. Thus, **total_count** stores the cumulative number of entered grades. Similarly, **total_sum** stores the total of all the entered grades. Thus, **running_average** stores the desired running average. Note that within the function static variables are used in exactly the same way as automatic variables.

Global Variables

In the last section we discussed pass by reference whereby the address of a variable was passed to a function. In that case, no memory space was reserved for that variable in the function. Instead, the variable in the function shared the memory space reserved for the variable in the calling program. Sometimes, a particular variable is used by many functions. Instead of repetitively passing the address of the variable in each function call, that variable can be declared to be a *global variable*, thus making its address accessible to all functions that include the proper declaration. In other words, that variable can then be accessed by such functions.

There is no special keyword used in conjunction with global variables. Rather, it is the location of its declaration that makes it global. The program in Figure 5–6 illustrates the use of global variables. This is a modification of the program in Figure 5–3 that utilized pass by reference. In the program in Figure 5–6 the same effect is achieved using global variables. Note the first lines of Figure 5–6a. They are

int x;	**5–20a**
float y;	**5–20b**
main()	**5–20c**

FIGURE 5–6 ■ An illustration of the use of global variables. (a) The main program with the global declaration; (b) the function.

```
/* an illustration of global variables */
#include <stream.h>
int x;
float y;
main()
{
    extern float square_cube_sum();
    float ans;
    cout << "\n enter x and y\n";
    cin >> x>> y;
    ans = square_cube_sum();
    cout << "\n x square = " << x << "    y cube = " << y;
    cout << "\nanswer = "  << ans;
}
```
(a)

```
float square_cube_sum()
{
    extern int x;
    extern float y;
    float result;
    x = x * x;
    y = y * y * y;
    result = float(x) + y;
    return result;
}
```
(b)

Because the variables **x** and **y** are declared *before* the main program begins, the compiler treats them as global variables. If the global declarations, the main program, and any functions are included in the same disk file, then there is no need for further declaration of these variables. They simply can be used in the main program and in the functions. Any use of **x** in the main program or in the functions refers to the same set of memory locations. Of course, the same statement can be made for **y**. If a program or function is not in the same disk file as the global declaration(s), then the **extern** declaration must be used. For instance, the function in Figure 5–6b contains the declarations

extern int x;   **5–21a**

extern float y;   **5–21b**

The **extern** declaration can be used even if the function is in the same file as the global declaration. The **extern** declarations can precede the line with the function name or be part of the function body. Figure 5–7 is a modification of Figure 5–6, in which the **extern** declarations preceded the line with the name of the function.

FIGURE 5–7 ■ A modification of the program in Figure 5–6. (a) The main program; (b) the function.

```
/* an illustration of global variables */
#include <stream.h>
int x;
float y;
main()
{
     extern float square_cube_sum();
     float ans;
     cout << "\n enter x and y\n";
     cin >> x>> y;
     ans = square_cube_sum();
     cout << "\n x square = " << x << "    y cube = " << y;
     cout << "\nanswer = "  << ans;
}
```

(a)

```
extern int x;
extern float y;
float square_cube_sum()
{
     float result;
     x = x * x;
     y = y * y * y;
     result = float(x) + y;
     return result;
}
```

(b)

Global variables can be initialized just as automatic and static variables are. For instance, 5–20a could be modified as

$$\text{int } x = 0;\hspace{6cm}\textbf{5-22}$$

If a global variable is not explicitly initialized, its initial value is unknown; different compilers function in different ways in this case.

Because calling programs and functions are often written in separate files and compiled separately, as shall be discussed in the next section, it is common practice to write all **extern** declarations for the global variables into a single file and then to **#include** that file at the beginning of any file containing the functions that use these global variables. This has the same effect as if the **extern** declarations were actually included in the files. The advantage of including a single file is that the chance for typographical error is reduced. If a program invokes many functions that are written in different files, then the use of the included file containing the **extern** declarations can be a great help. There is, however, a potential disadvantage to this procedure in that, although all the global variable names are written in a single file, not all these global variables are used by every function. If the name of one of these unused variables is accidentally used within a function without its being declared properly, the value assigned to the global variable could be changed inadvertently. This could result in a particularly hard-to-find bug. You should be very careful, therefore, when a file containing **extern** definitions is included. One other point should be made concerning included files: If the included file is modified, all functions that use that file should be recompiled.

Register Variables

There are a number of *registers* that are directly associated with the microprocessor, or central processor, of the computer. These registers can be used as memory locations. In general, operations involving registers are much faster than those involving ordinary memory. The processor uses many of its registers for its own internal operations. If, however, there are unused registers, these can be used for variable storage. The C++ keyword **register** allows you to declare a variable to be a *register variable*. This does not mean that it will definitely be stored in a register. If there is a register available, then the register variable will be stored in a register. However, if the register is not available, then the keyword **register** will be ignored, and the variable will be stored as an ordinary variable. Some typical declarations of register variables are

$$\text{register int x,}\hspace{5cm}\textbf{5-23a}$$
$$\text{register char ch;}\hspace{4.7cm}\textbf{5-23b}$$

A register variable cannot be a global variable, nor can its address be retrieved with the **&** operator.

5-4 ■ SCOPE

In a single program, or in a single function, a variable exists from the point of its definition to the end of the block in which it is defined. This range of existence is called the *scope* of the variable. We have considered some aspects of scope in Section 3–3, and we assume that the reader is familiar with that discussion. If a variable is declared in a main program and that variable's address is not passed to any function, the scope of that variable is only over the block of the main program in which it is defined. Such variables are called *local variables*. In a similar way, variables can be local to a block of the function in which they are defined. Thus, the discussion of local variables in functions follows the discussion in Section 3–3.

Now let us consider the scope of global variables. We start by considering the program in Figure 5–8. In that example the main program calls the

FIGURE 5–8 ■ A main program and two functions. (a) The main program; (b) the function **fun1**; (c) the function **fun2**.

```
/* an illustration of scope */
#include <stream.h>
int i;
main()
{
    extern int fun1();
    int ans;
    cout << "\nenter i\n";
    cin >> i;
    ans = fun1();
    cout << "\nanswer = " << ans;
}
```

(a)

```
extern int i;
int j;
int fun1()
{
    extern void fun2();
    j = 7 * i;
    fun2();
    return j;
}
```

(b)

```
#include <stream.h>
extern int j;
void fun2()
{
    cout << "\nj = " << j;
    return;
}
```

(c)

function **fun1**, which in turn calls the function **fun2**. In this discussion we assume that the main program, **fun1**, and **fun2**, as represented by Figures 5–8a, 5–8b, and 5–8c respectively, are each stored in a separate disk file. Each file is compiled separately, and finally, all three compiled files are linked to obtain the final program. Consult the documentation that comes with your system to determine the appropriate commands to accomplish this. An **extern** declaration in a file indicates to the compiler that the variable in question is defined elsewhere. During the linking process, the variable declared with the **extern** declaration is associated with the appropriate defined variable.

Let us clarify the meaning of the words *declare* and *define*. In Figure 5–8a the variable **ans** is defined in that the compiler reserves storage space for it. An initial value can be set up for this variable at this time. The defining statement is, in this case, also a declaration, in that it declares that a variable called **ans** is to be of type **int**. The first **extern** statement of Figure 5–8b is a declaration, but it is *not* a definition. Note that **i** is defined in Figure 5–8a. Note that there can be many declarations of a variable, but only one definition of it. That is, memory space is reserved only once.

Because the variable **i** is declared to be a global variable, any file with the declaration

extern int i;   **5–24**

can access it. Thus, the scope of **i** extends over the main program and over **fun1**. It does not extend over **fun2** because Statement 5–24 is not contained in the file represented by Figure 5–8c.

The variable **j** is also a global variable. The variable **j** is global because it is declared outside of the main program and outside of a function. Thus, any file, other than that of Figure 5–8b, in which the variable **j** is defined, can contain the statement

extern int j;   **5–25**

That statement extends the scope of **j** over that file. Thus, in the example, the scope of **j** is over Figures 5–8b and 5–8c. If the file represented by Figure 5–8a had Statement 5–25 included prior to **main()**, then the scope of **j** would extend over the main program as well. Note that global variables can be declared in any program module. However, in most cases it is a good idea to declare such variables in the file containing the main program. If all the global variables are declared in one place, it is easier to keep track of them.

If all three parts of Figure 5–8 were included in the same file and compiled together, the **extern** statements could be omitted. (Note, however, that there would be no problem in that case if they were present.) In this situation, the program and functions would be compiled at the same time, and the compiler would be aware of the global variables. When a function is compiled separately, the compiler has no way of "knowing about" any definitions in other files; therefore, in that case, the **extern** declarations must be present.

We have mentioned that no error occurs if functions that contain **extern** statements, and the main program that contains the global variable definitions, are in the same file and are compiled together. This is *not* the case, however, for the statement

#include <stream.h>

5–26

The header files usually contain definitions, i.e., **#define** statements. If the same header file is included twice in the same file, the C++ preprocessor will include the definitions into the file twice before passing it to the C++ compiler. This may cause a compiler error that aborts compilation. Whether or not this actually occurs depends upon the contents of the header file in question. If all three parts of Figure 5–8 are part of the same file, the Statement 5–26 should *not* be present in Figure 5–8c. On the other hand, if Figure 5–8a and Figure 5–8c are stored in different files, Statement 5–26 *must* be included in each of them, because each file is compiled separately, and the compiler is not able to compile the statements relating to stream input/output without the information in the header file. Note that Figure 5–8b does not contain 5–26, because no **stream** operation is performed in that function.

In Section 3–3 we discussed shadowing in conjunction with variables defined in different blocks of the same program. The same ideas carry over to functions. Figure 5–9 illustrates these ideas. Note that **i** is defined as a global variable in the main program in Figure 5–9a and is declared **extern** in the function in Figure 5–9b. Thus, the scope of **i** is over the main program and over

FIGURE 5–9 ■ An illustration of shadowing a global variable.

```
/* an illustration of shadowing */
#include <stream.h>
int i;
main()
{
    extern void fun();
    i = 5;
    fun();
    cout << "\nfrom main i = " << i;
}


extern int i;
void fun()
{
    i = 2 * i;  // global i;
    int i;  // global i shadowed
    i = 24;
    cout << "\nfrom function local i = " << i;
    ::i = 3 * ::i;  //global i assigned value based on global i
    cout << "\nfrom function local i = "  << i;
    return;
}
```

the function. The first executable statement of the function is

$$i = 2 * i;\qquad\qquad\qquad 5\text{--}27$$

This **i** refers to the global **i**. However, the next line of the program is

$$\text{int } i;\qquad\qquad\qquad 5\text{--}28$$

The variable **i** in 5–28 is local to the function. The scope of this **i** is from the point of its declaration to the end of the block in which it is declared—the end of the function, in this case. The local **i** shadows the global **i** for the rest of the function. Thus, all ordinary references to **i** following 5–28 are to the local **i**.

There are occasions when it is desirable to be able to refer specifically to a shadowed variable. This can be accomplished by preceding the variable by the C++ *scope-resolution operator* :: which in turn is preceded by a blank space. Note that this indicates to the compiler that the global **i** is meant. (We shall discuss other uses for the scope resolution operator subsequently.) The program in Figure 5–9 outputs the value of the local variable **i** twice while the function, **fun**, is executing; then it outputs the value of **i** (the global variable) from the main program. The numerical values that are output are 24, 24, and 30. Note that in the function, the local **i** is assigned the value 24. Then, because all subsequent assignments in the function involve the global variable ::**i**, the assignment of the local **i** is not changed. Thus, the value 24 is output twice when the function is executing. The global **i** is assigned the value 5 in the main program. Then the function is called and the global **i** is assigned twice its value, thereby becoming 10. Still later in the function global **i** is assigned the value equal to three times its currently assigned value, resulting in 30. Thus, the specified output is obtained.

Great care should be exercised when one variable shadows another one. The compiler will not be confused by this, but it is easy for programmers reading the program to mistake one variable for another. Duplicate names and shadowing should be avoided, if possible. Global variables can be convenient; however, the potential problems that result with shadowing and duplicate names should not be ignored. Thus, global variables should not be used indiscriminately.

5–5 ■ LIBRARIES

Groups of related functions are often combined into a single file called a *library*. Many C++ systems permit you to set up your own libraries. You need not concern yourself with the details of the structure of the libraries. The supplied library utilities set up the libraries for you in the proper form. In addition, all compiler systems provide their own libraries of commonly used functions. The user's manual should list the *library functions* that come with your system.

When a program is linked, the linker attempts to resolve all references to functions. If you write your own functions, the linker will search for them in the files provided in your instructions to the linker. If you have combined your functions into libraries, then instructions must be given to the linker to search these libraries. Similarly, instructions must be given to instruct the linker to search the system libraries. Because a library often contains many functions and any single program may use only a few of these functions, it would waste space if all the functions in a library were linked with each program. In most cases, the linker searches the library and extracts only those functions that the program requires. All of the required functions are combined with the main program.

Normally, the linker is supplied with the names of the file containing the main program, the files containing functions written for use with that program, and those containing the libraries. As each non-library is linked, the linker includes the functions that are on that file in the program. In addition, the linker sets up a list of all the functions *called* by routines that have been linked, but which have not as yet been found. A reference to a function not yet found is called a *forward reference*. Thus, the linker builds a list of forward references. A function that is referenced but never read from the disk is called an *unresolved reference*. If, after all the ordinary (non-library) files are read, unresolved references still exist, the specified libraries are searched in an attempt to resolve references.

Because the linker does not extract all the routines from every specified library, care must be taken to prevent referencing problems. Consider that there are two libraries, called A and B, that have been established to store various functions, and that a function in library A, named **funA**, calls a function in library B, called **funB**. Suppose that the linker is instructed to search library B before library A. The linker will not have **funB** on its list of references and therefore does not extract it from the library. Next, when library A is searched, **funB** will be placed on the list of referenced functions but, because library B has already been searched, **funB** is never found, and the program cannot be linked. This problem can be avoided by taking care to list the libraries in the proper order.

It is possible that a function in library A calls one in library B and a function in library B calls one in library A. In order to properly link a program that references these functions, the linker must be given instructions to search one library twice. Of course, this adds to the linking time. If possible, the contents of libraries should be set up so that multiple searches of the same library do not have to take place.

Although the details of your linker may not match this discussion exactly, the sequence in which libraries are searched will always be important. Consider this when you establish your own libraries and when you give the linker instructions relating to the sequence in which the libraries should be linked.

5–6 ■ RECURSION

Just as a function can call other functions, it can also call itself. This is termed a *recursive function call* or simply *recursion*. When a function calls another function, the scope of the local variables of the calling function do not extend over the called function, and vice versa. The same is true in a recursive call. In fact, the operation is the same as if the call were not recursive. That is, the operation would be exactly the same if, instead of calling itself, the function called a function that had a different name but contained the same statements as the calling function. For instance, suppose that a function named **test** has local variables **a**, **b**, and **c**, and that **test** calls itself recursively. The local variables in the calling **test** and the local variables in the called **test** are completely different. In particular, the scope of the **a**, **b**, and **c** in the calling test does not cover the called **test**. In addition, if **a**, **b**, and **c** are automatic variables, the **a**, **b**, and **c** of the calling function and those of the called function exist for different times. The calling function's variables will be in existence for the entire time during which both the calling function and the called function are being executed. However, the variables of the called function exist only while that (called) function is executing.

An example of a recursive function that calculates the factorial is shown in Figure 5–10. The main program (see Figure 5–10a) inputs and outputs the data and calls the function **factorial**. Figure 5–10b is the function **factorial**. Let us consider the executable statements of the function:

if(n <= 1)return 1;	**5–29a**
if(n >= 2)fact = n * factorial(n−1);	**5–29b**
return fact;	**5–29c**

Note that **factorial** is a function and **fact** is a variable. Factorial 0 is defined as 1. Thus, if the argument of factorial is 0 or 1, the function simply returns 1. Now suppose that the original call to factorial is

$$\text{factorial(3)} \qquad \textbf{5–30}$$

On the first evaluation of the function, the statement

$$\text{fact} = 3 * \text{factorial(2)}; \qquad \textbf{5–31}$$

is executed. Execution of this statement cannot be completed until **factorial(2)** is evaluated. Thus, a second instance of the **factorial** function is called. In this second instance,

$$\text{fact} = 2 * \text{factorial(1)}; \qquad \textbf{5–32}$$

is executed. Note that **fact** in 5–32 is a different variable from **fact** in 5–31. Again, execution of 5–32 cannot be completed until **factorial(1)** is evaluated.

FIGURE 5-10 ■ A function that computes the factorial. (a) The main program; (b) the function **factorial**.

```
/* an illustration of recursive function calls to compute the factorial */
#include <stream.h>
main()
{
    extern long factorial(int);
    long fact;
    int n;
    cout << "\nenter n\n";
    cin >> n;
    fact = factorial(n);
    cout << "\nfactorial " << n << " = " << fact;
}
```

(a)

```
long factorial(int n)
{
    long fact;
    if(n <= 1)return 1;
    if(n >= 2)fact = n * factorial(n-1);
    return fact;
}
```

(b)

Thus, a third instance of the **factorial** function is called. Now the argument of **factorial** is 1, thus the statement

$$\text{return 1;} \qquad\qquad \text{5-33}$$

is executed. Now, the second instance of **factorial** resumes execution and the execution of 5-32 can be completed; the value returned from the third call to **factorial** is multiplied by 2, resulting in an assignment of 2 to the variable **fact** in the second call of the function. The next statement executed in the second call to **factorial** is

$$\text{return fact;} \qquad\qquad \text{5-34}$$

The second instance of factorial then completes operation, and the value 2 is returned to the first call of **factorial**, which now resumes operation, and the execution of Statement 5-31 is completed. The value 6 is assigned to **fact**, and this value is returned to the calling program, where it is output.

In the example that we discussed, the first instance of **factorial** calls the second instance, which in turn calls the third instance. After the third instance completes execution, control is returned to the second instance, which then completes execution. Control then returns to the first instance, and its operation proceeds. Finally, control is returned to the main program. In other words, there were three instances of the **factorial** function. Remember that each instance is considered to be a different function, just as if each had a different name. The operation can be represented as follows:

$$\begin{array}{l} \text{enter factorial} \; - \; \text{argument(3)} \\ \quad \text{enter factorial} \; - \; \text{argument(2)} \\ \quad\quad \text{enter factorial} \; - \; \text{argument(1)} \\ \quad\quad \text{leave factorial} \; - \; \text{return 1} \\ \quad \text{leave factorial} \; - \; \text{return 2} \\ \text{leave factorial} \; - \; \text{return 6} \end{array}$$

5–35

The three **factorial** functions are indicated by the three levels of indentation, indicating the three separate calls to **factorial**. Thus, there are actually three different variables called **fact**.

Let us consider the steps of a general recursive procedure. First, define the operation in terms of a reduced form and simple operations. In the case of the function **factorial(n)**, the reduced form is **factorial(n−1)** and the simple operation is taking the product of the reduced form and **n**. Second, keep repeating the basic operation until the reduced form is so simple that the result is known. In the case of the **factorial**, the known form is **factorial(1)**, which results in 1. Third, recursion terminates, the reduced form is evaluated, and the result is built up from the reduced form. The condition that ends recursion is called a *boundary condition*. In Figure 5–10, the boundary condition occurs when **n** becomes less than or equal to 1, as indicated by

$$\text{if(n} <= 1)$$

5–36

A second example of a recursive function is shown in Figure 5–11. This procedure calculates the Fibonacci numbers. These numbers, consisting of an infinite sequence, appear in many mathematical calculations. The first few terms in the sequence are

$$1, 1, 2, 3, 5, 8, 13, 21, 34, 55, 89, \ldots$$

5–37

The first two Fibonacci numbers, f_0 and f_1, are each defined to be 1. Each remaining Fibonacci number is defined to be the sum of the two preceding numbers in the sequence, as represented by the relation:

$$f_n = f_{n-1} + f_{n-2} \qquad n = 2, 3, 4, \ldots$$

5–38

The executable statements in the function **fibonacci** are

```
if(n == 0)return 1;          5–39a
if(n == 1)return 1;          5–39b
fib = fibonacci(n − 1) + fibonacci(n−2);   5–39c
return fib;                  5–39d
```

FIGURE 5–11 ■ A recursive function that calculates the Fibonacci numbers. (a) The main program; (b) the function **fibonacci**.

```
/* recursive calculation of Fibonacci numbers */
#include <stream.h>
main()
{
     extern long fibonacci(int);
     long fb;
     int n;
     cout << "\nenter n\n";
     cin >> n;
     fb = fibonacci(n);
     cout << "\nThe " << n << " Fibonacci number = " << fb;
}
```

(a)

```
long fibonacci(int n)
{
     long fib;
     if(n == 0)return 1;
     if(n == 1)return 1;
     fib = fibonacci(n-1) + fibonacci(n-2);
     return fib;
}
```

(b)

The boundary condition consists of 5–39a and 5–39b. The value of the variable **fib** is the sum of the two preceding Fibonacci numbers. This operation is repeated recursively, until the boundary conditions are encountered. Then, successive results are returned until the value of **fib** in the original function call is obtained.

A recursive function is usually considerably shorter than a nonrecursive function that calculates the same quantity. For this reason, recursive functions are often easier to write and debug than are nonrecursive functions. The resultant machine language code is shorter when recursive functions are used. However, a recursive function often executes more slowly and requires more memory than does the corresponding nonrecursive function. Let us see why this is so. When a main program calls a function, control is transferred to the function. When the function completes operation, control must return to the statement in the main program immediately following the function call. When a program is executed, the instructions are fetched from memory and transferred to the central processor. Various values are stored in the registers of the processor. When a function call is encountered in a program, the address of the last instruction and all pertinent register values must be saved so that operation can resume correctly. Note that this information cannot be stored in the registers, because they have to be used to perform the calculations of the function. There is an area of memory called the *stack* that is used to store all this information. The values are said to be *pushed* onto the stack. After the execution of the function is complete, the values are retrieved from the stack and placed back into the appropriate registers. When they are retrieved, the values are said to be *popped* from the stack. If the function calls another function, then the calling function's values are pushed onto the stack as well. At this point, the stack is holding the pertinent values for both the main program and the function. The stack can hold only a specified amount of data. As values are pushed onto the stack, it fills; as values are popped off the stack, it empties. If there is an attempt to push too many values onto the stack, not enough stack space will be available. In this case, the program fails. In some cases, it may cause the entire computer system to crash. In addition, pushing values onto the stack and popping them off the stack consumes time.

When a nonrecursive function that does not call any other function is executed, values are pushed onto the stack and then popped off only once. When there is a recursive function call, it is as though there were many calls to different functions. Note that the number of calls to **fibonacci** varies as 2^n, where **n** is the Fibonacci number being computed. Thus, even a relatively small value of **n** may require more recursive calls than the stack can handle. The maximum value of **n** that can be accommodated differs from system to system. The number of recursive function calls that fills the stack depends upon the function. For instance, the number of recursive function calls to **factorial** (see Figure 5–10b) increases only as **n**, rather than as 2^n. Most C++ systems allow you to increase the stack size at the expense of other memory. Of course, if there are many function calls, operation of the program will be slowed by the pushes and pops even if there are no problems with the stack size. Usually, the same operations can be performed by more than one algorithm, some nonrecursive and some recursive. A nonrecursive algorithm usually runs faster and does not introduce the stack problems that we have discussed. However, programmers often prefer to write the shorter recursive function. There are some recursive functions that can be automatically converted into nonrecursive ones by some *optimizing* compilers. In that case, the programmer can write a short recursive program without having to pay the price of increased memory requirements and reduced speed.

Optimizing compilers cannot rewrite general recursive algorithms into nonrecursive ones. However, there is a certain form of recursion called *tail recursion* that always can be rewritten into a nonrecursive form. In tail recursion, no further computation is performed after the boundary condition is reached. For instance, the function in Figure 5–10 is not tail recursive because a multiplication is performed after each factorial function returns a value to the function that called it. The program of Figure 5–12, on the other hand, is a tail recursive algorithm that computes the factorial. In it, the function **factorial** calls itself recursively. Note that this is tail recursion because all computation is performed *before* the function is called recursively. Thus, once

FIGURE 5–12 ■ A tail recursive function that computes the factorial. (a) The main program; (b) the tail recursive function.

```
/* an illustration of tail recursive function calls to compute the factorial */
#include <stream.h>
main()
{
    extern void factorial(int,long&);
    long fact;
    int n;
    cout << "\nenter n\n";
    cin >> n;
    fact = (long)n;
    factorial(n-1,fact);
    cout << "\nfactorial " << n << " = " << fact;
}
```

(a)

```
void factorial(int n,long& fact)
{
    if(n < 1) {
        fact = 1;
        return;
    }   // end if(n < 1)
    if(n == 1)return;
    fact =  n * fact;
    if(n >= 2)factorial(n-1,fact);
    return;
}
```

(b)

the boundary condition is reached, each recursively called **factorial** simply returns, and no further computation is performed. Pass by reference is used for the variable named **fact**. Note that the function **factorial** is not completely self-contained in that some slight manipulation of the variables **fact** and **n** is performed in the main program. This could be eliminated if the main program called a new function that set **fact** equal to **n**, decremented **n**, and then called the function **factorial**.

5–7 ■ DEFAULT ARGUMENTS—VARIABLE NUMBER OF ARGUMENTS

C++ has several features that increase the versatility of functions. We shall consider two of them here. *Default values* can be specified for certain arguments. If values for these arguments are specified in the function call, then the defaults are ignored. On the other hand, if no values are specified for these arguments, then the default values are used. Default arguments are very convenient when a function is called many times and one or more of the arguments has the same value for most of those calls. Default values are specified when the function is declared in the main program. Thus, default values can be specified for existing functions that are defined elsewhere. For example, consider the following declaration:

$$\text{extern float test(int,int,int} = 3, \text{float} = 4.5) \qquad \textbf{5-40}$$

This declares that **test** is a function that is going to be used by the program. It returns a value of type **float** and has four arguments. The first three arguments are of type **int**, and the last is of type **float**. There are default values for the last two arguments. Specifically, the default value for the third argument is 3, and the default for the last argument is 4.5. If, when the function is called, values are specified for all four arguments, then the defaults are ignored. If values are specified for the first three arguments, the default value 4.5 is used for the fourth argument; if values are specified for the first two arguments, the default values are used for the last two arguments. Although default values can be specified for every argument, if they are specified for only some of the arguments, these arguments must be the last ones in the list. When a function is called, the specified arguments must form a continuous list. For instance, it would be improper to specify values for the first, second, and fourth arguments to function **test** in 5–40. Proper calls to **test** are

$$\text{w = test(a,b,c,d);} \qquad \textbf{5-41a}$$
$$\text{w = test(a,b,c);} \qquad \textbf{5-41b}$$
$$\text{w = test(a,b);} \qquad \textbf{5-41c}$$

where **a**, **b**, **c**, and **d** represent variables or constants that have been assigned values.

An example of the use of default arguments is shown in Figure 5–13. The function **check** (see Figure 5–13b) has four formal parameters. The first three are of type **int**, and the fourth is of type **char**. If the fourth argument is the character **'a'**, the function returns the maximum of the first three arguments. If the fourth argument is **'i'**, the function returns the minimum of the first three arguments.

The function **check** is declared in the main program with the statement

$$\text{extern int check(int,int,int,char} = \text{'a');} \qquad \textbf{5-42}$$

Thus, if no fourth argument is supplied, **check** returns the maximum of its first three arguments.

The first call to **check** is in the statement

$$\text{max = check(x,y,z);} \qquad \textbf{5-43}$$

FIGURE 5–13 ■ An illustration of the use of default arguments. (a) The main program; (b) the function.

```
/* illustration of default arguments */
#include <stream.h>
main()
{
      extern int check(int,int,int,char='a');
      int x,y,z,max,min;
      cout << "\nenter three numbers\n";
      cin >> x >> y >> z;
      max = check(x,y,z);
      min = check(x,y,z,'i');
      cout << "\nmax = " << max;
      cout << "\nmin = " << min;
}
```

(a)

```
int check(int a,int b,int c,char ch)
{
      int ans;
      if(ch == 'a')    {
         ans = a;
          if(ans < b)ans=b;
          if(ans < c)ans=c;
      }  // end if(ch == 'a')
      if(ch == 'i')    {
         ans = a;
          if(ans > b)ans=b;
          if(ans > c)ans=c;
      }  // end if(ch == 'i')
      return ans;
}
```

(b)

Because the fourth argument is not specified, the default, **'a'**, is used for the fourth argument, and **check** returns the maximum value of those assigned to **a**, **b**, or **c**. The second call to **check** is in the statement

$$max = check(x,y,z,'i');$$ **5–44**

Now, because the fourth argument is specified as **'i'**, the default is ignored, and **check** returns the minimum value of those assigned to **a**, **b**, and **c**. The use of default arguments can make programming less tedious in certain circumstances.

Arbitrary Number of Arguments

There are times when it is desirable to write functions that take an *arbitrary number of arguments*. Let us illustrate this with a simple example. Consider that a function is to be written that averages a set of grades; the grades are passed to it as arguments. If the number of arguments is fixed, a separate function of this type would have to be written for each possible number of grades. However, if the number of arguments were arbitrary, a single function would suffice for all sets of grades, no matter how many grades each set contained. The function that averages an arbitrary number of grades is shown in Figure 5–14. When an arbitrary number of variables is declared, the variable type is *not* specified. Normally, the C++ compiler checks that the type of the passed variables is proper. When an arbitrary number of variables is used, this type-checking is suspended. Thus, extra care must be taken to make sure that the correct variable types are involved.

An arbitrary number of variables is declared by an ellipsis, i.e., three periods (...). For instance, in the main program of Figure 5–14a we have

$$\text{extern float average(int ...);} \qquad \textbf{5–45}$$

This declares that the program calls a function named **average** that returns a value of type **float**. The first argument is of type **int**. This will be fol-

FIGURE 5–14 ■ An illustration of a function with an unspecified number of arguments. (a) The main program; (b) the function.

```
/* illustration of function with unspecified number of arguments */
#include <stream.h>
main()
{
    extern float average(int ...);
    float g1=80.0,g2=90.0,g3=100.0,g4=95.0,g5=100.0;
    float ave3,ave5;
    ave3 = average(3,&g1,&g2,&g3);
    ave5 = average(5,&g1,&g2,&g3,&g4,&g5);
    cout << "\naverage of first three = " << ave3;
    cout << "\naverage of first five = "  << ave5;
}
```

(a)

```
#include <stdarg.h>
float average(int n ...)
{
    va_list ap;
    va_start(ap,n);
    float sum=0.0,ave;
    int i;
    for(i=1;i<=n;i++)sum = sum + va_arg(ap,float&);
    va_end(ap);
    ave = sum/float(n);
    return ave;
}
```

(b)

lowed by an arbitrary number of arguments of unspecified type. Note that the unspecified list of arguments must *follow* the list of specifically declared arguments. When unspecified arguments are used, the addresses of the arguments must be passed to the functions. Thus, a number such as 23 cannot be passed in this way. Instead, 23 must be assigned to a variable or literal constant, e.g. **const int a = 23;**. The address of the variable or constant is then passed to the function. For instance, in the main program of Figure 5–14a, the two calls to average are

$$ave3 = average(3,\&g1,\&g2,\&g3); \qquad \textbf{5–46a}$$
$$ave5 = average(5,\&g1,\&g2,\&g3,\&g4,\&g5); \qquad \textbf{5–46b}$$

Note that because the first argument is specified, it can be passed as a simple value.

The function is shown in Figure 5–14b. The file **stdarg.h** must be included with functions that utilize an arbitrary number of arguments. Sometimes, this header file is called **stdargs.h** or **stdarg.hxx**. This file contains definitions and *macros* that must be used. We have not as yet considered macros. For the time being, consider that they act as functions. Macros are discussed later in this chapter. The first line of the function contains the three periods to indicate that an arbitrary number of arguments is to be used. In this case the function title is

$$float\ average(int\ n\ ...) \qquad \textbf{5–47}$$

Note that the usual formal parameter list is followed by three periods. In the body of the function, there is the declaration

$$va\_list\ ap; \qquad \textbf{5–48}$$

The **ap** is simply a variable name; any valid name could be used here, and **va_list** is a type and must be used as written here. The type **va_list** is defined in the header file **stdarg.h**. The variable **ap** is a pointer that is used to keep track of the arguments.

The macro **va_start** has two arguments: the first is **ap**, and the second is the name of the last-named argument in the formal parameter list, **n** in this case. When **va_start** is called, the first argument is assigned the address of the second argument. The arguments are stored in a contiguous section of memory. The macro **va_start** is used to find the end of those arguments that are specifically specified in the formal parameter list. For example, when

$$va\_start(ap,n) \qquad \textbf{5–49}$$

is executed, **ap** points to the address of the variable **n**. Now if the pointer **ap** is appropriately incremented it will point to each successive (unspecified) argument in turn.

The macro **va_arg** is used to access the unspecified arguments. It has two arguments: the first is the pointer to the arguments, **ap** in this example; the second argument is a type. The system has no idea of the type of the unspecified arguments. However, this type must be known if the arguments are to be properly accessed. It is for this reason that the type is specified as an argument of **va_arg**. If there are several calls to **va_arg**, then there can be different types specified as the second argument. In the example of Figure 5–14, the arguments are the addresses of variables of type **float**. Thus, the call to **va_arg** is

$$va\_arg(ap,float\&); \qquad\qquad 5\text{--}50$$

When this is executed, **va_arg** returns the value of the variable of type **float**, and **ap** is incremented to point to the next argument. Because the second argument is **float&**, the function returns a floating-point value. This is similar to the notation used in pass by reference.

In the function of Figure 5–14b, the number of values to be averaged is passed as the value **n**. Thus, after the execution of the loop

$$for(i=1;i<=n;i++)sum \ = \ sum \ + \ va\_arg(ap,float\&); \qquad 5\text{--}51$$

is completed, **sum** is assigned the sum of all the values that are to be averaged.

After all the unspecified arguments are used, the macro **va_end** is executed. Note that its argument is **ap**. The macros use the stack for some of their operations. The macro **va_end** properly restores the **stack**. It is necessary that this macro be invoked before the function terminates.

We have indicated that the use of an arbitrary number of arguments requires addresses to be passed. It is possible that in future versions of C++, actual values, rather than addresses, could be passed as well.

5–8 ■ OVERLOADED FUNCTIONS

Ordinarily, functions that perform similar operations on variables of different types are written separately and are given unique names. However, there are occasions when it is convenient, and less confusing, if these functions are given the same name, and the C++ system chooses the proper one to use. Consider that there are two functions that take the square root of a number. One, called **sqrt**, takes the square root of a number of type **float**, and the other, called **dsqrt**, takes the square root of a number of type **double**. It would be simpler for the programmer if both functions were called **sqrt**. C++ provides a feature, called *overloading*, that allows different functions to have the same name. The C++ compiler uses the types of the arguments to determine which function is to be used. For the square root example, an argument of type **float** indicates that the floating-point **sqrt** function is to be used. If, on the other hand, the argument is of type **double**, then the double-precision **sqrt** function is used.

Let us consider the rules by which the compiler matches overloaded functions with the appropriate function calls. Suppose that there are two functions called **test**. They are defined with the following argument types:

test(int,float,int);   5–52a

test(float,float,int);   5–52b

When there is a call to **test**, the compiler searches for an exact match in the argument types. For instance, if the arguments in the function call are of the types **float**, **float**, and **int**, in that order, then the function 5–52b would be used. If there is no exact match, then one or more of the arguments will be converted according to the usual rules. The first match found determines how the arguments are converted. For instance, if the list of arguments in the function call consists of the types **float**, **int**, and **int**, conversion of the first variable will not produce a match, but conversion of the second will. Thus, in this case, function 5–52b will be used. It should be noted that different systems may convert the types in different orders. Thus, in the interests of portability, ambiguous situations should be avoided. Casts should be used to establish definite matches with the specified types.

When user-defined functions are overloaded, the functions must be declared as such. For instance, suppose that there are two functions called **average_three**, each of which averages three numbers. One averages numbers of type **float**; the other averages numbers of type **int**. In addition to the usual declarations, these functions also must be declared to be overloaded. A typical declaration of these functions is

overload average_three;   5–53a

float average_three(float,float,float);   5–53b

int average_three(int,int,int);   5–53c

The functions are declared to be overloaded using the keyword **overload**. This declaration is followed by the usual function declarations.

Figure 5–15 illustrates the use of overloading. The functions **average_three** are used there. Figure 5–15a contains the main program and the declarations 5–53. In the main program, **average_three** is called with arguments of type **float**, and then it is called with arguments of type **int**. The two functions **average_three** are shown in Figures 5–15b and 5–15c. These functions are written in the usual way. When **average_three** is called with arguments of type **float**, the function in Figure 5–15b is used; when **average_three** is called with arguments of type **int**, the function of Figure 5–15c is used.

The program in Figure 5–15 is written assuming that all three functions are stored in the same file and compiled at the same time. If separate compilation is used, the statements must be modified slightly. These modifications

FIGURE 5-15 ■ An example of an overloaded function. (a) The main program; (b) one function **average_three**; (c) another function **average_three**.

```
/* an illustration of overloading */
#include <stream.h>
overload average_three;
float average_three(float,float,float);
int average_three(int,int,int);
main()
{
    float g1,g2,g3,ave;
    int x1,x2,x3,xave;
    cout << "\nenter three grades\n";
    cin >> g1 >> g2 >> g3;
    cout << "\nenter three integers\n";
    cin >> x1 >> x2 >> x3;
    ave = average_three(g1,g2,g3);
    xave = average_three(x1,x2,x3);
    cout << "\ngrade average = " << ave;
    cout << "\ninteger average = " << xave;
}
```
(a)

```
float average_three(float x,float y,float z)
{
    float average;
    average = (x + y + z)/3.0;
    return average;
}
```
(b)

```
int average_three(int x,int y,int z)
{
    int average;
    average = (x + y + z)/3;
    return average;
}
```
(c)

may vary from system to system. Consult your C++ manual to determine the exact statements used to overload functions contained in separately compiled files.

5-9 ■ POINTERS TO FUNCTIONS

When a program is run after having been compiled and linked, each function used by the program has a specific address in memory. C++ allows functions to be referenced by pointers to these addresses. A pointer to a function must be declared to be a pointer to the type returned by the function, e.g., **void**, **int**, **float**. In addition, the argument types of the function must also be specified when the pointer is declared. For instance, a pointer to a function that returns no value, and has two formal parameters of type **float** and one of type **int**, in that order, would be declared as

$$\text{void (*ptr1)(float,float,int);} \qquad \text{5–54}$$

The argument declaration is a list of types, separated by commas, and enclosed in parentheses. The pointer name is **ptr1** in this case. Any valid name could, in fact, be used. Note that the name and the de-referencing operator, *, are enclosed in parentheses and precede the list of argument types. The parentheses around the de-referenced variable name are required to make the proper declaration. Note that without the parentheses, ***ptr1(float, float,int)** would be interpreted as ***(ptr1(float,float,int))**, which is not the intent.

The pointer must be assigned the address of the function. This can be done with an ordinary assignment operation. For instance, suppose that the function **test** returns no value and has formal parameters of type **float,float**, and **int**. In this case, execution of

$$\text{ptr1 = \&test;} \qquad \text{5–55}$$

results in **ptr1**, as declared in 5–54, being assigned the address of the function **test**.

Figure 5–16 illustrates the use of pointers to functions. In this program there are two user-defined functions: **average_three**, which takes three arguments of type **float** and returns their average as type **float**, and **average_three_int**, which takes three arguments of type **int** and returns their average as type **int**. The two pointer declarations are

$$\text{float (*ptf)(float,float,float);} \qquad \text{5–56a}$$
$$\text{int (*ptf2)(int,int,int);} \qquad \text{5–56b}$$

Note that in Figure 5–16a, these declarations are included with the other declarations. The addresses of the functions are assigned by the statements

$$\text{ptf = \&average\_three;} \qquad \text{5–57a}$$
$$\text{ptf2 = \&average\_three\_int;} \qquad \text{5–57b}$$

The functions **average_three** and **average_three_int** are called by the statements

$$\text{ave = (*ptf)(g1,g2,g3);} \qquad \text{5–58a}$$
$$\text{xave = (*ptf2)(x1,x2,x3);} \qquad \text{5–58b}$$

FIGURE 5–16 ■ An illustration of pointers to functions. (a) The main program; (b) the function **average_three**; (c) the function **average_three_int**.

```
/* an illustration of pointers to functions */
#include <stream.h>
main( )
{
     extern float average_three(float,float,float);
     extern int average_three_int(int,int,int);
     float g1,g2,g3,ave,(*ptf)(float,float,float);
     int x1,x2,x3,xave,(*ptf2)(int,int,int);
     ptf = &average_three;
     ptf2 = &average_three_int;
     cout << "\nenter three grades\n";
     cin >> g1 >> g2 >> g3;
     cout << "\nenter three integers\n";
     cin >> x1 >> x2 >> x3;
     ave = (*ptf)(g1,g2,g3);
     xave = (*ptf2)(x1,x2,x3);
     cout << "\ngrade average = " << ave;
     cout << "\ninteger average = " << xave;
}
```

(a)

```
float average_three(float x,float y,float z)
{
     float average;
     average = (x + y + z)/3.0;
     return average;
}
```

(b)

```
int average_three_int(int x,int y,int z)
{
     int average;
     average = (x + y + z)/3;
     return average;
}
```

(c)

Note that the expression to the right of the assignment sign consists of the dereferenced pointer followed by a list of the arguments passed to the function enclosed in parentheses.

A pointer can be used to pass one function to another as an argument. Such an operation is illustrated in Figure 5–17. The main program (see Figure 5–17a) prompts the user for two numbers and then requests that a **p** or an **s** be entered. If **s** is entered, the sum of the two numbers is taken; if any other character is entered, the product of the two numbers is taken. This very simple operation illustrates the passing of a function as an argument of another function. The functions **sum** and **prod** (see Figures 5–17b and 5–17c) return the **sum** and **product** of their arguments, respectively.

FIGURE 5–17 ■ An illustration of passing a function as an argument. (a) The main program; (b) the function **sum**; (c) the function **prod**; (d) the function **do_it**.

```
/* an illustration of passing a function to another function */
#include <stream.h>
main()
{
    extern float sum(float,float);
    extern float prod(float,float);
    extern float do_it(float (*)(float,float),float,float);
    float x1,x2,ans,(*pf)(float,float);
    char ch;
    cout << "\nenter two numbers\n";
    cin >> x1 >> x2;
    cout << "\nenter p for product, s for sum\n";
    cin >> ch;
    if(ch == 's')pf = &sum;
    else pf = &prod;
    ans = do_it(pf,x1,x2);
    cout << "\nanswer = " << ans;
}
```

(a)

```
float sum(float x,float y)
{
    float ans;
    ans = x + y;
    return ans;
}
```

(b)

```
float prod(float x,float y)
{
    float ans;
    ans = x * y;
    return ans;
}
```

(c)

```
float do_it(float (*ptf)(float,float),float x,float y)
{
    float answer;
    answer = (*ptf)(x,y);
    return answer;
}
```

(d)

The function **do_it** is passed a pointer to either function **sum** or to function **prod** plus two arguments. It uses the pointer to call the appropriate function with the two arguments. Consider the main program. A pointer, **pf**, is declared to point to a function that returns a **float** and has two arguments of type **float**. The **if-else** construction is used to assign either the address of **sum** or the address of **prod** to **pf**. Then, **pf** is used as the first argument when **do_it** is called. Note the declaration of **do_it** in the main program:

$$\text{extern float do\_it(float (*)(float,float),float,float);} \qquad \textbf{5–59}$$

The first portion of the declaration, which is for the pointer, is

$$\text{float (*)(float,float)} \qquad \textbf{5–60}$$

This is similar in form to the other pointer declarations that we have considered. There is no variable name here, as is generally the case when functions are declared in the calling program. The first line of the function **do_it** is

$$\text{float do\_it(float (*ptf)(float,float),float x,float y)} \qquad \textbf{5–61}$$

Note that the declaration of the first formal parameter is of the form of 5–60 except that the variable name **ptf** is included here.

The function call within **do_it** is

$$\text{answer} = \text{(*ptf)(x,y);} \qquad \textbf{5–62}$$

Remember that the pointer to **sum** or **prod** is passed to **do_it** as the formal parameter **ptf**. Thus, this function call follows those discussed previously.

5–10 ■ MACROS AND INLINE FUNCTIONS

Usually, if the same sequence of steps has to be performed at several different points in a program, a function is written. That function is then called wherever the sequence of operations is needed. There is *time overhead* associated with function calls. For instance, it takes time to push values onto the stack and to pop them off the stack. If the sequences of instructions were written into the program wherever they occurred, the time overhead of the function calls would be eliminated. On the other hand, if these statements are written into the program at all the necessary points, the program is lengthened, and the amount of memory needed to store it is increased. In addition, it is tedious to retype program statements, and it also increases the chance of typographical errors. In general, function calls are used unless the sequence of steps is short and the time overhead is appreciable because the sequence is needed at many points in the program.

When it becomes advantageous to actually repeat the sequence of steps at many points in a program, one of several procedures can be used. Each of these procedures avoids the need for the programmer to actually type the steps more than once. The first procedure that we shall consider deals with writing *macros.* Macros require the use of the **#define** compiler directive. Remember that **#define** can be used to obtain a simple substitution. For instance, if the following compiler directive is written at the start of a file:

$$\text{\#define ABC the book} \qquad \textbf{5-63}$$

then every occurrence of **ABC** in the file will be replaced by the phrase **the book**. Although the **#define** compiler directive can be used to establish constants, it is better to use the **const** declaration, because the compiler's error-checking capabilities will verify that the constant is used correctly throughout the program. The general form for expressions of the type of 5–63 is

$$\text{\#define identifier token\_string} \qquad \textbf{5-64}$$

A *token string* is a string of characters. The compiler preprocessor replaces every occurrence of the identifier with the token string.

The **#define** compiler directive is more versatile than we have indicated thus far. Arguments can be included in the identifier in the **#define** statement. When the compiler preprocessor expands the identifier into the token string, these arguments can be modified. The general form of the **#define** compiler directive used with arguments is

$$\text{\#define identifier(arg1, \ldots ,argn) token string} \qquad \textbf{5-65}$$

Note that there is *no space* between the identifier and the parenthesis. The arguments **arg1**, ..., **argn** must be contained within the token string. The identifier, followed by a list of **n** arguments, can appear in the body of the program. The arguments in the program, in general, are different from those in the **#define** statement. The compiler preprocessor replaces every occurrence of the identifier and list of arguments by the token string. Wherever **arg1**, ..., **argn** appear in the token string, they are replaced by the corresponding arguments from the program. For example, suppose that the file containing a program begins with

$$\text{\#define test(a,b,c) a + b + c} \qquad \textbf{5-66}$$

In 5–66, **test** is the identifier, **a**, **b**, and **c** are the arguments, and **a + b + c** is the token string. Now suppose that the following statement is in the body of the program:

$$\text{sum} = \text{test(g,7,h);} \qquad \textbf{5-67a}$$

The compiler preprocessor will replace 5–67a with

$$\text{sum} = \text{g + 7 + h;} \qquad \textbf{5-67b}$$

test is a macro. Notice that, in some sense, it works as a function. If **test** is written at other points in the program with different arguments, the compiler preprocessor will expand it using the new arguments. Because macros can insert statements in a program, they achieve the desirable increase in speed of operation discussed at the start of this section.

An example of the use of a macro is shown in Figure 5–18. The macro **ave_three** is used to obtain the average of three numbers. The macro is defined by

$$\#define\ ave\_three(a,b,c)\ (a\ +\ b\ +c)/3.0 \qquad\qquad \textbf{5–68}$$

The macro is invoked in the program with the statement

$$average\ =\ ave\_three(x1,x2,x3); \qquad\qquad \textbf{5–69}$$

There are several problems associated with macros. Because they often are included in separate header files and do not appear explicitly in the program, the use of macros can produce programs that are difficult to read. Macros can be embedded within other macros resulting, at times, in code that is almost impossible to read. Also, subtle bugs may appear when macros are used. Consider the very simple macro that is used to take the product of two numbers:

$$\#define\ prod(a,b)\ a * b \qquad\qquad \textbf{5–70}$$

Now suppose that the macro is invoked with the statement

$$x\ =\ prod(a+1,b+1); \qquad\qquad \textbf{5–71a}$$

The compiler preprocessor will expand this as

$$x\ =\ a+1 * b+1; \qquad\qquad \textbf{5–71b}$$

which, because of hierarchy, is evaluated as

$$x\ =\ a\ +\ (1 * b)\ +\ 1; \qquad\qquad \textbf{5–71c}$$

which is probably not what is intended. Note that if **prod** were a function, then the result would be **(a+1)*(b+1)**. Another disadvantage of macros

FIGURE 5–18 ■ A simple macro.

```
/* an illustration of a macro */
#define ave_three(a,b,c) (a + b + c)/3.0
#include <stream.h>
main()
{
    float x1,x2,x3,average;
    cout << "\nenter three grades\n";
    cin >> x1 >> x2 >> x3;
    average = ave_three(x1,x2,x3);
    cout << "\naverage = " << average;
}
```

is that they cannot be manipulated with pointers in the way that functions can.

Macros are part of the C programming language, and are used extensively there. C++ provides a feature called an *inline function* that provides most of the features of macros without the disadvantages. The compiler replaces a call to an inline function with the actual steps of the inline function, with the appropriate argument substitution. However, an inline function *is* a true function. Its address can be taken and passed as a pointer. The problem with arguments that we discussed in relation to macros does not occur. The arguments are treated exactly as function arguments. Thus, in most instances it is preferable to use inline functions in place of macros. An inline function is written in the same way as an ordinary function, except that the first word in the function title is **inline**.

Figure 5–19 contains an example of an inline function. The function **ave_three** is written as an inline function. Note that the first line of this function is

$$\text{inline float ave\_three(float a,float b,float c)} \qquad \textbf{5--72}$$

The only difference between this and the first line of an ordinary function is the keyword **inline**. Note that the program in Figure 5–19 is written as a single file, and the inline function is written before the main program. This is done so that the compiler can actually place the function in line during compilation.

In many instances, the use of inline functions or macros does not substantially improve execution speed. In general, the use of user-defined inline functions and macros should be avoided unless there is a substantial improvement in performance. It should be noted that macros are commonly used in header files that are supplied with C++ systems.

FIGURE 5–19 ■ An inline function.

```
/* an illustration of an inline function */
inline float ave_three(float a,float b,float c)
{
    float ans;
    ans = (a + b + c)/3.0;
    return ans;
}
#include <stream.h>
main()
{
    float x1,x2,x3,average;
    cout << "\nenter three grades\n";
    cin >> x1 >> x2 >> x3;
    average = ave_three(x1,x2,x3);
    cout << "\naverage = " << average;
}
```

5–11 ■ STRUCTURED PROGRAMMING: MODULARIZATION

Unless a program is very short, it should be broken into short *modules*. This can be done by having one main program call several functions. One or more of these functions can, in turn, call other functions. In general, it is much easier to write and debug many short modules than a single long program. If possible, each module should not be more than about two pages in length. In Section 4–10 we considered some ideas of structured programming. The concept of modularization is also central to structured programming.

Structured programming techniques involve more than simply breaking a program into parts. There are various procedures for organizing the writing of programs. In one procedure, called *top-down programming*, the plan for the complete program is established first. The main program is written and tested *before* any of the functions. Because at this time no functions have as yet been written, special functions called *stubs* are written to test the main program. A stub is a function that performs no computation. It has the same arguments as the function it replaces, along with some simple statements. The main program is tested with all stubs in place. Each stub is used to verify that the appropriate transfer of data takes place between the main program and the functions. Next, the functions are written and tested. If these functions call other user-written functions, these are replaced by stubs. This procedure is repeated until the entire program is written.

In addition to making the program easier to write and debug, modular programming also allows a team of programmers to work on a project. Each member of the team works on one or more functions. When an organized approach such as top-down programming is used, each programmer can feel reasonably confident that, because the calling program will not be changed, the requirements of the module that he or she is writing will not change.

EXERCISES

Check any programs or functions that you write by running them on your computer. If necessary, write a main program to run the function.

1. Write a function that returns the smallest of four integers passed to it.
2. Modify the function of Exercise 1 to handle numbers of type **float**.
3. Modify the function of Exercise 1 so that it outputs the smallest number to the screen with suitable explanatory text. There should be no returned value.
4. What is the difference between pass by value and pass by reference?
5. Write a function that is passed a floating-point number and returns an integer value. The returned value should be equal to the rounded floating-point number. That is, if the fractional part of the floating-point number is less than 0.5, the fractional part of the number should be

discarded and the resulting integer returned. If the fractional part is 0.5 or more, then 1 should be added to the floating-point number, after which the fractional part is dropped, and the resultant integer is returned by the function. The value of the main program variable of type **float** that is the argument of the function should be set equal to the integer value returned by the function. Use pass by reference to modify the variable in the main program.

6. Repeat Exercise 5, but now use a different form of pass by reference.

7. Repeat Exercise 5, but now use a global variable.

8. Write a main program and function that illustrate the *scope* of variables in the main program and in the function.

9. Write a main program and function that illustrate the *shadowing* of global variables within the function.

10. Modify the program of Exercise 9 so that a global variable can be referenced after it has been shadowed.

11. Write a main program that calls a function four times. The function is to take four arguments of type **int**, and it is to return the smallest of those arguments. The function is also to output the smallest number that has been passed to it during the time that the main program has been running. This value is to be output each time the function is called.

12. What is meant by a recursive function call?

13. Write a function that is passed a positive integer argument **n**. The function is to return the sum of the first **n** integers. Use recursion.

14. Write a recursive function that computes the function

$$f(x) = 1 + (1/2x) + (1/2x)^2 + (1/2x)^3 + \ldots$$

where **x** is a positive integer. The summation is to terminate when $(1/2x)^n$ is less than some value called **err**. The values of **x** and **err** are to be passed to the function as arguments.

15. What is meant by tail recursion?

16. Modify the function of Exercise 13 so that it is tail recursive.

17. Write a main program that uses the function of Exercise 14. The value 0.0001 should be used as a default for **err**.

18. Write a function that averages an unspecified number of nonnegative floating-point numbers. The last-entered argument should be a negative number that is not included in the average.

19. Write a function that performs the same operation as that of Exercise 18, but for integers. Both functions should have the same name. Write a main program that calls both functions. Use overloading of functions here.

20. Modify Exercise 19 in the following way. Use different names for the functions. In the main program call the two functions using pointers.

21. Write a function that performs some unspecified operation on three integer variables. The operation to be performed is to be passed to the

function as an argument (i.e., a pointer to a function). Now write two functions: one that returns the smallest of its three integer arguments, and one that returns the largest of its three integer arguments. The main program is to obtain the maximum and minimum of three integers by calling the first function. The arguments of the first function are a pointer and three integers.

22. Write a macro that obtains the maximum of three numbers.

23. Repeat Exercise 22, but now use an inline function.

24. How can inline functions speed the operation of a program? Why should inline functions generally not be used?

25. Why, in general, is it preferable to use inline functions rather than macros?

26. What is meant by modular programming? What are its advantages?

27. What is meant by top-down programming?

CHAPTER 6
Arrays

Repetitive calculations often have to be performed on lists of data or tables. Such data can be stored conveniently in a form called an *array*. Data stored in arrays can be manipulated easily using looping. In this chapter we shall consider array operations.

6-1 ■ VECTORS: ONE-DIMENSIONAL ARRAYS

Computer programs often manipulate lists containing items of data that are all of the same type. For instance, there could be a list of the amounts of purchases made by customers in a store, or a list of grades of students in a class. Mathematics often deals with subscripted variables such as a_1, a_2, ... a_{10}. These are often analogous to a list. For instance, a_1 could refer to the first student's grades, a_2 to the second student's grades, and so forth. The procedures that we have discussed thus far are not well suited to manipulating lists of data. For instance, suppose that 20 grades have to be averaged. It would be tedious to write 20 different identifiers, one for each of the grades, in order to obtain their sum. Such a task essentially would be impossible if the sum of 10,000 customers' purchases were to be obtained. Fortunately C++, like other programming languages, provides a means for dealing with such data.

In C++, a list of variables of the same type can be set up; such a list is called an *array*. The variables in an array are subscripted. In this section, we shall consider arrays whose variables have only a single subscript. Such arrays are called *one-dimensional arrays*, *single subscript arrays*, or *vectors*. Each variable in an array is called an *element* of that array.

The compiler must reserve space for each element of an array, and the array declaration makes that possible. All the elements of an array must be

151

of the same type. A vector, or single-subscript array, is declared in a variable declaration as follows: the name of the variable is followed by a positive integer enclosed in square brackets. That integer specifies the number of elements in the vector (array) and is called the *dimension* of the vector. For instance, consider the following declaration:

$$\text{float grade[100];} \qquad\qquad \textbf{6--1}$$

Here **grade** is declared to be an array of 100 elements, each of which represents a variable of type **float**. The declaration of vectors can be included in the declaration of other variables, for instance,

$$\text{int name[25],date,purchases[100]} \qquad\qquad \textbf{6--2}$$

Now **name** is declared to be a vector of 25 integers, **date** is an ordinary integer variable, and **purchases** is a vector of 100 integers.

The subscripts of an array start with *zero* and are consecutive positive integers. An array element is referenced by writing the array name followed by a number enclosed in square brackets. For example, the elements of the **name** vector are: **name[0]**, **name[1]**, **name[2]**, ..., **name[24]**. Note that the largest subscript is always one less than the dimension of the vector. The number enclosed in square brackets following the variable name is called the *subscript*, or *index*, of the element. The subscript can be an integer variable or a simple expression that can be evaluated to an integer value during the *execution* of the program. In contrast, the dimension must be an integer or a constant expression that can be evaluated to an integer at *compilation*. That is, the compiler must have the actual numeric dimension available at compilation time. For instance, the following is a valid declaration:

$$\text{const int aaa=7;} \qquad\qquad \textbf{6--3a}$$
$$\text{float data[aaa*3];} \qquad\qquad \textbf{6--3b}$$

The **data** array has been declared to store 21 floating-point variables.

The subscripts of the elements of an array are often expressed in terms of a loop variable. In this manner, looping can be used effectively to perform operations on each element of an array. This combination is particularly powerful.

An example of vector manipulation is shown in Figure 6–1. The user enters a number of grades into an array, and then the average, maximum, and minimum grades are computed and output. This program could be written without arrays, and a single loop could be used. Written this way, however, it illustrates array operations. In addition, such a program illustrates practical procedures for programming with arrays. The program performs three distinct operations. The data is entered and stored in an array. This data could be entered over a period of time and stored in a file. (We shall discuss file operations in a subsequent chapter.) The file data could be read into an array and then the average taken at a later date. At some other time, the

FIGURE 6–1 ■ An example of vector manipulation.

```
/* an example of vector manipulations */
#include <stream.h>
main()
{
    const int array_size=100;
    float sum=0.0,max=0.0,min=100.0,grade[array_size],average;
    int i,numb;
    cout << "\nenter number of grades to be averaged\n";
    cin >> numb;
    if(numb > array_size)    {
        cout << "\nat most " << array_size <<" grades can be averaged\n";
        cout << "\nprogram terminating\n";
        exit(0);
    }   // end if(numb > array_size)
    for(i=0;i<numb;i++)   {
        cout << "\nenter grade number " << i+1 << ":   ";
        cin >> grade[i];
    }   // end for(i=0;i<numb;i++)
    /* obtain average */
    for(i=0;i<numb;i++)sum = sum + grade[i];
    average = sum/float(numb);
    cout << "\naverage = " << average;
    /* obtain maximum and minimum grade */
    for(i=0;i<numb;i++)    {
        if(grade[i]>max)max = grade[i];
        if(grade[i] < min)min = grade[i];
    }   // end for(i=0;i<numb;i++)
    cout << "\nmaximum grade = " << max;
    cout << "\nminimum grade = " << min;
}
```

maximum and minimum values could be calculated. The three parts of the program illustrate these operations. We shall now consider the details of the program.

The dimension of the array is specified in terms of a constant named **array_size**. This is desirable because the array dimension can be changed easily at a future time. Although other calculations utilize the value of **array_size**, that value can easily be changed wherever it is referenced in the program. If the dimension of the array has to be changed, then only a single line of the program has to be changed (i.e., the one containing the declaration of **array_size**) and that change will be reflected throughout the program.

Great care must be exercised when you work with arrays. If you dimension a vector to have 100 elements and then attempt to assign a value to an element whose subscript is 100 or greater, an error will result. However, neither the compiler nor the C++ system checks for this error. The elements of an array are stored in a contiguous block of memory. Suppose that the starting address of this block is designated by **start_block**. Assume that the array stores floating-point numbers, and that each number of type **float** is stored in four memory locations. Thus, the compiler will reserve 400 memory words starting at **start_block** to store the array. Assume that the array is called **grade**. An assignment such as

$$\text{grade[i]} = 97.0; \hspace{4cm} \text{6-4}$$

where **i** is 100 or more, will cause the assigned data, **97.0** in this case, to be written outside of the block of memory assigned to the array. For instance, if **i** is 109, the data will be written into the four memory words starting at **start_block + 440**. This may overwrite other program data, resulting in errors that are very hard to locate. Alternatively, parts of the stored program instruction or the operating system itself may be overwritten. This will cause the program to malfunction and may cause the computer system to crash. You must make sure that the subscript of an array member is neither less than zero nor greater than one less than the specified dimension.

In the program of Figure 6–1, the user enters the number of grades to be processed; this value is assigned to **numb** and must be less than the value assigned to **array_size**. This is checked in the statement sequence

if(numb > array_size) {	6–5a
cout << ”\nat most ” << array_size <<	
” grades can be averaged\n”;	6–5b
cout << ”\nprogram terminating\n”;	6–5c
exit(0);	6–5d
} // end if(numb > array_size)	6–5e

This routine is a simple form of *error-detecting* routine. If **numb** is greater than **array_size**, a warning message is printed, and the program is terminated. Consider the statement

$$\text{exit(0);} \hspace{4cm} \text{6-6}$$

The library function named **exit** terminates operation. Usually there are certain housekeeping operations that relate to the operating system that should be ended when a program ceases operation. These operations are usually performed by the **exit** function. The argument of **exit** (**0** in this case) is returned to the operating system. Consult your operating system manual to determine how these codes can be accessed after the program terminates. The code **0** usually signifies that there is no system error. There are programs that perform system manipulations. Errors in these programs can leave the system corrupted. Return codes other than **0** are used in conjunction with **exit()** in those cases. There is another routine, named **abort()**, that also terminates operation; **abort** differs from **exit** in that operation is terminated immediately without any normal exiting routines being carried out. Consult your operating system manual and your C++ manual to determine which of these routines should be used.

You must always check that the array subscript remains within bounds. If user-entered data can alter the range of the array subscript, then there must be some form of error-checking such as that illustrated in 6–5. The routine does not have to end the program; it could simply loop and request appropriate data from the user.

The first **for** loop is used to enter data. Its form is

$$\text{for}(i = 0; i < \text{numb}; i++)$$ 6-7a
    cout $\ll$ "\nenter grade number " $\ll$ i + 1
        $\ll$ ": "; 6-7b
    cin $\gg$ grade[i]; 6-7c
} // end for(i = 0; i < numb; i++) 6-7d

The user is prompted for each grade. After each grade is entered, it is stored in **grade[i]**. Of course, a different value of **i** is used for each grade. Note that, while it is conventional for people to number objects starting with 1, array subscripts start at 0; thus, grade i + 1 is stored in **grade[i]**. Notice how the use of looping in conjunction with arrays simplifies the manipulation of tabular data. If arrays were not used, there would have to be a separate variable associated with each grade.

The sum of all the grades is computed in the **for** loop:

$$\text{for}(i = 0; i < \text{numb}; i++)\text{sum} = \text{sum} + \text{grade[i]};$$ 6-8

After the looping is complete, each **grade[i]** (i=0, 1, ..., **numb −1**) will be added to **sum** so that, eventually, **sum** will be assigned the total of all the grades. In a similar way, after the third loop has cycled, **max** and **min** will be assigned the maximum and minimum, respectively, of all the entered grades. Note that the initial value of **sum** is 0.

Initial values can be established for an array in its declaration statement by following the array declaration with an equals sign and a list of constants, separated by commas and enclosed in curly braces. For instance, consider the declaration

$$\text{int item[4]} = \{ 1,2,7,9\}$$ 6-9

Here **item** has been declared to be a vector of **int**, with four elements. The initial values of the elements are **item[0]=1**, **item[1]=2**, **item[2]=7**, and **item[3]=9**. If there are fewer constants specified within the curly braces than there are elements in the array, all the remaining elements of the array are initialized to zero. Note that array variables are treated exactly as other variables. There is no standard for initial values of automatic variables. That is, if no initial value is specified, some compilers may initialize to zero, but others may not. Static variables are initialized to zero unless otherwise specified. This applies to array variables as well as to other variables.

6-2 ■ THE RELATIONSHIP BETWEEN VECTORS AND POINTERS

In Section 3-4 we discussed pointers and pointer arithmetic. In this section we shall demonstrate that certain basic array operations are essentially the same as pointer operations. This is done to provide additional insight into vector operations. Although array operations can be implemented as pointer operations, it is often more convenient to use arrays. We shall illustrate these ideas using the program in Figure 6–2, which is a modification of the program in Figure 6–1, using pointers in place of the array. Instead of declaring an array named **grade** in Figure 6–2, **grade** is declared to be a pointer. When the program is executed, **grade** will point at the first memory location in a block of memory that will be used to store all the **grade** data. Space is allocated for **grade** dynamically with **new**. That is,

$$\text{grade} = \text{new float[numb]} \qquad \qquad \textbf{6–10}$$

allocates enough contiguous memory to store **numb** variables of type **float**. Because the memory is allocated dynamically, rather than specifying a fixed dimension, no error-checking routine has to be included here to verify that the number of grades does not exceed some specified value. Note that **numb** is used to control the looping. Thus, the program cannot attempt to write outside of the available memory block. In other words, the logic of the program in Figure 6–2 prevents the writing of data in the wrong region of memory. Of course, the number of grades might be specified to be larger than available memory; in that case, **new** could not allocate the required memory block. However, error-checking is built into the **new** operation. If more memory than

FIGURE 6–2 ■ A modification of the program in Figure 6–1 using pointers instead of arrays.

```
/* an example of pointer manipulations */
#include <stream.h>
main()
{
    float sum=0.0,max=0.0,min=100.0,*grade,average;
    int i,numb;
    cout << "\nenter number of grades to be averaged\n";
    cin >> numb;
    grade = new float[numb];
    for(i=0;i<numb;i++)  {
        cout << "\nenter grade number " << i+1 << ":   ";
        cin >> *(grade + i);
    }  // end for(i=0;i<numb;i++)
    /* obtain average */
    for(i=0;i<numb;i++)sum = sum + *(grade + i);
    average = sum/float(numb);
    cout << "\naverage = " << average;
    /* obtain maximum and minimum grade */
    for(i=0;i<numb;i++)    {
        if(*(grade + i) > max)max = *(grade + i);
        if(*(grade + i) < min)min = *(grade + i);
    }  // end for(i=0;i<numb;i++)
    cout << "\nmaximum grade = " << max;
    cout << "\nminimum grade = " << min;
}
```

is available is requested, the operation of the program usually terminates. Some C++ systems allow you to modify the error-handling routine used by **new**. Check your C++ manual to determine the error-handling for **new** in your system.

Let us assume, for purposes of discussion, that a variable of type **float** is stored in four memory locations. In that case, after 6–19 is executed, the variable **grade** points at the first address in a block of memory that contains **4*numb** memory locations. Remember that C++ performs pointer arithmetic in a way that simplifies the operation for the programmer. For instance, if ***grade** represents the number of type **float** stored in the first group of four memory locations, then ***(grade+1)** represents the number of type **float** stored in the second group of four memory locations, ***(grade+2)** represents the number stored in the third group of four memory locations, and so forth. Thus,

$$*(grade + i) \hspace{4cm} \textbf{6–11a}$$

in Figure 6–2 is analogous to

$$grade[i] \hspace{4cm} \textbf{6–11b}$$

in Figure 6–1. Note that ***(grade+i)** simply replaces **grade[i]** in those parts of the program where computation is performed. Remember that incrementation and decrementation can be used in conjunction with pointers. For instance, ***(++grade)** is equivalent to ***(grade+1)**.

The name of an array is actually a pointer to the first element of an array. For instance, if the **grade** array is dimensioned as

$$float\ grade[100] \hspace{3cm} \textbf{6–12}$$

then **grade** is a pointer to the first element in the array named **grade**. For instance, the following two addresses are the same:

$$grade \hspace{5cm} \textbf{6–13a}$$
$$\&grade[0] \hspace{4.5cm} \textbf{6–13b}$$

The **&** operator is used to take the address of the first element in the array; this is the memory location pointed to by **grade**. In general, the following are equivalent:

$$grade[i] \hspace{4.5cm} \textbf{6–14a}$$
$$*(grade + i) \hspace{4cm} \textbf{6–14b}$$

That is, pointer arithmetic can be used in conjunction with the address of the first array element (the array name) to access the data in the array.

The program in Figure 6–3 illustrates these ideas. Note that the grade vector is declared just as it is in Figure 6–1. For this reason, the error-checking used in Figure 6–1 is incorporated in Figure 6–3. The form of 6–14b is used to enter and retrieve data from the array. Figure 6–3 is presented as an illustration. This mixed form should be used only in special cases.

FIGURE 6–3 ■ A program that uses an array declaration to declare the array and uses pointers to access the array. Note that this program is presented for illustrative purposes. The mixed form is used only in special cases.

```
/* an example of vector and pointer manipulations */
#include <stream.h>
main()
{
    const int array_size=100;
    float sum=0.0,max=0.0,min=100.0,grade[array_size],average;
    int i,numb;
    cout << "\nenter number of grades to be averaged\n";
    cin >> numb;
    if(numb > array_size)    {
        cout << "\nat most " << array_size <<" grades can be averaged\n";
        cout << "\nprogram terminating\n";
        exit(0);
    }  // end if(numb > array_size)
    for(i=0;i<numb;i++)  {
        cout << "\nenter grade number " << i+1 << ":   ";
        cin >> *(grade+i);
    }  // end for(i=0;i<numb;i++)
    /* obtain average */
    for(i=0;i<numb;i++)sum = sum + *(grade+i);
    average = sum/float(numb);
    cout << "\naverage = " << average;
    /* obtain maximum and minimum grade */
    for(i=0;i<numb;i++)    {
        if(*(grade+i)>max)max = *(grade+i);
        if(*(grade+i) < min)min = *(grade+i);
    }  // end for(i=0;i<numb;i++)
    cout << "\nmaximum grade = " << max;
    cout << "\nminimum grade = " << min;
}
```

6–3 ■ USING VECTORS WITH FUNCTIONS

When an array is the argument of a function, pass by reference must be used. In this case, the function can access all the data of the array and modify that data in the main program. Even though a function returns only a single value, pass by reference permits the array data to be modified in the main program. Figure 6–4 illustrates the passing of an array as an argument to a function. The function **sum_square** is passed two arguments: the first is the dimension of the vector, and the second is the vector itself. The function returns the sum of all the elements of the vector. After the sum is taken, each element of the vector is squared. This results in the squaring of each element of the original vector in the main program.

The function is declared in the main program as

extern int sum_square(int,int[ ]);   **6–15**

Note the declaration of the second argument; it is **int[ ]**. No numerical dimension is specified. The empty square brackets indicate that the second argu-

FIGURE 6–4 ■ An illustration of the use of a function with vectors. (a) The main program; (b) the function.

```
/* an illustration of passing an array to a function */
#include <stream.h>
main()
{
      extern int sum_square(int,int[]);
      int data[10],i,answer;
      for(i=0;i<10;i++)data[i] = i;
      answer = sum_square(10,data);
      cout << "\nsum of elements of array = " << answer;
      cout << "\nsquared array is\n";
      for(i=0;i<10;i++) cout << data[i] << "   ";
}
```

(a)

```
int sum_square(int dim,int numbs[])
{
      int total=0,i;
      for(i=0;i<dim;i++)  {
          total = total + numbs[i];
          numbs[i] = numbs[i] * numbs[i];
      }  // end for(i=0;i<dim;i++)
      return total;
}
```

(b)

ment is a vector. The dimension is not explicitly specified; we shall discuss this further when the function is considered. The function **sum_square** is called using the statement

$$answer = sum\_square(10,data);$$ 　　　　**6–16**

Because **data** is declared as a vector, the identifier **data** is the address of the first element of the data vector.

The first line of the function is

$$int \ sum\_square(int \ dim,int \ numbs[])$$ 　　　　**6–17**

The vector **numbs** is declared using empty square brackets to indicate that it is a vector. However, no dimension is given. Because this is a pass by reference, the memory has been reserved for the vector in the calling program. The fact that memory does not have to be reserved is a convenience. If a function could work with only one particular size of vector, then a separate function would have to be written every time that the vector dimension was changed.

There are times when a function uses arrays that are local to that function, although this is not the case in Figure 6–4. These arrays must be specifically dimensioned in the function. In many cases, the actual dimensions are not known, because many different programs, passing references to arrays of various sizes, may call the function. If this is so, these local vectors must be dimensioned large enough to accommodate any amount of data that could be passed to the function. This often results in a function that uses more memory than is needed for most situations. Local array variables, just as other variables, are automatic unless they are specifically declared to be static.

In the first computation performed by the function, the sum of all the elements of the vector is taken by the function; then each element of **numbs** is squared. This operation squares each element of the vector data in the main program because **numbs** and **data** represent the same memory locations.

Sometimes, program logic dictates that the elements of the vector in the calling program must not be changed by the function. The function can be prohibited from changing the data stored in an array by declaring that array to be a constant. For instance, a declaration in the main program might be

extern int test(int,const int[ ]);   6–18

The corresponding first line of the function would be

int test(int x,const int[] y)   6–19

Any attempt to change the values of the elements of the vector **y** in the main program would result in an error during compilation or linking.

Global variables can be used with arrays. Figure 6–5 is a modification of Figure 6–4, in which the array dimension and the array itself are a global

FIGURE 6–5 ■ An illustration of the use of array global variables.

```
/* an illustration of an array global variable */
#include <stream.h>
const int dim=10;
int data[dim];
main()
{
     extern int sum_square();
     int i,answer;
     for(i=0;i<10;i++)data[i] = i;
     answer = sum_square();
     cout << "\nsum of elements of array = " << answer;
     cout << "\nsquared array is\n";
     for(i=0;i<10;i++) cout << data[i] << "   ";
}

extern const int dim;
extern data[];
int sum_square()
{
     int total=0,i;
     for(i=0;i<dim;i++)   {
         total = total + data[i];
         data[i] = data[i] * data[i];
     }  // end for(i=0;i<dim;i++)
     return total;
}
```

constant and a global variable, respectively. The **extern** statement for the global array variable in the function is

extern data[ ];   **6–20**

Note that the numerical dimension is not specified in this statement because the data vector was dimensioned when it was originally defined. Remember that although a variable may be declared many times, it is defined only once. The details of the computations of Figure 6–5 follow those of Figure 6–4.

6–4 ■ MULTIDIMENSIONAL ARRAYS

A vector is a one-dimensional array that represents a list of individual data elements. At times, it is convenient to work with two-dimensional tables of data or with algebraic variables with two subscripts. Such data can be represented by *two-dimensional arrays*. A two-dimensional array, or any array for that matter, must be dimensioned so that the compiler can reserve storage space for it. A two-dimensional array is dimensioned by following its name by two pairs of square brackets, each bracket containing a positive integer or a constant expression that can be evaluated to a positive integer at *compile time*. For instance,

int test[4][3];   **6–21**

dimensions the **test** array to have 12 elements of type **int**. Considering that a two-dimensional array is made up of data elements arranged in a row-column table, the first number represents the number of rows and the second number represents the number of columns. Numbering starts with zero. Thus, the elements of the **test** array are

test[0][0]   test[0][1]   test[0][2]
test[1][0]   test[1][1]   test[1][2]   **6–22**
test[2][0]   test[2][1]   test[2][2]
test[3][0]   test[3][1]   test[3][2]

Another interpretation of a two-dimensional array is that it consists of a vector (one-dimensional array), each of whose elements is itself a vector. For instance, the **test** array could be considered to be a vector whose elements are **test[0]**, **test[1]**, **test[2]**, and **test[3]**. Each of these elements, in turn, is a vector of three elements. We shall consider this in greater detail in the next section.

Figure 6–6 illustrates the use of a two-dimensional array. This is a modification of the grade averaging program. The grades in three tests for up to 100 students are entered into a two-dimensional array. Each row of the array represents a particular student. The first three columns of each row store the grades in the three tests. The fourth column stores the computed average. The

FIGURE 6–6 ■ An example of the use of a two-dimensional array.

```
/* an example of a two-dimensional array */
#include <stream.h>
main()
{
    const int maxnumber=100;
    float grade[maxnumber][4];
    int i,j,numb;
    cout << "\nenter number of students\n";
    cin >> numb;
    while(numb > maxnumber)    {
        cout << "\n the maximum number of students is " << maxnumber;
        cout << "\nenter new number of students\n";
        cin >> numb;
    }  // end while(numb > maxnumber)
    /* data entry */
    for(i=0;i<numb;i++)    {
        cout << "\nenter three grades for student number " << i+1 << "\n";
        for(j=0;j<3;j++)cin >> grade[i][j];
    } // end for(i=0;i<numb;i++)
    /* initialize */
    for(i=0;i<numb;i++)grade[i][3]=0.0;
    /* compute averages */
    for(i=0;i<numb;i++)    {
        for(j=0;j<3;j++)grade[i][3] = grade[i][3] + grade[i][j];
        grade[i][3] = grade[i][3]/3.0;
    }  // end for(i=0;i<numb;i++)
    /* output */
    cout << "\nstudent    average\n\n";
    for(i=0;i<numb;i++)
        cout << i+1 << "            " << grade[i][3] << "\n";
}
```

number of the row of the array plus 1 is the student's ID number; e. g., row 0 has the data for student 1. After the averages are computed, the student's ID number and average are output.

The two statements at the start of the program dimension the array:

const int maxnumber=100;   6–23a
float grade[maxnumber][4];   6–23b

Thus, the array is dimensioned to have 100 rows and four columns. When the program is run, the user is prompted to enter the number of students. This number must be less than **maxnumber** (100). If this is not the case, the **while** loop cycles again, and the user is prompted to enter a smaller number.

The data is entered using a pair of nested loops. The pair of loops, without the prompting statements, is

for(i = 0;i<numb,i ++) {   6–24a
    for(j = 0;j<3;j ++)cin >> grade[i][j];   6–24b
}   // end for(i = 0;i<numb;i ++)   6–24c

Each cycle of the (outer) **i** loop corresponds to a row. Thus, three grades are entered for each row (student) entered; then the **i** loop cycles, and three grades are entered for the next student, and so forth. Note that one loop is often used to process a one-dimensional array, while a pair of nested loops is used to process a two-dimensional array.

The averages are stored in the fourth column of the array, and the next loop sets all these values to zero. A pair of nested loops then adds the values of the first three elements in each row, storing the sum in the fourth column, that is, in **grade[i][3]**. This value is then divided by 3.0 to obtain the desired average.

The average and the student's ID number are then output. The simple convention that the ID number is one more than the row number is used here. If arbitrary ID numbers were used, then the operation would be complicated somewhat. The grade array could be dimensioned to have an additional column to store the ID number. However, the ID number is an integer, while the grades are of type **float**. Because an array stores elements of the same data type, two arrays would have to be used. One would be the **grade** array as is used in Figure 6–6; the other would be a vector storing data of type **int**. The vector would store the ID numbers. Corresponding rows in each array would refer to the same student. This type of operation is awkward. Later in this book, we shall consider more convenient procedures for dealing with mixed data types.

Arrays can have more than two dimensions. The number of dimensions that a programmer would choose depends upon the programming application. The maximum allowable number of dimensions depends upon the compiler. Check your compiler manual to determine the maximum number of dimensions that are allowed. Of course, all arrays must be dimensioned. The procedures for dimensioning arrays always follow the same rules. For instance,

double aaa[20][10][5]   6–25

defines an array of 1000 elements, each of which stores a number of type **double**. The dimensions can be integers or integer constants that can be evaluated at compile time.

Storage Order

All arrays are stored in a contiguous block of memory with one item of data following the other. Thus, even multidimensional arrays can be considered to be lists of data. The *storage order* of a two-dimensional array is by rows. That is, the first row is stored, then the second row, and so forth. For instance, the storage order for the array defined in 6–21 is as shown in 6–22. That is, **test[0][0]**, **test[0][1]**, **test[0][2]**, **test[1][0]**, **test[1][1]**, **test[1][2]**, **test[2][0]**, **test[2][1]**, **test[2][2]**, **test[3][0]**, **test[3][1]**, and **test[3][2]**. If there are more than two dimensions, the storage order follows the same rules; that is, all indices start at 0. The rightmost index then cycles from 0 to its maximum value; then, the second-rightmost index is incremented by 1, and the rightmost index cycles again. This procedure is repeated until all the elements of the array have been stored.

Multidimensional Arrays as Arguments of Functions

When a multidimensional array is used as an argument of a function, the situation is somewhat different than that for a vector. Let us illustrate this with numbers of type **float**, which we assume are stored in four memory locations. Suppose that we are dealing with a vector called **test1** that is passed to a function. The function does not have to know the value of the dimension of **test1**. The function has the first address of the vector when its name, **test1** in this case, is passed to it. The type of data stored by the array is also known by the function; it knows, therefore, exactly how many memory locations are used to store each item of data. This is enough information to enable the function to access the elements of **test1**. For instance, **test1[0]** is stored in the first four memory locations, **test1[1]** is stored in the next four memory locations, and so forth. Now suppose that there is a two-dimensional array named **test2** that is dimensioned in the main program as **test2[100][2]**. The storage order for the first few elements is **test2[0][0]**, **test2[0][1]**, **test2[1][0]**, **test2[1][1]**, **test2[2][0]**, and so on. Now suppose that another two-dimensional array named **test3** is dimensioned as **test3[50][4]**. The storage order of the first few elements of **test3** is **test3[0][0]**, **test3[0][1]**, **test3[0][2]**, **test3[0][3]**, **test3[1][0]**, **test3[1][1]**, **test3[1][2]**, and so on. The arrays **test2** and **test3** each store 200 numbers of type **float**. However, because of the difference in the numbers of columns in each array, similarly named elements in each array are stored in different *relative* positions. For example, **test2[1][1]** is stored in the fourth block of four memory locations, whereas **test3[1][1]** is stored in the sixth block of four memory locations.

Now suppose that the only information passed to the function is the address of the first memory location of the block of memory storing the array, and the fact that the array has two dimensions. In this case, the function will not be able to access the data. For instance, it will not know where in the memory block **test2[1][1]** lies. For this reason, the *numerical* second dimension must be declared in the function. In general, *every dimension except the first must be declared in the function*. The first dimension is not needed to determine the position in the storage order of a particular element, and it must not be declared in the function. The first dimension is needed to allocate the block of memory to store the array. However, this is done by the calling program, not by the called function.

We shall illustrate these ideas with the program in Figure 6–7. This is a modification of the program in Figure 6–6. The test grades are entered into the **grade** array as before. Now, however, the function **average_all** is used to compute the averages and place them in the fourth column of the **grade** array.

FIGURE 6–7 ■ An example of a two-dimensional array being passed to a function.

```
/* an example of a two-dimensional array passed to a function */
#include <stream.h>
main()
{
    extern void average_all(float[][4]);
    const int maxnumber=100;
    float grade[maxnumber][4];
    int i,j,numb;
    cout << "\nenter number of students\n";
    cin >> numb;
    while(numb > maxnumber)    {
        cout << "\n the maximum number of students is " << maxnumber;
        cout << "\nenter new number of students\n";
        cin >> numb;
    }   // end while(numb > maxnumber)
    /* data entry */
    for(i=0;i<numb;i++)   {
        cout << "\nenter three grades for student number " << i+1 << "\n";
        for(j=0;j<3;j++)cin >> grade[i][j];
    } // end for(i=0;i<numb;i++)
    average_all(grade);
    /* output */
    cout << "\nstudent   average\n\n";
    for(i=0;i<numb;i++)
        cout << i+1 << "           " << grade[i][3] << "\n";
}

void average_all(float grade[][4])
{
    int i,j,numb=4;
    /* initialize */
    for(i=0;i<numb;i++)grade[i][3]=0.0;
    /* compute averages */
    for(i=0;i<numb;i++)   {
        for(j=0;j<3;j++)grade[i][3] = grade[i][3] + grade[i][j];
        grade[i][3] = grade[i][3]/3.0;
    }   // end for(i=0;i<numb;i++)
    return;
}
```

Consider the declaration of the **average_all** function in the main program. It is

$$\text{extern void average\_all(float[][4]);} \qquad \textbf{6–26}$$

Note that the second dimension is explicitly included here. The first line of the function also follows this form; it is

$$\text{void average\_all(float grade[][4])} \qquad \textbf{6 27}$$

The explicit declaration of dimensions does somewhat limit the versatility of functions, but is necessary for proper operation.

6–5 ■ THE RELATIONSHIP BETWEEN MULTIDIMENSIONAL ARRAYS AND POINTERS

In this section we shall demonstrate how multidimensional array operations can be implemented with pointers. This will provide additional insight into both arrays and pointers. A two-dimensional array can be represented using an *array of pointers*. As an example, the program in Figure 6–6 is modified in Figure 6–8 to utilize an array of pointers. The **grade** array is now a vector; however, it now stores pointers to numbers of type **float**. The declaration of the **grade** array is

$$\text{float}^* \ \text{grade[maxnumber];} \qquad\qquad \textbf{6–28}$$

where **maxnumber** is a constant. This statement indicates that each element of the **grade** array is a pointer that points to a number of type **float**. No memory space is reserved for the memory pointed to by these pointers during compilation. The memory is allocated dynamically during execution through

FIGURE 6–8 ■ An illustration of two-dimensional array operations using an array of pointers.

```
/* an example of an array of pointers */
#include <stream.h>
main()
{
    const int maxnumber=100;
    float* grade[maxnumber];
    int i,j,numb;
    for(i=0;i<maxnumber;i++)grade[i] = new float[4];
    cout << "\nenter number of students\n";
    cin >> numb;
    while(numb > maxnumber)    {
        cout << "\n the maximum number of students is " << maxnumber;
        cout << "\nenter new number of students\n";
        cin >> numb;
    }   // end while(numb > maxnumber)
    /* data entry */
    for(i=0;i<numb;i++)   {
        cout << "\nenter three grades for student number " << i+1 << "\n";
        for(j=0;j<3;j++)cin >> *(grade[i] + j);
    } // end for(i=0;i<numb;i++)
    /* initialize */
    for(i=0;i<numb;i++) {*(grade[i] + 3)=0.0;}
    /* compute averages */
    for(i=0;i<numb;i++)   {
        for(j=0;j<3;j++)*(grade[i] + 3) = *(grade[i] + 3) + *(grade[i] +j);
        *(grade[i] + 3) = *(grade[i] + 3)/3.0;
    }   // end for(i=0;i<numb;i++)
    /* output */
    cout << "\nstudent    average\n\n";
    for(i=0;i<numb;i++)
        cout << i+1 << "            " << *(grade[i] + 3) << "\n";
}
```

the use of **new**. That is, the statement

$$\text{for}(i = 0; i < \text{maxnumber}; i++)\text{grade}[i] = \text{new float}[4]; \qquad \textbf{6--29}$$

allocates space for four variables of type **float** corresponding to each pointer in the **grade** array.

Space has been allocated for **4*maxnumber** variables of type **float**. These variables can be accessed using the expression

$$*(\text{grade}[i] + j) \qquad \textbf{6--30}$$

where **i** can range between 0 and **maxnumber-1**, and **j** can range between 0 and 3. We shall again assume that a number of type **float** is stored in four consecutive memory locations. Then **grade[i]** points at the first memory location in block **i**, which was allocated in 6–29. Each block of memory allocated in 6–29 consists of 16 memory locations. Pointer arithmetic increments the pointer by four memory locations each time that **j** is increased by 1. The computation portion of the program in Figure 6–8 follows that of Figure 6–6, except that the array representation **grade[i][j]** of Figure 6–6 is replaced by the pointer representation of 6–30.

The program in Figure 6–8 always allocates the maximum amount of memory, no matter how many students' grades are to be entered. If there are only a few students, this is wasteful of both memory and of the time required to allocate the memory. If the memory is not allocated until after the number of students is entered, then 6–29 could be modified by replacing **maxnumber** with **numb**. If this is done, then only enough memory to store each student's grades and average would be allocated.

Now let us consider pointer operations applied to arrays. Figure 6–9, which is a modification of Figure 6–6, will be used as an example. The two-dimensional array **grade** is dimensioned as in Figure 6–6. The name **grade** serves as a pointer to the array. C++ pointer arithmetic as applied to multidimensional arrays requires some explanation. We shall consider the two-dimensional array **grade** here. Pointer arithmetic, when dealing with multidimensional arrays, considers that a fictitious vector of pointers is set up. When the de-referencing operation is applied to **grade**, i.e., ***grade**, the result is not the number stored in (row 0, column 0), but *another pointer*. This pointer points to the vector **grade[0]**, that is, to the first element (pointer) in the fictitious vector of pointers. Note that pointer arithmetic considers the two-dimensional **grade** array to be a vector, each of whose elements is itself a four-element vector. Thus, ***grade** points at the first four-element vector. That is, ***grade** is itself a pointer. If the *value* stored in the first element of the four-element vector is desired, the de-referencing operation must be applied again. Thus, ***(*grade)** is the value of the first (row 0, column 0) element in the **grade** array. The element that is in row **i** and column **j** of the **grade** array can be accessed with the expression

$$*(*\text{grade} + 4*i + j) \qquad \textbf{6--31}$$

FIGURE 6–9 ■ Pointer operations with a two-dimensional array.

```
/* an example involving a two-dimensional array and pointers */
#include <stream.h>
main()
{
      const int maxnumber=100;
      float grade[maxnumber][4];
      int i,j,numb;
      cout << "\nenter number of students\n";
      cin >> numb;
      while(numb > maxnumber)    {
           cout << "\n the maximum number of students is " << maxnumber;
           cout << "\nenter new number of students\n";
           cin >> numb;
      }  // end while(numb > maxnumber)
      /* data entry */
      for(i=0;i<numb;i++)   {
           cout << "\nenter three grades for student number " << i+1 << "\n";
           for(j=0;j<3;j++)cin >> *(*grade + 4*i + j);
      } // end for(i=0;i<numb;i++)
      /* initialize */
      for(i=0;i<numb;i++) *(*grade + 4*i + 3)=0.0;
      /* compute averages */
      for(i=0;i<numb;i++)   {
           for(j=0;j<3;j++)*(*grade + 4*i + 3) = *(*grade + 4*i + 3) +
                                                  *(*grade + 4*i + j);
           *(*grade + 4*i + 3) = *(*grade + 4*i + 3)/3.0;
      }   // end for(i=0;i<numb;i++)
      /* output */
      cout << "\nstudent    average\n\n";
      for(i=0;i<numb;i++)
           cout << i+1 << "            " << *(*grade + 4*i + 3) << "\n";
}
```

Note that because there are four elements in each row, the pointer must be incremented by 4 every time the row number is incremented. It is assumed that **j** can take on values 0 to 3, while **i** can take on values between 0 and **maxnumber-1**. An expression analogous to 6–31 is

$$*(*(grade + i) + j) \qquad\qquad \textbf{6–32}$$

Here **grade** is incremented *before* the de-referencing operation. Remember that **grade** is a pointer to the elements of the fictitious vector, each of whose elements is a four-element vector. Thus, each time **grade** is incremented by 1, it points at the next vector. The difference between 6–31 and 6–32 is as follows: in 6–31, grade is de-referenced before it is incremented; while in 6–32, grade is incremented before it is de-referenced. The arithmetic operations of Figure 6–9 are the same as those of Figure 6–6, except that the notation of 6–31 is used in Figure 6–9.

The ideas that we have discussed extend to arrays of more than two dimensions. For instance, a three-dimensional array can be considered to be a vector, each of whose elements is a two-dimensional array. Each two-dimensional array, in turn, can be considered to be a vector, each of whose elements is a vector. Thus, if the three-dimensional array is named **test**, *(*(*test)) represents the value of the first element, i. e., [0][0][0], of the array.

Array type operations can be implemented with pointers without declaring arrays as such, or using array notation. Figure 6–10, which is a modification of Figure 6–9, is an example of this. Instead of being declared as an array, **grade** is simply declared to be a pointer to type **float**. Then,

$$grade = new\ float[maxnumber*4];\qquad\qquad 6\text{--}33$$

is used to allocate space for the data. Each item of data is referenced using

$$*(grade + 4*i + j)\qquad\qquad 6\text{--}34$$

Note that this is similar to 6–31 except that the second de-referencing operation is omitted because there are no array operations involved.

FIGURE 6–10 ■ An implementation of two-dimensional array operations using pointers.

```
/* an example that relates two-dimensional array operations to pointers */
#include <stream.h>
main()
{
    const int maxnumber=100;
    float *grade;
    int i,j,numb;
    grade = new float[maxnumber*4];
    cout << "\nenter number of students\n";
    cin >> numb;
    while(numb > maxnumber)    {
        cout << "\n the maximum number of students is " << maxnumber;
        cout << "\nenter new number of students\n";
        cin >> numb;
    }  // end while(numb > maxnumber)
    /* data entry */
    for(i=0;i<numb;i++)    {
        cout << "\nenter three grades for student number " << i+1 << "\n";
        for(j=0;j<3;j++)cin >> *(grade + 4*i + j);
    } // end for(i=0;i<numb;i++)
    /* initialize */
    for(i=0;i<numb;i++) *(grade + 4*i + 3)=0.0;
    /* compute averages */
    for(i=0;i<numb;i++)    {
        for(j=0;j<3;j++)*(grade + 4*i + 3) = *(grade + 4*i + 3) +
            *(grade + 4*i + j);
        *(grade + 4*i + 3) = *(grade + 4*i + 3)/3.0;
    }  // end for(i=0;i<numb;i++)
    /* output */
    cout << "\nstudent    average\n\n";
    for(i=0;i<numb;i++)
        cout << i+1 << "             " << *(grade + 4*i + 3) << "\n";
}
```

Usually, straightforward array operations, rather than pointer manipulations, are used because there is less detail for the programmer to keep track of. However, pointer operations can be used to make multidimensional array operations more versatile. In the last section we indicated that all dimensions, except the first, had to be explicitly declared in a function. This limits the versatility of the function because specific dimensions must be used. Functions involving multidimensional arrays would be more versatile if all the dimensions could be passed as arguments to the function. Pointer operations can be used to provide this versatility. An illustration of this is shown in Figure 6–11 which is still another modification of the grade-averaging program.

FIGURE 6–11 ■ An illustration of the use of pointers to pass array dimensions to a function.

```
/* an example illustrating the passing of array data using pointers */
#include <stream.h>
main()
{
    extern void ave_general(float*,int,int);
    const int maxnumber=10;
    float grade[maxnumber][4];
    int i,j,numb;
    cout << "\nenter number of students\n";
    cin >> numb;
    while(numb > maxnumber)    {
        cout << "\n the maximum number of students is " << maxnumber;
        cout << "\nenter new number of students\n";
        cin >> numb;
    }   // end while(numb > maxnumber)   /* data entry */
    for(i=0;i<numb;i++)    {
        cout << "\nenter three grades for student number " << i+1 << "\n";
        for(j=0;j<3;j++)cin >> grade[i][j];
    } // end for(i=0;i<numb;i++)
    ave_general(&grade[0][0],4,numb);
    /* output */
    cout << "\nstudent    average\n\n";
    for(i=0;i<numb;i++)
        cout << i+1 << "              " << *(*grade + 4*i + 3) << "\n";
}


void ave_general(float* grade,int tests,int numb)
{
    int i,j;
    /* initialize */
    for(i=0;i<numb;i++) *(grade + tests*i + 3)=0.0;
    /* compute averages */
    for(i=0;i<numb;i++)    {
        for(j=0;j<3;j++)*(grade + tests*i + 3) = *(grade + tests*i + 3) +
                                    *(grade + tests*i +j);
        *(grade + tests*i + 3) = *(grade + tests*i + 3)/3.0;
    }  // end for(i=0;i<numb;i++)
    return;
}
```

The main program utilizes the two-dimensional array **grade**. The function, **ave_general**, is passed the address of the first element in the array and the pertinent dimensions of the array. The formal parameters corresponding to the dimensions are **tests** and **numb**. Note that **numb** does not represent the row dimension of the array but, rather, the number of rows that are actually used. The first argument of **ave_general** is an ordinary pointer to type **float**, not an array pointer. Thus, the address of the first element is explicitly passed to the function. Pointers, rather than arrays, are used to perform the calculations within the function. Thus, the convenience of array operations is not utilized within the function.

6–6 ■ EVALUATION ORDER

When used in conjunction with array operations, the increment and decrement operators can lead to unpredictable results. Let us illustrate this with some examples. Suppose that **i** has been declared to be an integer, **test** has been declared to be an array of integers, and the following statements are executed.

i = 3;	6–35a
test[i] = i++;	6–35b

Because the increment operator **++** follows the **i**, after 6–35b is executed, **i** is assigned the value 4, and an element of **test** is assigned the value 3. However, *the C++ standards do not define whether that element is **test[3]** or **test[4]**. The evaluation order* is not defined in this case. The rules relating to whether the increment or decrement operators precede or follow a variable, do not apply to the case in question. That is, if the **++** or **– –** symbol is to the right of the assignment operator, its effect on a variable to the left of the assignment operator is undefined. You should always write code that is unambiguous. For instance, in 6–35, suppose that **test[3]** is the element to be assigned a value. An appropriate sequence of statements would be

i = 3;	6–36a
test[i] = i;	6–36b
i++;	6–36c

If the increment operator preceded the **i**, then an appropriate sequence of statements would be

i = 3;	6–37a
test[i] = i + 1;	6–37b
i++;	6–37c

In this case, the terseness of C++ *must* be avoided if the program is to be unambiguous. Of course, readability should not be sacrificed in the interests of terseness.

Do not be tempted to test your compiler to determine how it operates with statements such as 6–35 with the idea of using these statements in your program. There is no guarantee that a new release of your compiler will function in the same way as the old one. You should always write code that is portable and clear.

6–7 ■ STRINGS

The basic ideas of characters and strings were introduced in Section 3–1. Because strings are collections of characters that are stored in a vector, we can now discuss some additional string manipulations. Strings are often variable in length. For instance, string data could be a name entered from the keyboard by the person running the program. The vector that stores such a string must be dimensioned so that it can store the largest possible entered string. However, because it may store strings that are shorter than that dimension, there must be some way of indicating the end of the string. For instance, suppose that a vector is dimensioned to have 100 elements. If this vector stores a string of 20 characters, there must be some way of indicating that the remaining 80 characters are not part of the string. The ASCII character 0, or '\0', is used as the string terminator. Remember that characters are stored as integers. The integer that is the ASCII code usually is used to represent each character. If the integer 0 is stored in one of the elements of the vector, the string is assumed to end at that point. Often, a **#define** compiler directive is contained in one of the header files that is present when string operations are carried out. This statement is

$$\#\text{define NULL } 0 \qquad \textbf{6–38}$$

Thus, when such a compiler directive is used, **NULL** is equivalent to 0. C++ defines **NULL** as 0, and we shall use 0 in the programs and functions of this section. Remember that if **NULL** is used, the appropriate **#define** statement must be included. The advantage of using **NULL** is that its value can be changed simply by changing the statement in the header file and recompiling. However, as mentioned earlier, 0 is the standard string terminator in C++, as well as being the de facto standard in C. For this reason, we shall use 0 explicitly.

There are various ways that a string can be established. For instance,

$$\text{char name[81]} \qquad \textbf{6–39}$$

sets up a string called **name** that can store 80 characters plus the 0 terminator. An alternative procedure is

$$\text{char *name;} \qquad \textbf{6–40a}$$
$$\text{name } = \text{ new char[81];} \qquad \textbf{6–40b}$$

Here **name** is declared to be a pointer to a variable of type **char**, and **new** is used to allocate space for the **name** string. In either case, **name** represents a pointer to the start of the string. Of course, 6–39 represents memory that is allocated at compile time (if the declaration statement is in the main program), while 6–40 allocates memory dynamically.

String *constants* are established by enclosing the string within double quotation marks, and can be assigned to string *pointers* but *not* to vectors. For instance, we can write

$$\text{name} = \text{"bill smith"}; \qquad\qquad \textbf{6–41}$$

Remember that in many systems this will establish an 11-character string. There must be space available for the 0 terminator, even though it is not written.

Strings can be entered from the terminal with **cin** and the $\gg$ operator as with other predefined data types. However, a problem arises with string entry. The normal input operator uses any *whitespace* as a terminator. A whitespace is either a blank, a carriage return (ENTER or RETURN, represented by ASCII 13), or a line feed (ASCII 10). This is convenient for many applications. For instance, consider the statements

$$\text{cin} \gg \text{i}; \qquad\qquad \textbf{6–42a}$$
$$\text{cin} \gg \text{j}; \qquad\qquad \textbf{6–42b}$$
$$\text{cin} \gg \text{k}; \qquad\qquad \textbf{6–42c}$$

where **i**, **j**, and **k** are variables of type **int**. The user of the program can enter the data in several ways. All three numbers can be entered on one line separated by blank spaces; all three numbers can be entered on separate lines; two numbers can be entered on one line and one on another; and so forth. This convenience causes some problems when strings are entered. For example, suppose that **name** is declared as before, and

$$\text{cin} \gg \text{name}; \qquad\qquad \textbf{6–43}$$

is executed. If the person running the program enters

bill smith

the blank will be taken as a delimiter, and **name** will store the string **bill**, but **smith** will be held for the next data input. Thus, a statement of the form of 6–43 is useful only for one-word strings. The function **cin.get** supplied in the **string.h** header file overcomes this problem. (Do not consider the notation involving the period here; the notation will be discussed in a later chapter.) The function is used as follows:

$$\text{cin.get(str,length,term\_char)}; \qquad\qquad \textbf{6–44}$$

where **str** is a string variable (e.g., **name** in the previous examples), **length** is an integer constant or variable that indicates the maximum number of characters that will be read, and **term_char** is a character constant or variable that specifies the terminating character, or delimiter. The terminating character for the input of 6–43 is the whitespace. When **cin. get** is used, the programmer specifies the terminating character. For example, when

$$cin.get(str,80,'\backslash n');$$ **6–45**

is executed, operation pauses until the person running the program enters a string, terminated with a newline. The string will be stored in the string variable **str**. No more than 79 characters can be read using 6–45.

Figure 6–12 illustrates some of the ideas that we have been discussing. In addition, a function named **string_length** that determines the length of a string is included there. Note that **str** is dimensioned to store 81 characters. Statement 6–45 is used to input the string. The length of the input string is obtained with the function **string_length**. Note that the variable **length** is incremented until a 0 is encountered; length is then incremented once more to account for the space in the string occupied by the 0. It may seem as though **sizeof** could be used to determine the length of the string. However **sizeof(str)** results in 81, the total space dimensioned for the **str** vector.

The string that is input is output by the statement

$$cout << "\backslash n" << str;$$ **6–46**

FIGURE 6–12 ■ A function that returns the length of a string.

```
/* a function that returns the length of a string */
#include <stream.h>
main()
{
    extern int string_length(char[]);
    int len;
    char str[81];
    cout << "\nenter string\n";
    cin.get(str,80,'\n');
    len = string_length(str);
    cout << "\nstring length is " << len;
    cout << "\n" << str;
}

int string_length(char st[])
{
    int length=0;
    while(st[length] != 0)length++;
    length++;
    return length;
}
```

Note that there is no problem with whitespace here because the $\ll$ operator uses ASCII 0, not whitespace, to delimit the string.

There are times when one string must be assigned the value of another string. The function **string_assign** (see Figure 6–13) can be used for this purpose. A typical use of this function is

string_assign(str2,str1);   **6–47**

After execution of 6–47, **str2** stores the string assigned to **str1**. The assignment of **str1** is unchanged by this execution. Note that **str2** must be large enough to hold the string stored in **str1**. The programmer must be careful that the vector stored in **str1** is not too large to be adequately stored in **str2**. If the string is too large, then data, the program, or the operating system may be overwritten. This, of course, should always be avoided. The function simply copies each character of **str1** into **str2** until a 0 is reached in **str1**. The **while** loop then terminates and, finally, a 0 is copied into the next position of **str2**. If **str2** is dimensioned to be longer than the string that is copied into it, the data beyond the terminating 0 will be unpredictable, but this is generally of no consequence because the 0 usually terminates all reading of the string data.

If **st1** in Figure 6–13 does not have a 0 (because of error), the function **string_assign** loops indefinitely. A statement could be included to terminate operation if the value assigned to **i** exceeded a specified value.

The function **string_compare** in Figure 6–14 is used to *lexicographically* compare two strings. Two strings are lexicographically ordered if they are in alphabetical order. The function **string_compare** returns 0 if the two strings that are its arguments are the same; it returns a positive number if the first argument would follow the second argument in an alphabetical list; it returns a negative number if the first argument would precede the second argument in an alphabetical list. The function compares two strings on a character-by-character basis. When two unequal characters are found in the same character position, looping terminates. The ASCII codes for the two characters are

FIGURE 6–13 ■ A function that assigns one string to another.

```
void string_assign(char st2[],char st1[])
{
     int i=0;
     while(st1[i] != 0) {
          st2[i] = st1[i];
          i++;
     }
     st2[i] = 0;
     return;
}
```

FIGURE 6–14 ■ A function that lexicographically compares two strings.

```
int string_compare(char st1[],char st2[])
{
    int i=0,j;
    while(st1[i] != 0)  {
        if(st1[i] != st2[i])break;
        i++;
    } // end while(st1[i] != 0)
    j = st1[i] - st2[i];
    return j;
}
```

subtracted. Because the letters further along in the alphabet have higher ASCII codes, the desired results are obtained. The looping terminates when the end of the first string is reached. When this occurs, the ASCII code that is used for the first string in the subtraction is 0. The string **compare** in Figure 6–14 is *case sensitive*. That is, the ASCII codes for the uppercase letters are 32 less than the ASCII codes for the corresponding lowercase letters. Thus, any uppercase letter will be alphabetized before the corresponding lowercase letter. The routine can be made *case insensitive* by checking the ASCII codes of the characters and subtracting 32 from those that lie between 97 and 122, inclusive.

A program that alphabetizes a list of names is shown in Figure 6–15. This program makes use of the functions **string_assign** and **string_compare**. The **name** array is an array of pointers, each of which points to one of the names to be alphabetized. Two strings, **tmp** and **last**, are also established. Note that **last** is set up equal to a string of 19 **z**'s. Thus, it will be the last item in any alphabetized list. The value of **last** is established by looping and assigning a **'z'** to the first 19 elements of **last**; a 0 is assigned to element 20. Alternatively, the **last** array could be initialized in its declaration.

The person running the program is prompted to enter the number of names to be alphabetized, and then **new** is used to allocate memory space for those names. The names are then entered. We assume that only a single name is entered, i. e., a last name. Because only a single name is entered, whitespace is sufficient to indicate the end of the entry, and therefore, the statement

$$cin \gg name[i];$$ 6–48

can be used to enter data.

The actual alphabetizing is done in a pair of nested loops. Consider the inner loop. It finds the name that is alphabetically first. Note that **tmp** has been assigned the string **last**. Now **tmp** is compared with each string in the **name** array. If the string assigned to **name[j]** lexicographically precedes that assigned to **tmp**, then **tmp** is assigned **name[j]**; in addition, **hold** is

FIGURE 6–15 ■ An alphabetizing program.

```
/* an alphabetizing program */
#include <stream.h>
main()
{
    extern void string_assign(char[],char[]);
    extern int string_compare(char[],char[]);
    char *name[100],tmp[20],last[20];
    int numb,i,j,hold;
    for(i=0;i<19;i++)last[i] = 'z';
    last[19] = 0;
    /* input data */
    cout << "\nenter number of names\n";
    cin >> numb;
    /* set up string space in memory */
    for(i=0;i<numb;i++)name[i] = new char[20];
    for(i=0;i<numb;i++)  {
        cout << "\nenter name " << i+1 << ":   ";
        cin >> name[i];
    }
    /* alphabetize */
    string_assign(tmp,last);
    for(i=0;i<numb;i++)  {
        /* find leading name */
        for(j=0;j<numb;j++)  {
            if(string_compare(tmp,name[j]) > 0)  {
                string_assign(tmp,name[j]);
                hold = j;
            } //end if(tmp > name[j])
        } // end for(j=0;j<numb;j++)
        /* output leading name and set leading name last */
        cout << "\n" << name[hold];
        string_assign(name[hold],last);
        string_assign(tmp,last);
    }   // end for(i=0;i<numb;i++0
}
```

assigned the value of **j**. After the loop has cycled completely, **tmp** stores the name that is lexicographically first, and **hold** stores its index. That name, **name[hold]**, is then output. Next, **name[hold]** and **tmp** are each assigned the value of the string **last**, i.e, the string of **z**'s. Therefore, the name that was lexicographically first becomes a string of 19 **z**'s, thus insuring that the program does not pick it again. The outer loop cycles again. This causes the inner loop to cycle, and the name that is lexicographically first in the modified list is output. After the outer loop cycles **numb** times, the complete alphabetized list has been output.

The alphabetizing routine of Figure 6–15 is an example of a very simple *sort*. It contains two loops, each of which cycles **numb** times. Thus, if there are n names in the list, the time required to sort the list varies as n^2. If the list is long, the time required for the sort can become excessive. We now consider some additional sorting techniques that are usually faster than the one in Figure 6–15.

A simple sorting technique called a *ripple sort* is shown in Figure 6–16. In this sorting technique a name in the list, which we shall call the *test name*, is compared with the one preceding it in the list. If the two names are not in alphabetical order, then they are interchanged. If an interchange has been made, then the test name becomes the first in the pair. Now the test name is compared with the new name that now precedes it in the list. This operation continues until the test name reaches a point in the list where it alphabetically follows the one with which it is tested. At this point, the next name in the list, following the original position of the test name, becomes the test name, and the operation is repeated.

The form of the procedure that we shall use places a dummy name "A" in the zero position of the list. This will always be alphabetically first. The procedure starts by using term number one, which is in the second position of

FIGURE 6–16 ■ An example of a ripple sort.

```
/* a ripple sort */
#include <stream.h>
main()
{
    extern void string_assign(char[],char[]);
    extern int string_compare(char[],char[]);
    char *name[100],sub[20];
    int numb,i,j;
    /* input data */
    cout << "\nenter number of names\n";
    cin >> numb;
    /* set up string space in memory */
    for(i=0;i<=numb;i++)name[i] = new char[20];
    for(i=1;i<=numb;i++)  {
        cout << "\nenter name " << i << ":  ";
        cin >> name[i];
    }
    /* ripple sort */
    string_assign(name[0],"A");
    for(i=1;i<=numb;i++)  {  // outer loop starts
        j = i;
        while(string_compare(name[j],name[j-1])<0)  {    // inner loop starts
            /* interchange */
            string_assign(sub,name[j]);
            string_assign(name[j],name[j-1]);
            string_assign(name[j-1],sub);
            j--;
        } // end while - end inner loop
    } // end for -end outer loop
    /* output data */
    for(i=1;i<=numb;i++)cout << "\n" << name[i];
}
```

the list, as the test name, and continues until the last name in the list is used as the test name. Thus, when the procedure is complete, the list is sorted. In this type of sort, names "ripple" up the list, hence the term ripple sort. Note that the 0 position of the loop is not output. The dummy name "A" is used to ensure that every name in the list is used, in turn, as the test name.

In the program in Figure 6–16, the test name is selected in the outer loop. The first test name is the second name in the list, counting **name[0]** as the first name. The inner loop performs the sort with each of the chosen test names. Then, after the test name is moved as far as possible toward the top of the list, the inner loop terminates. Then operation proceeds with the next test name (the third one in the list). After the outer loop has cycled completely, the list will be ordered alphabetically. The ripple sort requires fewer operations than the simple sort in Figure 6–15. In general, if there are **n** terms in the list, then there will be, at most, **n(n + 1)/2** comparisons performed in the ripple sort. Thus, if **n** is considerably greater than 1, the ripple sort requires approximately half the number of operations of the simple sort in Figure 6–15. Note that if the list were completely sorted at the start of the procedure, there would be only **n** comparisons performed. Therefore, a ripple sort is particularly fast if the list presented to it is almost sorted.

Another type of sort, called a *shell sort*, named after the man who developed it, takes advantage of the fact that the ripple sort will be fast if the list sorted is short and/or if the list is almost ordered. In the shell sort, small sublists within the original list are sorted with a ripple sort. Then, larger sublists are picked and ordered. At each stage, the list becomes more and more ordered so that even though the lists sorted by the ripple sorts become longer, each sort proceeds rapidly. In the last step, the entire list is sorted with a ripple sort and, because this list is almost ordered, the ripple sort proceeds rapidly.

The diagrams in Figures 6–17a through 6–17e illustrate these ideas. A list of 10 letters is shown. The first sorting interval is 4. The four sublists are illustrated in Figure 6–17b. Each list is shown on a separate horizontal line. Each sublist is sorted with a ripple sort. The result of these sorts is shown in Figure 6–17c. The list now looks like the one shown in Figure 6–17d. The next sorting interval is 1. That is, the entire list is ripple sorted. Because the list in Figure 6–17d is almost completely sorted, the final ripple sort will be rapid. The completely sorted list is shown in Figure 6–17e.

The spacing that is used to pick elements of the sublists affects the speed of the sort. It has been experimentally determined that the following algorithm is a good one to use. The final interval is always 1. (The complete list is sorted.) Each preceding interval is three times the preceding one plus 1. For instance, if there are four intervals selected, they will be 1, 4, 13, and 40. Of course no interval can be longer than the list itself.

A program that implements the shell sort is shown in Figure 6–17f. The **do-while** loop is used to pick the intervals according to the algorithm of the previous paragraph. The actual sorting is done in the nested loops. The spacing is established in the outer loop, and the ripple sorts are performed in the two inner loops.

A very fast sorting technique is the *quick sort.* The basis for this procedure is that a list can be sorted into two lists quickly. The first list contains all of the items that precede a certain element of the list, called the *pivot value*, and the second contains all the items that follow the pivot value. The procedure is then applied recursively to each of the two sublists. As the procedure is repeated, the lists involved become successively shorter. Eventually, the entire list is sorted. Because successively shorter lists are involved, the operation is fast. The operation of a quick sort is illustrated in Figure 6–18a. The pivot value is arbitrarily chosen to be the last item in the list. The procedure starts at the beginning of the list and compares each element in turn with the pivot value. When an element that *follows* the pivot is found, that element is marked. This occurs when the letter **H** is encountered in the list in Figure 6–18a. Now the operation transfers to the end of the list. Working backwards, each element in turn is compared with the pivot. When an element that *precedes* the pivot is found, that element is marked. In Figure 6–18a that is the value **F**. Now the two marked values are interchanged (**H** and **F**). The operation then transfers to the position of the first marked element where **H** used to

FIGURE 6–17 ■ A shell sort. (a)–(e) A representation; (f) a program that uses a shell sort.

```
J  I  H  G  F  E  D  C  B  A
```

(a)

```
J           F           B
   I           E           A
      H           D
         G           C
```

(b)

```
B           F           J
   A           E           I
      D           H
         C           G
```

(c)

```
B  A  D  C  F  E  H  G  J  I
```

(d)

```
A  B  C  D  F  F  G  H  I  J
```

(e)

```
/* a shell sort */
#include <stream.h>
main()
{
    extern void string_assign(char[],char[]);
    extern int string_compare(char[],char[]);
    char *name[100],sub[20];
    int numb,numb_int,space,i,j,k;
    int interval[50];
    /* input data */
    cout << "\nenter number of names\n";
    cin >> numb;
    /* set up string space in memory */
    for(i=0;i<=numb;i++)name[i] = new char[20];
    for(i=1;i<=numb;i++)   {
        cout << "\nenter name " << i << ":   ";
        cin >> name[i];
    }
    /* shell sort */
    string_assign(name[0],"A");
    numb_int = 1;
    interval[1] = 1;
    do   {
        interval[numb_int+1] = 3*interval[numb_int] + 1;
        numb_int = numb_int + 1;
    } while(2*interval[numb_int] < numb); // end do while
    for(i=numb_int;i>=1;i--)   {   // outer loop
        j = i;
        space = interval[i];
        while(j+space<=numb)   {   // middle loop
            k = j + space;
            while((string_compare(name[k],name[k-space])<0)&&(k-space>=0))   {
                // inner loop
                /* interchange */
                string_assign(sub,name[k]);
                string_assign(name[k],name[k-space]);
                string_assign(name[k-space],sub);
                k = k - space;
            }   // end while - inner loop
            j = j + 1;
        }   // end while - middle loop
    }   // end for - outer loop
    /* output data */
    for(i=1;i<=numb;i++)cout << "\n" << name[i];
}
```

(f)

be and **F** is now. Successive values of the list are checked until one that
follows the pivot is found and marked. In Figure 6–18a, it is **I**. Operation
transfers to the second marked element (originally **F** and now **H**). Proceeding
backwards, successive elements are checked until one that precedes the pivot
is found; in this case it is **A**. The new pair of marked values is interchanged.
Operation continues in this manner until the position of the second marked
value passes (in the reverse direction) the position of the first marked value.
Notice that, for simplicity, we are assuming that there are no duplicate names

in the list. Now the list is broken into two lists, with the division between the last two marked values. Now the quick sort procedure is applied, in turn, to each of the two sublists, and it is repeated recursively until all of the sublists are reduced to either single lists or to sorted two-element lists. Once this is done, the complete list is sorted.

A program that implements the quick sort is shown in Figure 6–18b. The procedure **quicksort** is implemented as a function so that it can be called recursively. The last name in the list is, arbitrarily, chosen as the pivot and is

FIGURE 6–18 ■ A quick sort. (a) A representation; (b) a program that uses a quick sort.

(a)

```
/* a quick sort alphabetizing routine */
#include <stream.h>
main()
{
    extern void quicksort(int,int,char*[]);
    char* name[100];
    int numb,i;
    cout << "\nEnter number of names\n";
    cin >> numb;
    /* set up string space in memory */
    for(i=0;i<numb;i++)name[i] = new char[20];
    /* enter names */
    for(i=0;i<numb;i++)    {
        cout << "\nenter name " << i+1 << ":   ";
        cin >> name[i];
    }
    quicksort(0,numb-1,name);
    for(i=0;i<numb;i++)cout << "\n" << name[i];
}
```

```
void quicksort(int i,int j,char* name[])
{
    extern void string_assign(char[],char[]);
    extern int string_compare(char[],char[]);
    int ii,jj;
    char test[20],sub[20];
    if(i<j)   {
        ii = i - 1;
        jj = j;
        string_assign(test,name[j]);
        while(ii<jj)  {
            while((string_compare(name[ii+1],test)<0)&&(ii<=j-1))ii++;
            if(ii<j)ii++;
            while((string_compare(name[jj-1],test)>=0)&&(jj>=ii-1)&&
                (jj>i+1))jj--;
            if(jj>i)jj--;
            /* interchange */
            if(jj>ii)   {
                string_assign(sub,name[ii]);
                string_assign(name[ii],name[jj]);
                string_assign(name[jj],sub);
            } // end if(jj>ii)
        }   // end while(ii<jj)
        /* move ii to bottom of first list and jj to top of second */
        if(ii>jj)  {
            ii--;
            jj++;
        }  // end if(ii>jj)
        /* if pivot first in list then move to first position */
        if(jj==i)   {
            jj = i+1;
            ii = i;
            /* interchange */
            string_assign(sub,name[i]);
            string_assign(name[i],name[j]);
            string_assign(name[j],sub);
        }  // end if(jj==1)
        /* recursive calls */
        quicksort(i,jj-1,name);
        quicksort(jj,j,name);
    }   // end if(i<j)
    return;
}
```

(b)

assigned the value **test**. The two **string_compare** functions are used to mark
the list as previously discussed. The marked values are then interchanged.
Note that when **jj** becomes equal to or greater than **ii**, the searching of the
list terminates.

In the actual implementation of the program, only one list is used. The
first and second arguments of the function **quicksort** indicate the location
(starting and end points) of the sublist within the original list. Thus, the list
is sorted in place, and when the recursive procedure terminates, the list is
sorted.

We have illustrated sorting using alphabetization. Of course, this need not be the case, and these procedures could be applied to numerical lists as well.

6–8 ■ COMMAND LINE ARGUMENTS

Normally a program is invoked by typing its name followed by RETURN (ENTER). For example, suppose that you write a program called **sum** that adds an arbitrary number of integers. The program is stored in a file called **sum**, or possibly, **sum.com** or **sum.exe**. The program is invoked by entering the word **sum** followed by RETURN (ENTER). Using previously discussed procedures, the person running the program would be prompted for the numbers and would enter them. When experienced persons run programs, it is often convenient for them to be able to enter some or all of the data on the same line that invokes the program. For instance, suppose that the program **sum** was to add the numbers 10, 20, and 30. The following could be entered

$$\text{sum 10 20 30} \hspace{3cm} \textbf{6–49}$$

followed by RETURN. The line that invokes the program is called a *command line*, and the items of data following the program name are called *command line arguments*.

Arguments on the command line can be passed to the main program in a manner similar to the passing of arguments to a function. In all the programs considered thus far, we have written the word **main** followed by a pair of empty parentheses. The parentheses need not be empty and, in fact, are not empty when arguments are to be passed on the command line. When command line arguments are used, a specific formal parameter list is included within the parentheses that follow **main**. The first formal parameter is always an integer that is assigned the number of arguments passed to the program; the second formal parameter is an array of pointers, in which each pointer points to a string. Each string stores one command line argument. When command line arguments are used, the first line of the main program is

$$\text{main(int argc,char* argv[ ])} \hspace{2.5cm} \textbf{6–50}$$

The variable names **argc** and **argv** are arbitrary, but these particular names are widely used. The first command line argument passed to the program is always the program name. Thus, if 6–49 were the command line, there would be four arguments passed to **main**. For this reason, **argc** would be assigned 4, while **argv[0]** would be assigned the string **"sum"**, **argv[1]** would be assigned the string **"10"**, and so forth.

The command line arguments are stored in the form of strings. If these strings are numerical data to be manipulated by the program, then the string data must be converted into the appropriate numerical data types. Most C++

systems have functions that convert numbers in string form into the appropriate numerical types. These functions are usually called **atoi**, **atol**, and **atof**. The argument of each of these is a string representation of a number; each of these functions returns a number of type **int**, **long**, or **float** respectively. Consult your manual to determine the functions that are provided with your system and the header files that must be included when they are used.

Figure 6–19 is a program that outputs the sum of the integers that are entered on the command line. The first line of the program is 6–50. The integers entered as strings on the command line are converted to type **int** and are stored in the **data** vector, and this vector is output, by the statements

$$\text{for(i = 0;i<argc − 1;i ++) \{} \qquad\qquad \textbf{6–51a}$$
$$\text{data[i] = atoi(argv[i + 1]);} \qquad \textbf{6–51b}$$
$$\text{cout << data[i] << "   ";} \qquad\qquad \textbf{6–51c}$$
$$\text{\} // end for(i = 0;i<argc − 1;i ++);} \qquad \textbf{6–51d}$$

Note that each string is converted to type **int** and then is assigned to an element of the **data** vector. The statements 6–51 are not an essential part of the program, but are included as an example. The desired sum is obtained in the single line

$$\text{for(i =1;i<argc;i ++)sum = sum + atoi(argv[i]);} \qquad \textbf{6–52}$$

Throughout the book we have used streams to input and output data. Data that is input from the keyboard, or output to the screen, is always in string form. When data is input, the string is automatically converted to the correct data type. For instance, if the data is read into a variable of type **int**, then the string representation of the integer is converted into the appropriate binary representation of the integer. In a similar way, when data is output, the data type is automatically converted to a string. Streams can be used to convert data that is stored in a string just as if that data was entered as a string from the keyboard. The name of the string array and the name of the

FIGURE 6–19 ■ A program that utilizes command line arguments.

```
/* illustration of the use of command line arguments */
#include <stream.h>
main(int argc,char* argv[])
{
     extern int atoi(char[]);
     int sum=0,data[20],i;
     for(i=0;i<argc-1;i++)    {
         data[i] = atoi(argv[i+1]);
         cout << data[i]  << "   ";
     } // end for(i=0;i<argc-1;i++)
     for(i=1;i<argc;i++)sum = sum + atoi(argv[i]);
     cout << "\nsum = " << sum;

}
```

stream must be related. This is done with the C++ function **istream**. The form of its use is

$$\text{istream cinx(str\_len,str);} \qquad \qquad \textbf{6-53}$$

Here **str_len** is an integer that specifies the maximum length of the string, **str** is the name of the string, and **cinx** is the stream name. Note that any valid name could be used here; the name need not be **cinx**. Now, if

$$\text{cinx} \gg \text{b;} \qquad \qquad \textbf{6-54}$$

is executed, the string assigned to **str** will be converted to the type of **b**, and then assigned to **b**. For instance, if **b** is of type **int**, and the string **str** stores the string **"10"**, then, after execution of 6-54, **b** is assigned the integer value 10.

Figure 6-20 is a modification of Figure 6-19. Now streams are used to convert the string data to type **int**. The loop that corresponds to 6-51 is

```
for(i = 0;i<argc −1;i++) {                                    6-55a
    istream cinx(string_length(argv[i+1]) ,argv[i+1]);       6-55b
    cinx >> data[i];                                         6-55c
    cout << data[i] << "     ";                              6-55d
    sum  =  sum + data[i];                                   6-55e
} // end for(i = 0;i<argc −1;i++)                            6-55f
```

The function **string_length** (see Figure 6-12) is used to determine the length of the string. Alternatively, a number that is equal to or greater than the length of the largest string could be used in place of the first argument. For instance, 6-55b could be written as

$$\text{istream cinx(81,argv[i+1]);} \qquad \qquad \textbf{6-56}$$

Note that the function **istream** must be invoked separately for each string. In the case of 6-55, there are **argc − 1** strings, and therefore, **istream** is invoked on each pass through the loop.

FIGURE 6-20 ■ An illustration of the use of command line arguments and strings.

```
/* illustration of the use of command line arguments */
#include <stream.h>
main(int argc,char* argv[])
{
    extern int string_length(char[]);
    int sum=0,data[20],i;
    for(i=0;i<argc-1;i++)    {
        istream cinx(string_length(argv[i+1]),argv[i+1]);
        cinx >> data[i];
        cout << data[i] << "     ";
        sum = sum + data[i];
    }   // end for(i=0;i<argc-1;i++)
    cout << "\nsum = " << sum;
}
```

EXERCISES

Check any programs that you write by running them on your computer. If you write functions, your answers should include the main programs that run them.

1. Why is it necessary to dimension an array?
2. Write a program that stores up to 100 nonnegative floating-point numbers in a *vector*. The numbers are to be entered by the person running the program. Input is to be terminated when a negative number is entered. The average of all the entered positive numbers is to be output.
3. Repeat Exercise 2, but now use pointers to access the data stored in the vector.
4. Repeat Exercise 2 but, instead of declaring a vector, use **new** to obtain the storage space for the numerical data.
5. Write a function that divides each element of the vector of Exercise 2 by the average of all the elements.
6. Modify the function of Exercise 5 as follows. The vector in the main program that calls the function is to be unchanged; a second vector, declared in the main program, should contain the divided elements.
7. Write a function that returns the largest element in a vector of integers.
8. Repeat Exercise 5, but now use global variables to pass the data to and from the function.
9. Repeat Exercise 6, but now use global variables to pass the data to and from the function.
10. Write a program that stores up to 100 students' grades in a two-dimensional array and the students' ID numbers in a vector of integers. Each student takes four tests. Corresponding rows in the array and in the vector are to store data for the same student. The student's averages are to be computed and stored in the two-dimensional array. Each student's ID number and average are to be output.
11. Repeat Exercise 10, but now have the averaging performed in a function.
12. Repeat Exercise 10, but now have all data entry, output, and calculations performed in separate functions.
13. Repeat Exercise 10, but now use pointers to access all data.
14. Repeat Exercise 10, but now use an array of pointers to implement the data storage of the grades and averages.
15. Repeat Exercise 12, but now the functions should be able to work with a two-dimensional array of arbitrary dimensions.
16. Write a program that sets the initial value of all the elements in an array of two rows and three columns to 6.5.
17. Write a function that returns the number of words in a string. Assume that adjacent words are separated by a blank space.
18. Write a function whose arguments are two strings. The function should return 0 if the first string is not contained within the second string; if the first string is contained in the second string, it should return the starting position of the first string in the second string.

19. Repeat Exercise 10, but now have the output in order of the students' averages, highest average first.
20. Write a program that is passed a string on its command line. The input string should be output by the program, all in capital letters, even if the corresponding letters in the input string were lowercase.
21. Write a program that outputs the name of the file that stores the program.
22. Write a program that outputs the product of the floating-point numbers that are entered on the *command line*. Use the function **atof** to convert the *command line arguments* to floating-point numbers.
23. Repeat Exercise 22, but now use *streams* to perform the data conversion.
24. Write a program that inputs an arbitrary number of integers and then sorts the list using a shell sort.
25. Repeat Exercise 24, but now use a quick sort.

CHAPTER 7
Elementary Structures and Other User-Defined Data Types

An array can have many elements, but each must store data of the same type. In this chapter, we introduce a data type, called a *structure*, that can store different types of data. For instance, we could set up a data structure that stores a student's name, ID number, and grades. Thus, a string, an integer, and a number of floating-point numbers could be stored in a single data element. Because arrays of structures can be set up, versatile data storage results. Data storage can be even more general than we have indicated here. In this chapter we introduce some elementary ideas about structures and other forms of data storage. In the next chapter, we shall extend and generalize these concepts.

7–1 ■ STRUCTURES

It is often convenient to have a data type whose elements store several *different* types of data. For instance, suppose that data for students in a class is to be manipulated. Items of interest are: each student's name, ID number, grades in four tests, and average grade. It would be convenient to use an array to store the class data. However, the student's name is a string, the ID number is an integer, and the grades and averages are floating-point numbers. Because an array stores only one data type, a single array cannot store all the required information. However, C++ allows users to define a data type, called a *structure*, that can store different data types. For instance, we can set up a structure that stores a string, an integer, and four floating-point numbers. The structure is a user-defined data type, and an array of such structures could be set up. Thus, the desired form of storage would be accomplished.

Structures are established with the keyword **struct**. For example, suppose that a structure called **student** is to be set up to contain a student's name, ID number, grade in three tests, and average. The following declaration accomplishes this:

```
struct student{                                  7–1a
      char name[40];  //student's name           7–1b
      int id_numb;   // ID number                7–1c
      float grades[3];  // test grades           7–1d
      float average;   // average of tests       7–1e
};                                               7–1f
```

The declaration of the structure consists of the keyword **struct** followed by the *structure tag*, **student**. The structure tag is the *name* associated with this particular user-defined data type, **student** in this case. The structure tag is followed by a pair of curly braces containing declarations of all the data types contained in the structure. The declarations follow the usual form. For instance, the **student** structure contains a string array of 40 characters called **name**, an integer called **id_numb**, a vector of three elements of type **float** called **grades**, and a floating-point number called **average**. Optional comments have been included to identify the variables. The components of a structure are called the *fields* of the structure. Note the semicolon following the closing brace. Usually, semicolons do not follow closing braces in C++, but structure declarations are an exception, and a semicolon is included.

Once a data type has been established, variables can be declared to be of this data type, just as we do with standard data types. For instance, following 7–1, we can write

```
student stu1,stu2,programming[100];              7–2
```

Here we have declared 102 structures of type **student**. These are **stu1**, **stu2**, **programming[0]**, **programming[1]**, . . . , **programming[99]**.

A variable in a structure is specified by writing the structure variable name, followed by a period or dot (.), followed by the element of the structure that the variable represents. This is called *dot notation*. For instance, consider the following:

```
cin >> stu1.name;                                7–3a
```

or

```
programming[5].grades[2]  =  100.0;              7–3b
```

In 7–3a the single-word string entered from the keyboard has been assigned to the **name** field of the **stu1** structure. Similarly, the execution of 7–3b results in 100.0 being assigned to the third element of the **grades** vector field in the **programming[5]** structure.

A program illustrating the use of structures is shown in Figure 7–1. The **student** structure is set up as in Statement 7–1. The array called **programming** is set up to store data of type **student**. That is, each element of the

FIGURE 7–1 ■ An example of basic structure manipulation.

```
/* an example of basic structure manipulation */
#include <stream.h>
main()
{
    struct student {
        char name[40];   // student's name
        int id_numb;     // ID number
        float grades[3]; // test grades
        float average;   // average of tests
    };
    const int max_number = 10;
    student programming[max_number];
    int i,j,numb;
    /*   enter data   */
    cout << "\nenter number of students\n";
    cin >> numb;
    while(numb > max_number)   {
        cout << "\nnumber too large\nonly " << max_number;
        cout << " students allowed";
        cout << "\nenter number of students\n";
        cin >> numb;
    }   // end while(numb > max_number)
    for(i=0;i<numb;i++)   {
        cout << "\nstudent number " << i+1;
        cout << "\nenter name\n";
        cin >> programming[i].name;
        cout << "\nenter ID number\n";
        cin >> programming[i].id_numb;
        cout << "\nenter grades in three tests\n";
        for(j=0;j<3;j++)cin >> programming[i].grades[j];
    }   // end for(i=0;i<numb;i++)
    /* compute averages */
    for(i=0;i<numb;i++)    {
        programming[i].average = 0.0;
        for(j=0;j<3;j++)programming[i].average += programming[i].grades[j];
        programming[i].average /= 3.0;
    }   // end for(i=0;i<numb;i++)
    /*   output data   */
    cout <<"\nName    ID number   Average\n";
    for(i=0;i<numb;i++)   {
        cout << "\n" << programming[i].name << "     ";
        cout << programming[i].id_numb << "       ";
        cout << programming[i].average;
    }   // endfor(i=0;i<numb;i++)
}
```

programming array is a structure of type **student**. The fields of each element of the vector are referenced with dot notation. For instance, the name is entered into element **i** with the statement

$$\text{cin} >> \text{programming[i].name;} \qquad \text{7–4}$$

This statement is in a **for** loop that cycles **numb** times, where **numb** is the number of students in the class. We assume here that a single name is entered without whitespace. If this were not the case, the **cin.get** function should be used here (see Figure 6–12).

Data for the grades is entered with the nested **for** loop

for(j = 0; j<3; j ++)cin >> programming[i].grades[j];   **7–5**

Dot notation is used to reference the appropriate element.

The averages are computed in the nested loops

```
for(i = 0;i<numb;i ++) {                                          7–6a
    programming[i].average  =  0.0;                              7–6b
    for( j = 0; j<3; j ++)
        programming[i].average  +=  programming[i].grades[j];    7–6c
    programming[i].average /= 3.0;                               7–6d
}  // end for(i = 0;i<numb;i ++)                                 7–6e
```

Note that **programming[i].average** is set equal to zero before the appropriate grades are added to it. This could have been done by initializing the **programming** array. However, the entire structure would have to be specified for each element of the **programming** array, which would have been very tedious. In the next chapter we shall consider procedures for initializing structures. We have used += and \= rather than the somewhat more readable equivalent forms. This was done because of the length of the variable names involved.

Variables representing the *same* structure type can be used on either side of an assignment. For instance, if the declaration of 7–2 has been made, then the following are valid:

stu1 = programming[3];   **7–7a**

programming[3] = stu2   **7–7b**

The variables on either side of the assignment sign must be of the same user-defined structure type. For instance, suppose that we declare a structure called **learner** whose field declarations are *identical* to those of 7–1 except that the tag **student** has been replaced by the tag **learner**. A variable of type **learner** *cannot* be used in an assignment with a variable of type **student**.

The operation **sizeof** can be used with structures just as it is with standard data types. For example, the following are valid:

i = sizeof(student);   **7–8a**

i = sizeof(programming[1]);   **7–8b**

In either case, **i** is assigned the number of bytes required to store the specified structure. Remember, that where **sizeof** is concerned, a byte is the amount of storage required to store a data item of type **char**.

7–2 ■ STRUCTURES, POINTERS, AND FUNCTIONS

In this section we shall discuss the relationship between structures and pointers. In addition, we shall consider the use of structures with functions. It should be noted that this discussion is not complete. The discussion of classes in the next chapter will treat these topics in a more general fashion. Classes are an important feature of C++, and the discussions in this chapter provide only an introduction to this major topic.

Pointers to structures can be declared in essentially the same way as are pointers to other variables. For instance, if the **student** structure is declared as in 7–1, then the following would be a valid declaration:

$$\text{student *programming;} \hspace{3cm} \textbf{7–9}$$

Now **programming** is a pointer to a data item of type **student**. When the program is run, memory is reserved for the data dynamically, using **new**. For instance, suppose that **numb** is an integer variable, and that memory space is to be reserved for **numb** variables of type **student**. The following will accomplish this:

$$\text{programming = new student[numb];} \hspace{2cm} \textbf{7–10}$$

Pointer arithmetic works with user-defined data types just as it does with the built-in data types. For instance, **programming** points at the first set of data of type **student**, **programming +1** points at the second set of data, and so forth.

Data can be referenced using dot notation in conjunction with pointers. For example, the execution of

$$\text{(*(programming+1)).average = 100.0;} \hspace{2cm} \textbf{7–11}$$

causes 100.0 to be assigned to the **average** variable field of the second set of **programming** data. Note that the two pairs of parentheses are necessary to cause the operations to be carried out in the proper order.

Figure 7–2 is a modification of the program in Figure 7–1. In it, the data is referenced using pointers and no array is declared. The **programming** pointer is set up using Statement 7–9. The memory required for data storage is allocated dynamically using 7–10. Dot notation is used to reference the data. The actual computational details of the program follow those of Figure 7–1.

When pointers are involved using dot notation to reference the variables (see 7–11), the notation is cumbersome. The operator −> can be used to simplify the notation. Note that the operator is written by entering a minus sign and a greater-than symbol with no intervening space. Using this operator, Statement 7–11 would be written as

$$\text{(programming+1)−>average = 100.0;} \hspace{2cm} \textbf{7–12}$$

Note that typing the asterisk, one pair of parentheses, and the dot is avoided when the −> operator is used. Figure 7–3 is a modification of Figure 7–2, where the −> operator is used when the structure data is referenced.

Structures and Functions

Structures can be passed to functions just as the built-in data types can. When this is done, all the specifics of the structure must be made available to the

FIGURE 7–2 ■ An example of pointer manipulations with structures.

```
/* an example of pointer manipulations and structures */
#include <stream.h>
main()
{
    struct student {
        char name[40];   // student's name
        int id_numb;     // ID number
        float grades[3]; // test grades
        float average;   // average of tests
    };
    student *programming;
    int i,j,numb;
    /*   enter data   */
    cout << "\nenter number of students\n";
    cin >> numb;
    /* allocate space for structure */
    programming = new student[numb];
    for(i=0;i<numb;i++)   {
        cout << "\nstudent number " << i+1;
        cout << "\nenter name\n";
        cin >> (*(programming+i)).name;
        cout << "\nenter ID number\n";
        cin >> (*(programming+i)).id_numb;
        cout << "\nenter grades in three tests\n";
        for(j=0;j<3;j++)cin >> (*(programming+i)).grades[j];
    }  // end for(i=0;i<numb;i++)
    /* compute averages */
    for(i=0;i<numb;i++)   {
        (*(programming+i)).average = 0.0;
        for(j=0;j<3;j++)(*(programming+i)).average +=
                             (*(programming+i)).grades[j];
        (*(programming+i)).average /= 3.0;
    }  // end for(i=0;i<numb;i++)
    /*   output data   */
    cout <<"\nName    ID number    Average\n";
    for(i=0;i<numb;i++)   {
        cout << "\n" << (*(programming+i)).name << "    ";
        cout << (*(programming+i)).id_numb << "    ";
        cout << (*(programming+i)).average;
    }  // endfor(i=0;i<numb;i++)
}
```

function. Remember that because a new definition of an identical structure is considered to be a different data type, the structure cannot be declared again in the function. However, if the declaration of the structure is global, only a single declaration exists. We shall illustrate this discussion with the program in Figure 7–4. This program works with a single structure, rather than with an array of structures. This is done to illustrate the actual passing of structure data, rather than the passing of an array (pointer). The **student** structure is used (see 7–1). Data is entered and the average of the grades is computed by the function **set_average**. Because pass by reference is used, the data in the main program is modified by the function.

FIGURE 7–3 ■ A modification of Figure 7–2. The $->$ operator is used here.

```
/* an example of pointer manipulations and structures */
#include <stream.h>
main()
{
    struct student {
        char name[40];   // student's name
        int id_numb;     // ID number
        float grades[3]; // test grades
        float average;   // average of tests
    };
    student *programming;
    int i,j,numb;
    /*  enter data  */
    cout << "\nenter number of students\n";
    cin >> numb;
    /* allocate space for structure */
    programming = new student[numb];
    for(i=0;i<numb;i++)  {
        cout << "\nstudent number " << i+1;
        cout << "\nenter name\n";
        cin >> (programming+i)->name;
        cout << "\nenter ID number\n";
        cin >> (programming+i)->id_numb;
        cout << "\nenter grades in three tests\n";
        for(j=0;j<3;j++)cin >> (programming+i)->grades[j];
    }  // end for(i=0;i<numb;i++)
    /* compute averages */
    for(i=0;i<numb;i++)   {
        (programming+i)->average = 0.0;
        for(j=0;j<3;j++)(programming+i)->average +=
            (programming+i)->grades[j];
        (programming+i)->average /= 3.0;
    }  // end for(i=0;i<numb;i++)
    /*  output data  */
    cout <<"\nName    ID number    Average\n";
    for(i=0;i<numb;i++)  {
        cout << "\n" << (programming+i)->name << "      ";
        cout << (programming+i)->id_numb << "      ";
        cout << (programming+i)->average;
    }  // endfor(i=0;i<numb;i++)
}
```

The structure is declared globally by placing its declaration before the start of the main program. The function is declared in the main program with the statement

$$\text{extern void set\_average(student\&);} \qquad \textbf{7–13}$$

Note that the user-defined **student** data type is treated exactly the same as a built-in data type. The function is called by the statement

$$\text{set\_average(jim);} \qquad \textbf{7–14}$$

FIGURE 7–4 ■ An illustration of the use of a structure in a pass by reference.

```
/* an example of passing a structure to a function */
#include <stream.h>
struct student {
      char name[40];   // student's name
      int id_numb;     // ID number
      float grades[3]; // test grades
      float average;   // average of tests
};
main()
{
      extern void set_average(student&);
      student jim;
      int j;
      /*  enter data  */
      cout << "\nenter name\n";
      cin >> jim.name;
      cout << "\nenter ID number\n";
      cin >> jim.id_numb;
      cout << "\nenter grades in three tests\n";
      for(j=0;j<3;j++)cin >> jim.grades[j];
      set_average(jim);
      /*  output data  */
      cout <<"\nName    ID number   Average\n";
      cout << "\n" << jim.name << "       ";
      cout << jim.id_numb << "        ";
      cout << jim.average;
}

extern struct student;
void set_average(student& person)
{
      int j;
      /* compute averages */
      person.average = 0.0;
      for(j=0;j<3;j++)person.average += person.grades[j];
      person.average /= 3.0;
      return;
}
```

Note that **jim** is the name of the variable that stores the structure. The first two lines of the function are

$$\text{extern struct student;} \qquad \textbf{7–15a}$$
$$\text{void set\_average(student\& person)} \qquad \textbf{7–15b}$$

Because we assume that the function and the main program are stored in separate files, the **extern** declaration is necessary. After the user-defined data type is declared globally, the passing of data to and from the function follows the details of data passing with built-in data types. We have illustrated these ideas using pass by reference. However, pass by value could be used as well.

Figure 7–5 illustrates the passing of an array of structures to a function. Again, the ideas follow the passing of data with the built-in types, except that

FIGURE 7–5 ■ A program that passes an array of structures to a function.

```
/* an example of passing an array of structures to a function */
#include <stream.h>
struct student {
     char name[40];  // student's name
     int id_numb;    // ID number
     float grades[3]; // test grades
     float average;  // average of tests
};
main()
{
     extern void make_average(student[],int);
     const int max_number = 10;
     student programming[max_number];
     int i,j,numb;
     /*  enter data  */
     cout << "\nenter number of students\n";
     cin >> numb;
     while(numb > max_number)  {
         cout << "\nnumber too large\nonly " << max_number;
         cout << " students allowed";
         cout << "\nenter number of students\n";
         cin >> numb;
     }  // end while(numb > max_number)
     for(i=0;i<numb;i++)  {
         cout << "\nstudent number " << i+1;
         cout << "\nenter name\n";
         cin >> programming[i].name;
         cout << "\nenter ID number\n";
         cin >> programming[i].id_numb;
         cout << "\nenter grades in three tests\n";
         for(j=0;j<3;j++)cin >> programming[i].grades[j];
     }  // end for(i=0;i<numb;i++)
     /* compute averages */
     make_average(programming,numb);
     /*  output data  */
     cout <<"\nName    ID number   Average\n";
     for(i=0;i<numb;i++)  {
         cout << "\n" << programming[i].name << "     ";
         cout << programming[i].id_numb << "        ";
         cout << programming[i].average;
     }  // endfor(i=0;i<numb;i++)
}


extern struct student;
void make_average(student group[],int numbr)
{
     int i,j;
     for(i=0;i<numbr;i++)   {
         group[i].average = 0.0;
         for(j=0;j<3;j++)group[i].average += group[i].grades[j];
         group[i].average /= 3.0;
     }  // end for(i=0;i<numb;i++)
     return;
}
```

the structure is declared globally. We shall extend the ideas introduced here in the next chapter.

7-3 ■ MEMORY-SAVING OPERATIONS

In this section we discuss some procedures that can be used to conserve the amount of memory used to store data. In particular, we shall discuss the use of *fields* and *unions*.

Fields

The smallest standard data type is the **char**. Normally, eight bits are used to store a **char**. However, there are occasions when not all eight bits are needed to store the data. For instance, suppose a variable can represent one of only two values, such as true or false. Only one bit would be needed to store such a value. If it were stored in a variable of type **char**, seven bits would be wasted. Similarly, an unsigned integer lying between 0 and 7 requires only three bits for storage. In general, when reduced bits are used, the stored data represents an **unsigned** integer. C++ allows the programmer to restrict the number of bits used to store the data in an **unsigned** integer field of a structure. (Some systems do not restrict the data type to **unsigned**, but many do.) This is done by following the name of the field with a colon and an integer. The integer specifies the number of bits to be used to store the named data item. For example, consider the following structure declaration:

struct restricted {	7–16a
unsigned abc:1;	7–16b
unsigned def:3;	7–16c
unsigned ghi:2;	7–16d
};	7–16e

The type **restricted** contains three **unsigned** integers: **abc** is stored in one bit, **def** is stored in three bits, and **ghi** is stored in two bits.

The program in Figure 7–6 uses **unsigned** integers, each of which is stored in a single bit. Such integers can represent either 0 or 1 and are called *flags*. The structure type flags has four one-bit fields. In the program, the variable **flg** is declared to be of type **flags**, and all of the fields of **flg** are set equal to 0. The user enters a number between 0 and 15, and some logical operations are performed that may change the values of one or more of **flg.fl1**, **flg.fl2**, **flg.fl3**, and **flg.fl4** from 0 to 1. These values are then output. Actually the logic of the program is such that the output number, made up of the four flags in sequence, is the binary representation of the input number. If integers, instead of one-bit numbers, were used in this program, the logic would be unchanged; storage space is saved, however, when one-bit fields are used.

FIGURE 7–6 ■ An illustration of the use of bit fields.

```
/* an illustration of the use of fields */
#include <stream.h>
main()
{
    struct flags {
        unsigned fl1:1;
        unsigned fl2:1;
        unsigned fl3:1;
        unsigned fl4:1;
    };
    unsigned i;
    flags flg;
    flg.fl1 = flg.fl2 = flg.fl3 = flg.fl4 = 0;
    cout << "\nenter number between 0 and 15\n";
    cin >> i;
    if (i > 7)  {
        flg.fl4 = 1;
        i = i - 8;
    }  // end if(i > 7)
    if (i > 3)  {
        flg.fl3 = 1;
        i = i - 4;
    }  // end if(i > 3)
    if ( i > 1)  {
        flg.fl2 = 1;
        i = i - 2;
    }  // end if(i > 1)
    if (i > 0)flg.fl1 = 1;
    cout << "\n" << flg.fl4 << flg.fl3 << flg.fl2 << flg.fl1;
}
```

Although the use of reduced bit fields can save storage space, it does have disadvantages. Often, such use may cause the program logic to become more complex, and the space saved by the reduced bit fields is offset by the additional space required to store the program. Reduced bit operations often require more time to execute than do operations using standard data types. In addition, undetected errors can occur with any integer overflow, and in the case of reduced bit operations, very small numbers can produce overflow. For instance, if the number 2 is assigned to any of the one-bit variables of Figure 7–6, an overflow results.

Unions

Sometimes a variable is used in only one part of a program and is never used again. If there is a pressing need to conserve memory, such a variable could be reused later in the program to store other data. If both data items are the same type, then this can be done easily; the variable is simply used again. On the other hand, it might be convenient for a single variable to store data of different types in different parts of the program. There is a storage type called a *union* that allows this to be done. The use of unions can substantially reduce the readability of programs, and can result in bugs that are hard to detect. For these reasons, unions should *not* be used unless there is a pressing need to do so.

Unions are declared with the keyword **union**; for example,

$$\begin{array}{ll} \text{union multi\_store \{} & \textbf{7--17a} \\ \quad\text{float flt;} & \textbf{7--17b} \\ \quad\text{int in;} & \textbf{7--17c} \\ \quad\text{char ch;} & \textbf{7--17d} \\ \text{\};} \end{array}$$

Here we have declared a data type called **multi_store**. A variable of type **multi_store** is allocated only enough memory to store a single variable. The amount of storage allocated depends on the declared data type in the union that requires the most memory for its storage. In the case of **multi_store**, the data type that requires the most storage space is type **float**. Thus, variables of type **multi_store** will occupy the same memory space as do ordinary variables of type **float**. Note that the construction of 7–17 is the same as that for a structure except that the keyword **union** is used in place of **struct**. The names used for the tag of the union and for the variables can be any valid names.

A program that uses the **multi_store** union is shown in Figure 7–7. Notice that **x** is declared to be of type **multi_store**. Consider the statement

$$x.in \;=\; 123; \hspace{3cm} \textbf{7--18}$$

The variables of the union are referenced using dot notation, just as the variables of a structure are. Of course, in the structures that we have considered, the data for each field is stored in a separate memory location. In the case of the union, the data for all the fields for a given variable is stored in the same

FIGURE 7–7 ■ An illustration of **union** operations.

```
/* an example of a union */
#include <stream.h>
main()
{
    union mult_store  {
        float flt;
        int in;
        char ch;
    };
    mult_store x;
    x.in = 123;
    cout << "\ninteger " << x.in;
    x.flt = 54.2344;
    cout << "\nfloating point " << x.flt;
    cout << "\nerror " << x.in;
    x.ch = 'w';
    cout << "\ncharacter " << x.ch;
}
```

memory locations (but not at the same time). After 7–18 is executed, the value of **x.in** is output. The compiler must know how to interpret the data stored in the memory locations so that it can convert it into a string for output. The variable **x.in** is of type **int**, and thus, the integer is converted into a string. After the output of the integer data, the statement

$$x.flt \ = \ 54.2344; \qquad\qquad \text{7–19}$$

is executed. This floating-point number is then output. Next the statement

$$\text{cout} \ll \text{"\textbackslash nerror "} \ll x.in; \qquad\qquad \text{7–20}$$

is output. This results in meaningless data. The floating-point number 54.2344 is stored in the memory locations reserved for **x**. When 7–20 is executed, the bit patterns stored are interpreted as an integer, and that value is output. Integers and floating-point numbers are stored in different amounts of storage space and in different ways. Thus, 7–20 results in the output of a meaningless integer. It is the responsibility of the programmer to keep track of the type of data "currently" stored by the union. Note that it is easy to lose track of this, and as mentioned, unions should be used only when absolutely necessary.

Unions can be used within structures and, when this is done, the union is not named; for example,

structure test {	7–21a
int aaa;	7–21b
float def;	7–21c
union {	7–21d
float ghi;	7–21e
char jkl;	7–21f
};	7–21g
};	7–21h

In this case the field **ghi** and **jkl** share the same memory locations. Dot notation is used as usual. For instance, suppose that **bbb** has been declared to be of type **test**. Then **bbb.ghi** would reference data of type **float**, while **bbb.jkl** would reference data of type **char**.

EXERCISES

Check any programs that you write by running them on your computer.

1. Modify the program of Exercise 10 of Chapter 6. Now, the student's name and ID number are also to be entered. In addition, a letter grade is to be computed and stored. The letter grade is to be based on the student's average according to the following rule. If the average is 90 or higher, the grade is A; if the average is less than 90, but equal to or greater than 80, the grade is B; if the average is less than 80, but equal to or

greater than 70, the grade is C; if the average is less than 70, but equal to or greater than 60, the grade is D; if the average is less than 60, the grade is F. All the data for a single student is to be stored in a single structure.

2. Modify the program of Exercise 1. Now have the data output in alphabetical order according to the students' names.

3. Repeat Exercise 1, but do not store the data in an array. Use pointers to reference the data.

4. Modify the program in Figure 7–4. Now, use pass by value. The function should return the average.

5. Modify the program of Exercise 1. The averages and the student's grades should be computed in functions that modify the value of the data in the main program.

6. Repeat Exercise 5. Now the functions should return the average and grade, but they should not modify the data in the main program.

7. Modify the program of Figure 7–4. Now, use pointers to pass the data.

8. Write a program that inputs a decimal number that lies between 0 and 127, and returns its binary representation. Each binary digit should be stored in one bit. Compare this with a program that stores each binary digit in a variable of type **unsigned**.

9. Test your system to determine the output when the integers 0, 1, 2, and 3 are each assigned to a one-bit variable.

10. Write a program that stores data of types **double**, **long**, and **char** in the same set of memory locations. Check the output that occurs when the data is misinterpreted. For example, output the type **double** after a type **long** has been stored.

CHAPTER 8
Classes

The structure discussed in the last chapter is an example of a user-defined data type. However, the concept of a user-defined type can be extended in very powerful ways. When a new data type is defined, it is usually desirable to define functions to operate on that new data type. The functions can be made part of the structure so that, if a structure is provided to a program, the functions that operate on it are supplied as well. Operators can also be provided with the structure. The ability to provide functions and operators as part of the structure is an important feature of C++.

Ideally, the functions that are supplied with a structure should be debugged thoroughly. If we assume that this has been done, then the manipulation of the data by these functions should be error-free. If that structure were part of a large program being worked on by many programmers, then as long as the structure data is manipulated using the functions built into the structure, there should be no errors in that large program. Of course, the overall algorithms that use the built-in functions could have bugs, but these would be relatively easy to find. On the other hand, if the functions that directly manipulate the data have errors, the debugging process could become very difficult. For instance, although a programmer might assume that the bug was in the code that he or she was writing, the error could actually be in one of the functions that directly manipulated the data. We assume that the supplied functions that manipulate the data are error-free. Suppose, however, that one programmer writes a function that directly manipulates the data, but does not test it thoroughly, so that it contains a bug. That function, with its bug, could then be distributed to all the programmers working on the large program. If that function is used, with the assumption that it is error-free, then the nasty bugs discussed previously would result. For this reason, such functions that directly manipulate the data should be written only by the programmer(s) whose responsibility it is to maintain the structure. (It is assumed that the associated responsibility ensures that the functions will be tested thoroughly.)

Similarly, errors can result if a programmer writes a statement in the main program that directly changes the data of the structure. For instance, suppose that in a charge account program, there are two variables: one representing total purchases and the other the outstanding balance. If the value of the total-purchases variable is increased, the outstanding balance should be increased by the same amount. Any function supplied with the structure that increases the total-purchases variable would automatically increase the outstanding-amount value as well. Suppose that a programmer writes a statement in the main program that directly changes the value assigned to the total-purchases variable without changing the outstanding balance; then the entire data structure is in error. This is an intolerable situation. Of course, it would be just as intolerable if the programmer wrote a function that changed the total purchases without changing the outstanding balance. It is simple to tell programmers not to write functions that directly manipulate the data of the structure. However, the temptation to directly manipulate the data may be very strong. For this reason, it is desirable if the programming language has a feature that prevents programmers from either directly manipulating certain data, or from writing functions that directly manipulate that data. In this case, the data is said to be *private*, and only certain specified functions can manipulate it. The data in a structure is *public*; that is, all functions can manipulate it, and the data can be directly accessed and changed from the main program. The idea of a structure can be generalized to a *class* that has private elements that can be accessed only by functions and operators that are part of the **class**. The only difference between a structure and a **class** is the idea that some of the elements of a **class** can be made private; that is, a **class** can provide privacy. Note that an element of a **class** can be a variable, a function, or an operator. Any of these can be made private.

Classes have other important advantages. When a **class** containing data and its associated data-manipulating functions is supplied to a programmer, that programmer does not have to be concerned with the details of manipulating the data. Instead, he or she can concentrate on the larger programming problem. In addition, the **class** is itself a smaller module that can be written and debugged once, and then supplied to many programmers. Another advantage is that one **class** can be made part of a larger **class** without having to rewrite code. The properties of classes that we have discussed fall into the general concept of *object-oriented programming,* which greatly facilitates the development of large, complex programs.

8–1 ■ CLASSES

As we discussed in the introduction to this chapter, it is often desirable for a structure to contain the functions that operate on its data. Figure 8–1 contains such a structure, and we shall use it as an example in our discussion.

The structure is called **checking**, and in a very simple way, it could model a system used to maintain the checking accounts of a bank's depositors. A complete banking system would obscure the discussion with unnecessary details. However, there are enough details in the program in Figure 8–1 so that the discussion can be complete.

The three items of data in the structure **checking** are: **name**, the depositor's name; **act_no**, the depositor's account number; and **balance**, the current balance in the account. There are five functions associated with the structure. Each of these functions takes a single argument, the depositor's account number. The functions are: **make_deposit** which is used to credit a deposit to the depositor's account; **debit_check**, which is used to subtract the amount of a check from the depositor's balance; **service_charge**, which is used to subtract a service charge from the depositor's account; **open_account**, which is used to open an account for a new depositor; **output_data**, which outputs a depositor's data to the screen.

Note that the structure is written as we discussed in Chapter 7, except that the functions are declared within the structure definition; that is,

struct checking {	8–1a
char name[81];	8–1b
int act_no;	8–1c
float balance;	8–1d
void make_deposit(int);	8–1e
void debit_check(int);	8–1f
void service_charge(int);	8–1g
void open_account(int);	8–1h
void output_data(int);	8–1i
};	8–1j

The declaration of the functions is the same as the declaration of functions in a main program.

The functions themselves are defined in the usual way. A complex program could contain several structures, each containing functions with the same name. The definitions of the functions that belong to the various structures have been written outside of the body of the structure; there must be some way, therefore, to associate the function with its corresponding structure. This is done with the *scope-resolution operator* ::. For instance, the first line of the **make_deposit** function is

void checking::make_deposit(int acc_numb)   8–2

Remember that we previously used the scope-resolution operator in conjunction with global variables. In that case the operator was preceded by a blank space; in the present instance it is not.

The function could be defined within the body of the structure. In this case the scope, the resolution operator, and its preceding structure tag would not be used. For instance, the single line 8–1e could be replaced by

void make_deposit(int acc_numb)	8–3a
if(acc_numb == act_no) {	8–3b
cout << "\nenter amount of deposit\n";	8–3c
cin >> amount;	8–3d
balance += amount;	8–3e
} // end if(acc_numb == act_no)	8–3f
else cout << "\n wrong depositor\n"	8–3g
return;	8–3h
}	

That is, the single line 8–1e is replaced by the complete function as defined in 8–3. When a function is written within the body of the structure it becomes an inline function (see Section 5–10) so that, unless the function is very short, it is better to write and compile the functions separately. Also note that certain C++ compilers will not allow inline functions to contain loops.

The compiler must know the form of the structure. This is usually accomplished by placing the structure declaration (see 8–1) at the start of any file that is to be compiled. A convenient way to do this is to write the structure declaration into a header file and use the **#include** compiler directive to include the structure definition in all files that are to be compiled.

The main program is illustrated in Figure 8–1b; it simulates a banking operation. In such an operation, the data for a depositor would be read from a disk file and stored in the variables of the program. We shall consider file operations later in the book. In the program in Figure 8–1, the initial data for a depositor is set up by statements within the main program. In this case, the depositor's name is **smith**, the account number is **11**, and the balance is **1050**. Note that the program only stores a single account at any one time. We shall extend these ideas subsequently.

The remainder of the program consists of an endless loop. The user is prompted to enter the account number. Each of the functions checks that this

---

FIGURE 8–1 ■ (a) The structure **checking** and its member functions; (b) a main program that uses the structure. (pp. 206–208).

```
/* an illustration of a structure containing functions */
#include <stream.h>
struct checking {
     char name[81];
     int act_no;
     float balance;
     void make_deposit(int);
     void debit_check(int);
     void service_charge(int);
     void open_account(int);
     void output_data(int);
};
```

```
void checking::make_deposit(int acc_numb)
{
    float amount;
    if(acc_numb == act_no)  {
            cout << "\nenter amount of deposit\n";
            cin >> amount;
            balance += amount;
    }  // end if(acc_numb == act_no)
    else cout << "\nwrong \n";
    return;
}


void checking::debit_check(int acc_numb)
{
    float amount;
    cout << "\nenter amount of check\n";
    cin >> amount;
    if(acc_numb == act_no)balance -= amount;
    else cout << "\nwrong \n";
    return;
}

void checking::service_charge(int acc_numb)
{
    float amount;
    cout << "\nenter amount of service charge\n";
    cin >> amount;
    if(acc_numb == act_no)balance -= amount;
    else cout << "\nwrong depositor\n";
    return;
}

void checking::open_account(int acc_numb)
{
    float amount;
    if(acc_numb != 0)    {
        cout << "\check account number\n";
        return;
    }  // end if(acc_numb !=0)
    cout << "\nenter account number\n";
    cin >> act_no;
    cout << "\nenter name\n";
    cin >> name;
    cout << "\nenter initial deposit\n";
    cin >> amount;
    balance = amount;
    return;
}

void checking::output_data(int acc_numb)
{
    if(acc_numb == act_no)  {
        cout << "\naccount number " << act_no;
        cout << "\n" << name;
        cout << "\nbalance " << balance;
    } // end if(acc_numb == act_no) start else
    else cout << "\nwrong depositor\n";
    return;
}
```

(a)

FIGURE 8–1 ■ (*continued*)

```
main()
{
    extern void exit(int);
    checking depositor;
    char ch;
    int account_numb;
    /* simulation of data input from disk or tape */
    depositor.name[0] = 's';
    depositor.name[1] = 'm';
    depositor.name[2] = 'i';
    depositor.name[3] = 't';
    depositor.name[4] = 'h';
    depositor.name[5] = 0;
    depositor.act_no = 11;
    depositor.balance = 1050.00;
    /* end of data input simulation */
    for( ; ; ) {
        cout << "\nenter account number; enter 0 for new account\n";
        cin >> account_numb;
        cout << "\nMenu\n";
        cout << "\nm make deposit";
        cout << "\nd debit check";
        cout << "\ns service charge";
        cout << "\no open account";
        cout << "\nx output data";
        cout << "\nz end program\n";
        cin >> ch;
        switch(ch) {
            case 'm':
                depositor.make_deposit(account_numb);
                break;
            case 'd':
                depositor.debit_check(account_numb);
                break;
            case 's':
                depositor.service_charge(account_numb);
                break;
            case 'o':
                depositor.open_account(account_numb);
                break;
            case 'x':
                depositor.output_data(account_numb);
                break;
            case 'z':
                exit(0);
                break;
            default:
                cout << "\nwrong entry\n";
                break;
        }  // end switch
    } // end for( ; ; )
}
```

(b)

is the same as the account number for the stored data. Next, a menu is output, and the user is prompted to enter a letter corresponding to a desired function. The entered character is used to pick a branch in a **switch-case** construction. Each branch consists of a call to one of the functions of the structure. The next-to-last branch of the **switch-case** construction terminates the program, and the last branch is the default.

The structure variable is declared with the statement

$$\text{checking depositor;} \qquad \textbf{8-4}$$

That is, **depositor** is declared to be a variable of type **checking**. The variables are referenced using dot notation. For instance,

$$\text{depositor.name[0]} \ = \ \text{'s';} \qquad \textbf{8-5a}$$
$$\text{depositor.act\_no} \ = \ 11; \qquad \textbf{8-5b}$$

The functions of Figure 8–1 verify that the account number is correct, and then prompt for an amount that is added to or subtracted from the balance. An exception is the **open_account** function, which prompts for a new account number, name, and balance, and then stores this data in the appropriate variables of the **depositor** structure. The **output_data** function simply outputs the depositor's data, if the account number entered in response to the prompt is the same as that stored in the **depositor** structure.

Note that the functions are called with dot notation. For instance, the **make_deposit** is called with the statement

$$\text{depositor.make\_deposit(account\_numb);} \qquad \textbf{8-6}$$

The function call in this case differs from others that we have considered. The structure variable name, **depositor** in this case, is part of the function call. Because **depositor** is a variable of type **checking**, this indicates to the compiler that **make_deposit** is a function that belongs to the structure **checking**. In addition, the word **depositor** indicates to the compiler that the function is to operate data contained in the structure called **depositor**. This is equivalent to passing the address of the **depositor** structure to the function so that 8–6 is actually a pass by reference and the function can modify the variables contained in the **depositor** structure. In other words, because this is a pass by reference, the values stored in the **depositor** structure can be modified by the function **make_deposit**. In the last chapter, we used the structure variable name as one of the arguments of the function when a pass by reference was used. There are two reasons for not using the structure variable name, **depositor**, here. First, it is not necessary to do so because, as we have stated, the dot notation makes the structure variable name (address) available. This permits the function to access the structure. Furthermore, if the structure variable name were provided as an argument, the function would be provided with two different "copies" (one via dot notation and the other via the argument) of the depositor structure address. Errors can result in this case, and it should be avoided.

Note that there could be more than one structure variable. For instance, the program might have the declaration

checking depositor,person;   8–7

In this case, both **depositor** and **person** are variables of type **checking**. The variables

depositor.act_no   8–8a

and

person.act_no   8–8b

are different and are stored in different structures. In addition, the statement

depositor.make_deposit(account_numb);   8–9a

calls the function **make_deposit**, which manipulates variables of **depositor**, while the statement

person.make_deposit(account_numb)   8–9b

calls the function **make_deposit**, which manipulates variables of **person**. The manipulations of structures that contain functions are similar to those of structures that do not contain them, except that dot notation must be used to call the contained functions, and the referencing of the structure variables is somewhat different.

In the introduction we discussed the need for privacy. C++ implements this with an additional data type called a *class*. A class is the same as a structure except that some or all of its variables and functions can be made private. In fact, a structure is simply a class with all of its components public. The form of the declaration of a class is very similar to that of a structure. The word **struct** is replaced by **class**, and the word **public** appears within the declaration. The program in Figure 8–2 performs essentially the same operations as that in Figure 8–1 except that a class is used in place of a structure. The notation and operations used with a class are essentially the same as those used with a structure.

The class **checking** is declared with these statements:

```
class checking {                               8–10a
    char name[81];                             8–10b
    int act_no;                                8–10c
    float balance;                             8–10d
public:                                        8–10e
    void make_deposit(int);                    8–10f
    void debit_check(int);                     8–10g
    void service_charge(int);                  8–10h
    void open_account(int);                    8–10i
    void output_data(int);                     8–10j
    void simulate_input(int);                  8–10k
};                                             8–10l
```

This is essentially the same as the structure of 8–1 except for line 8–10e which consists of **public:** and line 8–10k that declares the function **simulate_input**. All variables and functions of a class that are written before **public:** are private. Private variables and functions can be accessed *only* by functions that are members of the class. (We shall modify this statement somewhat

FIGURE 8–2 ■ (a) The class **checking** and its member functions; (b) a main program that uses the class. (pp. 211–213).

```
/* an illustration of a class */
#include <stream.h>
class checking {
     char name[81];
     int act_no;
     float balance;
public:
     void make_deposit(int);
     void debit_check(int);
     void service_charge(int);
     void open_account(int);
     void output_data(int);
     void simulate_input();
};

void checking::make_deposit(int acc_numb)
{
     float amount;
     if(acc_numb == act_no)  {
              cout << "\nenter amount of deposit\n";
              cin >> amount;
              balance += amount;
     }  // end if(acc_numb == act_no)
     else cout << "\nwrong depositor\n";
     return;
}


void checking::debit_check(int acc_numb)
{
     float amount;
     cout << "\nenter amount of check\n";
     cin >> amount;
     if(acc_numb == act_no)balance -= amount;
     else cout << "\nwrong depositor\n";
     return;
}

void checking::service_charge(int acc_numb)
{
     float amount;
     cout << "\nenter amount of service charge\n";
     cin >> amount;
     if(acc_numb == act_no)balance -= amount;
     else cout << "\nwrong depositor\n";
     return;
}
```

FIGURE 8–2 ■ *(continued)*

```
void checking::open_account(int acc_numb)
{
     float amount;
     if(acc_numb != 0)   {
         cout << "\check account number\n";
         return;
     }   // end if(acc_numb !=0)
     cout << "\nenter account number\n";
     cin >> acc_numb;
     act_no = acc_numb;
     cout << "\nenter name\n";
     cin >> name;
     cout << "\nenter initial deposit\n";
     cin >> amount;
     balance = amount;
     return;
}

void checking::output_data(int acc_numb)
{
     if(acc_numb == act_no)   {
         cout << "\naccount number " << act_no;
         cout << "\n" << name;
         cout << "\nbalance " << balance;
     } // end if(acc_numb == act_no) start else
     else cout << "\nwrong depositor\n";
     return;
}

void checking::simulate_input()
{
     name[0] = 's';
     name[1] = 'm';
     name[2] = 'i';
     name[3] = 't';
     name[4] = 'h';
     name[5] = 0;
     act_no = 11;
     balance = 1050.00;
     return;
}
```

(a)

subsequently.) For the case of the class **checking**, the variables **name**, **act_no**, and **balance** can be read and modified only by the functions of the class. If 8–10 contained additional function declarations that were written before the word **public:**, these additional functions could be called only by themselves or by the functions declared on lines 8–10f to 8–10k. In particular, private variables and functions cannot be accessed directly from the main program.

FIGURE 8–2 ■ *(continued)*

```
main()
{
    extern void exit(int);
    checking depositor;
    char ch;
    int account_numb;
    depositor.simulate_input();
    for( ; ; )  {
        cout << "\nenter account number; enter 0 for new account\n";
        cin >> account_numb;
        cout << "\nMenu\n";
        cout << "\nm make deposit";
        cout << "\nd debit check";
        cout << "\ns service charge";
        cout << "\no open account";
        cout << "\nx output data";
        cout << "\nz end program\n";
        cin >> ch;
        switch(ch) {
            case 'm':
                depositor.make_deposit(account_numb);
                break;
            case 'd':
                depositor.debit_check(account_numb);
                break;
            case 's':
                depositor.service_charge(account_numb);
                break;
            case 'o':
                depositor.open_account(account_numb);
                break;
            case 'x':
                depositor.output_data(account_numb);
                break;
            case 'z':
                exit(0);
                break;
            default:
                cout << "\nwrong entry\n";
                break;
        }  // end switch
    } // end for( ; ; )
}
```

(b)

In the program in Figure 8–1, the initial input was simulated by a set of statements in the main program that directly manipulated the variables of the **depositor** structure. The variables of the **depositor** class, however, are not directly accessible from the main program. Therefore, we have added the function called **simulate_input**, which is a public function, to establish the initial values of the **depositor** class variables. This function is called from the main program with the statement

depositor.simulate_input();   8–11

Note that this function takes no arguments. The remainder of the program in Figure 8–2 is the same as that in Figure 8–1. Remember that the only difference between a structure and a class is that variables and functions can be made private in a class. However, this difference often reduces the number of errors that occurs in programs.

8–2 ■ ARRAYS OF CLASSES–CONSTRUCTORS AND DESTRUCTORS–ASSIGNMENT

In the example in Figure 8–2 there was a single *instantiation*, or specific occurrence, of the class **checking**. That instantiation was called **depositor**. We shall next consider examples where there are many instantiations of the class. In fact, we shall set up an array of classes.

Often certain operations are always performed when each instantiation of a class is established. This is called *initialization*. These operations could be written into a function that is called by the program that declares the instantiation of the class. For instance, in Figure 8–2, the instantiation of **depositor** to be of the class **checking** occurred in the declaration

checking depositor;   8–12

The initializing function should be called immediately after the declaration. (Note that instantiations of classes can occur either in functions or in the main program. For purposes of this discussion, we shall assume that the instantiation occurs in the main program.) A problem can arise. Suppose that the person writing the main program forgets to write the call to the initializing function. A hard-to-find error could occur. It would be better if the initializing function were called automatically whenever an occurrence of the class was established. Such an automatically called initializing function is called a *constructor*.

A constructor is simply a function of the class. It is distinguished as a constructor by having the *same* name as the class. The constructor is never specifically called; thus it returns no value, and no return value, not even **void**, is listed in its declaration or body. Arguments can be specified for constructors unless an array of the class is declared. The first example that we shall consider will use an array of the class **checking** so that the constructor will take no arguments. Later in this section we shall consider an example of a constructor with arguments. Figure 8–3 includes a constructor for the **checking** class. It is declared in the class as

checking( );   8–13

The actual body of the constructor is listed as

checking::checking( )	8–14a
{	8–14b
balance = 0.00	8–14c
cout << "***********initialized*********";	8–14d
}	8–14e

Statement 8–14d would not be included in an actual constructor; its only purpose is to print out a line each time that the constructor is called. If you include such a line, you can verify the operation of the constructor. Statement 8–14d should be removed after the program is debugged.

After a program (or function) that uses a class has finished its operations, there are often "clean-up" operations that must be performed. For instance, some programs may modify characteristics of the operating system to enhance their operations. If the program simply terminated, leaving the operating system in the modified state, all subsequent computer operations would be disrupted. Thus, it is desirable to have a function that is automatically called whenever an instantiation of a class goes out of existence. Such a function is called a *destructor*. Just as the constructor, a destructor also has the same name as the class, except that it is preceded by the *tilde*, ~. A destructor cannot have arguments. Figure 8–3 contains an example of a destructor. Its declaration within the class is

~checking( );   8–15

The actual body of the destructor is

checking::~checking( )	8–16a
{	8–16b
cout << "\n**********finished**********";	8–16c
}	8–16d

In this example, the destructor simply outputs the line containing the word **finished**. In practice, this line would be replaced by one or more statements that perform some operation. Both constructors and destructors can be defined within the body of the class.

If a variable is declared within a block, then its scope is over that block. The constructor will be called at that point in the block when the variable is declared, and the destructor will be called at the end of the block. It is said that the constructor is called when the variable "goes out of scope."

The main program in Figure 8–3 sets up an array of classes. The declaration is

$$\text{checking depositor[total\_depositors];} \qquad \text{8–17}$$

where **total_depositors** is a constant of type **int**, that has been assigned the value 10. Thus, 8–17 sets up 10 variables of type **checking**. When the program is run, the word initialized will be output 10 times, and the value assigned to **balance** in each instantiation of the class will be set equal to 0.0.

The functions of the class are called by preceding the function name with **depositor[i]**, where **i** represents an integer variable or value in the range

FIGURE 8–3 ■ An illustration of a class constructor. (a) The class; (b) the main program that sets up an array, each of whose elements is of type **checking**. (pp. 216–218).

```
/* an illustration of class constructors and destructors */
#include <stream.h>
class checking {
     char name[81];
     int act_no;
     float balance;
public:
     int find_depositor(int);
     void make_deposit(int);
     void debit_check(int);
     void service_charge(int);
     void open_account(int);
     void output_data(int);
     checking();
     ~checking();
};

checking::checking()
{
     balance = 0.00;
     cout << "\n***********initialized*********";
}

checking::~checking()
{
     cout << "\n***********finished*********";
}

int checking::find_depositor(int acc_numb)
{
     int ans=0;
     if(acc_numb == act_no)ans = 1;
     return ans;
}
```

```
void checking::make_deposit(int acc_numb)
{
     float amount;
     if(acc_numb == act_no)   {
               cout << "\nenter amount of deposit\n";
               cin >> amount;
               balance += amount;
     }  // end if(acc_numb == act_no)
     else cout << "\nwrong depositor\n";
     return;
}


void checking::debit_check(int acc_numb)
{
     float amount;
     cout << "\nenter amount of check\n";
     cin >> amount;
     if(acc_numb == act_no)balance -= amount;
     else cout << "\nwrong depositor\n";
     return;
}


void checking::service_charge(int acc_numb)
{
     float amount;
     cout << "\nenter amount of service charge\n";
     cin >> amount;
     if(acc_numb == act_no)balance -= amount;
     else cout << "\nwrong depositor\n";
     return;
}

void checking::open_account(int acc_numb)
{
     float amount;
     if(acc_numb != 0)   {
         cout << "\check account number\n";
         return;
     }  // end if(acc_numb !=0)
     cout << "\nenter account number\n";
     cin >> acc_numb;
     act_no = acc_numb;
     cout << "\nenter name\n";
     cin >> name;
     cout << "\nenter initial deposit\n";
     cin >> amount;
     balance = amount;
     return;
}

void checking::output_data(int acc_numb)
{
     if(acc_numb == act_no)   {
         cout << "\naccount number " << act_no;
         cout << "\n" << name;
         cout << "\nbalance " << balance;
     } // end if(acc_numb == depositor>act_no) start else
     else cout << "\nwrong depositor\n";
     return;
}
```

(a)

FIGURE 8–3 ■ *(continued)*

```
main()
{
     extern void exit(int);
     const int total_depositors=10;
     int is_depositor = 0,i,actual_depositors=0,ender=0;
     checking depositor[total_depositors];
     char ch;
     int account_numb;
     while(ender == 0)  {
          cout << "\nenter account number\nenter 0 for new account";
          cout << "\nenter -1 to terminate program\n\n";
          cin >> account_numb;
          if(account_numb < 0)break;
          for(i=0;i<total_depositors;i++)  {
               if(account_numb == 0)break;
               is_depositor = depositor[i].find_depositor(account_numb);
               if(is_depositor == 1)break;
          } // end for(i=0;i<total_depositors;i++)
          if((is_depositor == 0)&&(account_numb != 0))continue;
          cout << "\nMenu\n";
          cout << "\nm make deposit";
          cout << "\nd debit check";
          cout << "\ns service charge";
          cout << "\no open account";
          cout << "\nx output data";
          cout << "\nz end program\n";
          cin >> ch;
          switch(ch) {
               case 'm':
                    depositor[i].make_deposit(account_numb);
                    break;
               case 'd':
                    depositor[i].debit_check(account_numb);
                    break;
               case 's':
                    depositor[i].service_charge(account_numb);
                    break;
               case 'o':
                    if(actual_depositors == total_depositors) {
                         cout << "\nnot enough space for new account\n";
                         break;
                    }  // end if(actual_depositors == total_depositors)
                    depositor[actual_depositors].open_account(account_numb);
                    actual_depositors++;
                    break;
               case 'x':
                    depositor[i].output_data(account_numb);
                    break;
               case 'z':
                    ender = 1;
                    break;
               default:
                    cout << "\nwrong entry\n";
                    break;
          }  // end switch
     } // end while(ender == 0)
}
```

(b)

of 0 to **total_depositors − 1**. For example, the **make_depositor** function is called with the statement

depositor[i].make_deposit(account_numb);   8–18

When there are many instantiations of a class, space is reserved for the variables of *each* instantiation. However, only *one* set of functions is stored. An exception to this is the case of inline functions. This corresponds to the case of ordinary functions.

Because the program in Figure 8–3 stores data for more than one **depositor**, we have changed it from the program in Figure 8–1. There is no initialization of the data for a single **depositor**. The data for the depositors is entered from the keyboard. Several depositors can have their data stored simultaneously in different elements of the **depositor** array. We have added the function **find_depositor**. This function takes an account number as an argument, and returns 0 if the argument does not correspond to the **act_no** stored for the **depositor** that is the (implied) argument of the function. The function returns 1 if the argument does correspond to the stored account number. For instance, if the function call is

x = depositor[3].find_depositor(22);   8–19

then **x** is assigned 1 if **depositor[3].act_no** is assigned 22, and **x** is assigned 0 if **depositor[3].act_no** is assigned any other value.

The loop within the endless loop of the main program is used to find a depositor that corresponds to a given account number. This loop scans through all entered accounts until **find_depositor** returns 1. The value of the corresponding index of the depositor array can then be used to identify the desired depositor. If the specified account number is not found, the user is prompted to enter a new account number.

We have replaced the endless **for** loop of Figure 8–2 with a **while** loop. This loop continues to cycle as long as the variable **ender** is assigned the value 0. This value is not changed unless the z option of the menu is picked. At that time, **ender** is assigned the value 1, and both the looping and the program terminate. This modification is used so that the program would have a normal termination. It insures that the destructor is called **total_depositors** times before the program ends. If **exit()** were used, the destructor might not be called; therefore, we have modified the loop.

The program in Figure 8–4 includes a constructor and destructor that perform more meaningful operations. Instead of storing the depositor's names in a declared array, a **char*** pointer is declared. Space is reserved by **new** in the constructor. When the program terminates, space is freed by **delete**. Space is reserved for each instantiation of structure by the statement

name = new char[81];   8–20

and that space is deallocated by

delete name;   8–21

FIGURE 8–4 ■ A further illustration of constructors.

```
/* an illustration of class constructors and destructors */
#include <stream.h>
class checking {
     char* name;
     int act_no;
     float balance;
public:
     int find_depositor(int);
     void make_deposit(int);
     void debit_check(int);
     void service_charge(int);
     void open_account(int);
     void output_data(int);
     checking();
     ~checking();
};

checking::checking()
{
     balance = 0;
     name = new char[81];
     cout << "\n***********initialized*********";
}

checking::~checking()
{
     delete name;
     cout << "\n***********finished*********";
}
```

Figure 8–4 illustrates the structure declaration and the constructor and destructor. The remainder of the program is the same as that in Figure 8–3.

Constructors with Arguments

Constructors, but not destructors, can have arguments when an array of class is not used. The arguments are passed when the class variable is declared. An illustration of this is shown in Figure 8–5, which is a modification of Figure 8–1. Two constructors are declared in the body of the class declaration; they are

$$checking(int);$$ **8–22a**

and

$$checking(int,float)$$ **8–22b**

We have declared two functions called **checking**. These are overloaded functions (see Section 5–8). The keyword **overload** is not used when functions are declared within the body of a class. The two **checking** functions are listed in Figure 8–5. If the constructor is called with a single integer argument, the **act_no** variable is assigned the value of the argument. On the other hand, if

FIGURE 8–5 ■ An illustration of a constructor with arguments.

```
/* an illustration of a constructor with arguments */
#include <stream.h>
class checking {
      char name[81];
      int act_no;
      float balance;
public:
      void make_deposit(int);
      void debit_check(int);
      void service_charge(int);
      void open_account(int);
      void output_data(int);
      checking(int);
      checking(int,float);
};

checking::checking(int acc_numb)
{
      act_no = acc_numb;
}

checking::checking(int acc_numb,float bal_start)
{
      act_no = acc_numb;
      balance = bal_start;
}
```

the constructor is called with arguments of type **int** and type **float**, **act_no** will be assigned the value of the argument of type **int**, and **balance** will be assigned the value of the argument of type **float**.

The constructors are called when the class variables are declared in the main program. For instance, the declaration could be

$$\text{checking depositor(21),person(35,5000.00);} \qquad \textbf{8–23}$$

Note that the variables are declared with arguments. In this case, **depositor.act_no** is assigned 21, **person.act_no** is assigned 35, and **person-.balance** is assigned 5000.00.

When class variables are declared, their arguments must match the arguments in the constructor(s). For instance, for the program in Figure 8–5 it would be improper to declare a variable of type **checking** without specifying either a single argument of type **int** or two arguments of type **int** and type **float**.

Assignment of Variables

Variables of a **class** type can be assigned. For instance, for the variables declared in 8–23 a valid statement is

$$\text{person} = \text{depositor;}$$

Now all of the fields of **person** become equal to those of **depositor**.

A variable can be declared at any point in the program. For instance, we can write:

$$\text{checking abc} = \text{person};$$

Let us assume that the constructors of Figure 8–5 are used here. The variable **abc** is declared without arguments, while all the constructors have arguments. This would generate an error in a simple declaration statement. However, because this is an assignment, no error will be generated. This could cause a problem if the constructor allocated space for variables (see Figure 8–4). If **abc** was listed with a proper argument(s), then the constructor would be called. Destructors have no arguments, so they will be called whenever a variable goes out of scope. Thus, the destructor, if it exists, will be called when **abc** goes out of scope. In a given program it is possible that there will be more calls to a destructor than there are calls to a constructor. This may not be a problem; however, programmers should be aware of this type of operation.

8–3 ■ this: A POINTER

There is a C++ keyword **this** that provides a pointer to the current instantiation of the class. This pointer is generally used within one of the functions of the class. For instance, in the last chapter we demonstrated that if **test** is a pointer to a structure, and **aaa** is a variable of that structure, then the variable could be referenced by

$$(*(\text{test})).\text{aaa} \qquad\qquad \textbf{8–24a}$$

or equivalently by

$$\text{test} -> \text{aaa} \qquad\qquad \textbf{8–24b}$$

When a function of a class or a structure is being executed, the keyword **this** points at that instance of the class that is referenced by the function. For instance, in the program in Figure 8–4, if the function call

$$\text{depositor[3].make\_deposit(5.00)}; \qquad\qquad \textbf{8–25}$$

is being executed, then within the body of the **make_deposit** function, **this** is a pointer to **depositor[3]**. Because **this** is a keyword, it does not have to be declared; in fact, it cannot be declared.

Although it is correct to use **this** as a pointer to the variables of the class within a function of the class, it is not necessary to do so. For instance, the statement of **make_deposit** that upgrades the amount stored in the variable **balance** of the current instantiation of the class could be written either as

$$\text{this.balance} += \text{amount}; \qquad\qquad \textbf{8–26a}$$

or as

balance += amount;   **8–26b**

It is not necessary to include **this** because the referenced class variable always belongs to the instantiation of the class that was specified by the dot notation in the function call.

Suppose that we modify the program in Figure 8–3 in the following way. When a new depositor is added, the data for the last-entered depositor is output. This guarantees that a new-depositor number is used and also permits the user to review the data of the last new depositor. The modified program is shown in Figure 8–6. Note that we have not written the complete program in Figure 8–6; only the modifications and additions to Figure 8–3 are shown.

The **open_account** function now returns a pointer to type **checking**. The only modifications to this function occur in the declaration of the function in the body of the class and in the first line of the body of the function, where **void** is replaced by **checking***. In addition, the return statement is

return this;   **8–27**

Thus, the function returns a pointer to the instantiation of the class on which it has just completed operation.

A new function called **output_old_data** has been added. This function is very similar to **output_data**, except that the new function takes no argument and does not check to see if the current account number is correct. A current account number would have no meaning in this case.

Now consider the main program. A variable of type **checking***, called **old**, is declared. That is, the type of **old** is a pointer to **checking**. Now consider the operations in case 'o' of the **switch-case** construction. The statement

if(actual_depositor > 0)old − >output_old_data();   **8–28**

causes the function **output_old_data** to be called. The instantiation of **checking** that is passed to the function is that pointed at by **old**. The **if** statement prevents **output_old_data** from being called for the first depositor because, in that case, there is no old data.

The value of **old** is assigned when the function **open_account** is called. This occurs in the statement

old = depositor[actual_depositors].open_account
                              (account_number);   **8–29**

The next time that the add depositor choice is picked from the menu, **old** points at the instantiation of **checking** that was last used to store new account data. Thus, the execution of 8–28 results in the output of the desired data.

In this particular example, we could have avoided the use of **this** by storing the index of the last-used depositor array element. However, there would have been no advantage in doing so. In addition, such an index may not be available in all cases; **this**, therefore, can be very useful.

FIGURE 8–6 ■ An illustration of the use of the keyword **this**. Only the modifications to Figure 8–3 are shown.

```
/* an illustration of the use of this */
#include <stream.h>
class checking {
     char name[81];
     int act_no;
     float balance;
public:
     int find_depositor(int);
     void make_deposit(int);
     void debit_check(int);
     void service_charge(int);
     checking* open_account(int);
     void output_data(int);
     void output_old_data();
     checking();
     ~checking();
};

checking* checking::open_account(int acc_numb)
{
     float amount;
     if(acc_numb != 0)    {
         cout << "\check account number\n";
         return this;
     }  // end if(acc_numb !=0)
     cout << "\nenter account number\n";
     cin >> acc_numb;
     act_no = acc_numb;
     cout << "\nenter name\n";
     cin >> name;
     cout << "\nenter initial deposit\n";
     cin >> amount;
     balance = amount;
     return this;
}

void checking::output_old_data()
{
         cout << "\naccount number " << act_no;
         cout << "\n" << name;
         cout << "\nbalance " << balance;
     return;
}


main()
{
     extern void exit(int);
     const int total_depositors=10;
     int is_depositor = 0,i,actual_depositors=0,ender=0;
     checking depositor[total_depositors];
     checking* old;
```

```
      char ch;
      int account_numb;
      while(ender == 0)   {
          cout << "\nenter account number\nenter 0 for new account";
          cout << "\nenter -1 to terminate program\n\n";
          cin >> account_numb;
          if(account_numb < 0)break;
          for(i=0;i<total_depositors;i++)   {
              if(account_numb == 0)break;
              is_depositor = depositor[i].find_depositor(account_numb);
              if(is_depositor == 1)break;
          } // end for(i=0;i<total_depositors;i++)
          if((is_depositor == 0)&&(account_numb != 0))continue;
          cout << "\nMenu\n";
          cout << "\nm make deposit";
          cout << "\nd debit check";
          cout << "\ns service charge";
          cout << "\no open account";
          cout << "\nx output data";
          cout << "\nz end program\n";
          cin >> ch;
          switch(ch) {
              case 'm':
                  depositor[i].make_deposit(account_numb);
                  break;
              case 'd':
                  depositor[i].debit_check(account_numb);
                  break;
              case 's':
                  depositor[i].service_charge(account_numb);
                  break;
              case 'o':
                  if(actual_depositors == total_depositors) {
                      cout << "\nnot enough space for new account\n";
                      break;
                  }   // end if(actual_depositors == total_depositors)
                  cout <<"\ndata for last new depositor is\n";
                  if(actual_depositors > 0)old->output_old_data();
                  old = depositor[actual_depositors].open_account(account_numb);
                  actual_depositors++;
                  break;
              case 'x':
                  depositor[i].output_data(account_numb);
                  break;
              case 'z':
                  ender = 1;
                  break;
              default:
                  cout << "\nwrong entry\n";
                  break;
          } // end switch
      } // end while(ender == 0)
}
```

8–4 ■ FRIENDS

There are occasions when it would be convenient if a single function could access, and possibly modify, the private variables of two different classes. One procedure for doing this would be to define (public) member functions in each of the classes to provide access to their variables. However, this defeats the advantages of privacy, because then anyone could use these functions to modify the private variables directly. Because a single function cannot be a member of two classes, the procedures that we have discussed thus far cannot be used to write a function to access the private variables of more than one class. C++ provides the keyword **friend** to provide a solution to this dilemma.

A function can be declared to be a *friend of a class*. Although this function is not a member of that class, it can access the private variables, and functions, of the class. Note that because a **friend** function is not a member of the class, it cannot use **this**, unless the **friend** function is itself a member of another class so that **this** points to the instantiation of the other class.

We shall illustrate the use of a **friend** function by extending the banking program that we have been discussing. The class **checking** has been used to simulate checking account operations. Suppose that a second class, called **savings**, is set up to simulate saving account operations. The program in Figure 8–7 includes such a class. Functions to open an account, add deposits, subtract withdrawals, add interest, and output data are written for this class. In the interests of brevity, these functions are not shown in Figure 8–7. To keep matters simple, assume that each person has a checking account and a savings account, and furthermore, that each account has the same account number. There should be no confusion here because one account number belongs to **class checking** while the other belongs to **class saving**.

FIGURE 8–7 ■ An illustration of the use of the keyword **friend**. Only the pertinent functions are listed here. (pp. 226–228).

```
/* an illustration of friend */
#include <stream.h>

class saving;

class checking {
    char name[81];
    int act_no;
    float balance;
public:
    int find_depositor(int);
    void make_deposit(int);
    void debit_check(int);
    void service_charge(int);
    checking* open_account(int);
    void output_data(int);
    void output_old_data();
    void transfer_funds(saving&);
};
```

```
class saving {
     char name[81];
     int act_no;
     float balance;
public:
     int find_depositor(int);
     void make_deposit(int);
     void make_withdrawal(int);
     void add_interest(int);
     saving* open_account(int);
     void output_data(int);
     void output_old_data();
friend void checking::transfer_funds(saving&);
};

void checking::transfer_funds(saving& sav_pt)
{
     float amount;
     cout << "\nenter amount to be transferred\n";
     cin >> amount;
     sav_pt.balance -= amount;
     balance += amount;
     return;
}

/* other functions written here */
main()
{
     extern void exit(int);
     const int total_depositors=10;
     int is_depositor = 0,i,actual_depositors=0,ender=0;
     checking depositor[total_depositors];
     saving person[total_depositors];
     checking* old_checking;
     saving* old_saving;
     char ch;
     int account_numb;
     while(ender == 0)  {
          cout << "\nenter account number\nenter 0 for new account";
          cout << "\nenter -1 to terminate program\n\n";
          cin >> account_numb;
          if(account_numb < 0)break;
          for(i=0;i<total_depositors;i++)  {
               if(account_numb == 0)break;
               is_depositor = depositor[i].find_depositor(account_numb);
               if(is_depositor == 1)break;
          } // end for(i=0;i<total_depositors;i++)
          if((is_depositor == 0)&&(account_numb != 0))continue;
          cout << "\nMenu\n";
          cout << "\nfor checking\n";
          cout << "\nm make deposit";
          cout << "\nd debit check";
          cout << "\ns service charge";
          cout << "\nt transfer funds from savings to checking";
          cout << "\no open both savings and checking accounts";
          cout << "\nx output data";
          cout << "\nz end program\n";
          cout << "\nfor savings\n";
          cout << "\n1 make deposit";
```

FIGURE 8–7 ■ *(continued)*

```
        cout << "\n2 make withdrawal";
        cout << "\n3 add interest";
        cout << "\n4 output data\n";
        cin >> ch;
        switch(ch) {
            case 'm':
                depositor[i].make_deposit(account_numb);
                break;
            case 'd':
                depositor[i].debit_check(account_numb);
                break;
            case 's':
                depositor[i].service_charge(account_numb);
                break;
            case 'o':
                if(actual_depositors == total_depositors) {
                    cout << "\nnot enough space for new account\n";
                    break;
                }  // end if(actual_depositors == total_depositors)
                cout << "\ndata for last new depositor is\n";
                if(actual_depositors > 0)  {
                    old_checking->output_old_data();
                    old_saving->output_old_data();
                } // end if(actual_depositors > 0)
                old_checking =
                    depositor[actual_depositors].open_account(account_numb);
                old_saving =
                    person[actual_depositors].open_account(account_numb);
                actual_depositors++;
                break;
            case 't':
                depositor[i].transfer_funds(person[i]);
                break;
            case 'x':
                depositor[i].output_data(account_numb);
                break;
            case '1':
                person[i].make_deposit(account_numb);
                break;
            case '2':
                person[i].make_withdrawal(account_numb);
                break;
            case '3':
                person[i].add_interest(account_numb);
                break;
            case '4':
                person[i].output_data(account_numb);
                break;
            case 'z':
                ender = 1;
                break;
            default:
                cout << "\nwrong entry\n";
                break;
        }  // end switch
    } // end while(ender == 0)
}
```

Suppose that a function is to be written to transfer funds from a person's savings account to his or her checking account. The function is called **transfer_funds**, and it is a member of **class checking**. The function **transfer_funds** subtracts an amount from a person's savings account balance, and adds that amount to the person's checking account balance. Thus, **transfer_funds**, a member of **class checking**, must be able to access data of **class saving**.

Consider Figure 8–7. The function **transfer_funds** is declared in **class checking** as

$$\text{void transfer\_funds(saving\&);} \qquad \text{8–30}$$

Thus, its argument is an address of a variable of type **saving**. In other words, this is a pass by reference. A slight problem arises here. The class **saving** is declared after the declaration of class **checking** in the program. When the compiler reads 8–30, it does not yet know of the existence of **class saving** and does not know the meaning of the word **saving**. This is termed a *forward reference*. The difficulty is resolved by preceding the declaration of **class checking** with the statement

$$\text{class saving;} \qquad \text{8–31}$$

which indicates to the compiler that a declaration of **class saving** will follow. Future modifications of the compiler could eliminate the need for statements such as 8–31, because the compiler could make an extra pass through the code to determine all types declared there.

The function **transfer_funds** must be declared to be a **friend** of the class **saving**. This is done within the body of the declaration of **class saving** with the statement

$$\text{friend void checking::transfer\_funds(saving\&);} \qquad \text{8–32}$$

It is not necessary for a **friend** function to belong to any class. If it does not, the class name (e.g., **checking**) and the scope-resolution operator would not be written in 8–32.

The function **transfer_funds** is defined as is

```
void checking::transfer_funds(saving& sav-pt)          8–33a
{                                                       8–33b
    float amount;                                       8–33c
    cout << "\nenter amount to be transfered\n";        8–33d
    cin >> amount;                                      8–33e
    sav_pt.balance -= amount;                           8–33f
    balance += amount;                                  8–33g
    return;                                             8–33h
}                                                       8–33i
```

Note that this is a pass by reference. The argument of the function will be the name of the appropriate instantiation of **saving**. The variable **sav_pt** is used to reference the **balance** variable in the desired instantiation of **saving**. As usual, the variable **balance** in Statement 8–33g does not require dot notation because **transfer_funds** is a function of **class checking** and has been called by a member of that class.

Now consider the main program. Two arrays of **class** are set up, each having **total_depositors** elements. The declaration statements are

checking depositor[total_depositors];   8–34a
saving person[total_depositors];   8–34b

The actual call to **transfer_funds** is

depositor[i].transfer_funds(person[i]);   8–35

Note that the address of the data of type **saving** is provided by **person[i]**, and the address of the data of type **checking** is provided by **depositor[i]**.

More than one function of a class can be a friend of another class. In fact, it is common that all the functions of one class are friends of another class. C++ provides a shorthand notation for this particular case to avoid the need to write a long list of friends into the class declaration. For instance, suppose that all the functions of **class checking** are to be friends of **class saving**. The following statement, included in the declaration of **class saving**, would accomplish this.

friend class checking;   8–36

Remember that a **friend** function need not be a member of another class; it could be an ordinary function of the program.

8–5 ■ STATIC FIELD VARIABLES

When different instantiations of a class are declared, each has its own memory locations. If we assume that the class **checking** is as shown in Figure 8–7, the declaration

checking aaa,bbb;   8–37

causes a set of memory locations to be set up to store the **name**, **act_no**, and **balance** fields for **aaa**, and a different set of memory locations to store the corresponding fields for **bbb**. That is, **aaa** and **bbb** do not share any memory locations.

If a class field variable is declared to be **static**, then every instantiation of that class shares the *same* memory location for the **static** field variable. That is, the **static** variable is common to all the instantiations. The **static** field variable acts as a global variable over all instantiations of the class.

In Figure 8–8, we have modified the program in Figure 8–6 to include a variable in type **checking**, called **service_charge_amt**, that represents the amount of service charge that is charged to an account. Furthermore, we assume that all accounts are charged the same amount so that this variable can be shared by all variables of type **checking**. This is done by declaring **service_charge_amt** to be **static**. The declaration of the class **checking** in Figure 8–8 is

class checking {	8–38a
char name[81];	8–38b
int act_no;	8–38c
float balance;	8–38d
static float service_charge_amt;	8–38e
public:	8–38f
int find_depositor(int)	8–38g
void make_deposit(int);	8–38h
void debit_check(int);	8–38i
void service_charge(int);	8–38j
checking* open_account(int);	8–38k
void output_data(int);	8–38l
void output_old_data( );	8–38m
void set_service_charge_amt( );	8–38n
checking( );	8–38o
~checking( );	8–38p
};	8–38q

The **static** variable is declared in Statement 8–38e. A function that assigns a value to **service_charge_amt** is declared in Statement 8–38n. This function, **set_service_charge_amt()**, is listed in Figure 8–8. Note that the account number is not passed to this function as an argument because the variable **service_charge_amt** is global to all variables of type **checking**. There is no reason, therefore, to check the account number.

Because of the presence of the **static** variable, the **service_charge** function is modified in this program. It no longer prompts for a service charge amount. Instead, the variable **service_charge_amt** is used.

In both of these functions, the variable **service_charge_amount** is treated as though it were an ordinary field variable. Of course, the address of the variable **service_charge_amt** is the same for every variable of type **checking**.

The value of **service_charge_amt** is assigned in case 'w' of the main program. The function call is

depositor[i].set_service_charge_amt();   8–39

Although **depositor[i]** is a particular variable of type **checking**, **service_charge_amt** is common to all variables of type **checking**. Any **depositor[i]** could be used in Statement 8–39.

FIGURE 8–8 ■ An illustration of a **static class** field variable. Only the modifications to Figure 8–6 are shown.

```
/* an illustration of a static class variable */
#include <stream.h>
class checking {
    char name[81];
    int act_no;
    float balance;
    static float service_charge_amt;
public:
    int find_depositor(int);
    void make_deposit(int);
    void debit_check(int);
    void service_charge(int);
    checking* open_account(int);
    void output_data(int);
    void output_old_data();
    void set_service_charge_amt();
    checking();
    ~checking();
};

void checking::set_service_charge_amt()
{
    cout << "\nenter service charge amount\n";
    cin >> service_charge_amt;
}

void checking::service_charge(int acc_numb)
{
    if(acc_numb == act_no)balance -= service_charge_amt;
    else cout << "\nwrong depositor\n";
    return;
}


main()
{
    extern void exit(int);
    const int total_depositors=10;
    int is_depositor = 0,i,actual_depositors=0,ender=0;
    checking depositor[total_depositors];
    checking* old;
    char ch;
    int account_numb;
    while(ender == 0)  {
        cout << "\nenter account number\nenter 0 for new account";
        cout << "\nenter -1 to terminate program\n\n";
        cin >> account_numb;
        if(account_numb < 0)break;
        for(i=0;i<total_depositors;i++)  {
            if(account_numb == 0)break;
            is_depositor = depositor[i].find_depositor(account_numb);
            if(is_depositor == 1)break;
        } // end for(i=0;i<total_depositors;i++)
        if((is_depositor == 0)&&(account_numb != 0))continue;
        cout << "\nMenu\n";
        cout << "\nm make deposit";
        cout << "\nd debit check";
```

```
cout << "\ns service charge";
cout << "\no open account";
cout << "\nw set service charge for all depositors";
cout << "\nx output data";
cout << "\nz end program\n";
cin >> ch;
switch(ch) {
    case 'm':
        depositor[i].make_deposit(account_numb);
        break;
    case 'd':
        depositor[i].debit_check(account_numb);
        break;
    case 's':
        depositor[i].service_charge(account_numb);
        break;
    case 'o':
        if(actual_depositors == total_depositors) {
            cout << "\nnot enough space for new account\n";
            break;
        }   // end if(actual_depositors == total_depositors)
        cout <<"\ndata for last new depositor is\n";
        if(actual_depositors > 0)old->output_old_data();
        old = depositor[actual_depositors].open_account(account_numb);
        actual_depositors++;
        break;
    case 'w':
        depositor[i].set_service_charge_amt();
        break;
    case 'x':
        depositor[i].output_data(account_numb);
        break;
    case 'z':
        ender = 1;
        break;
    default:
        cout << "\nwrong entry\n";
        break;
    }   // end switch
} // end while(ender == 0)
}
```

8–6 ■ CLASSES AND UNIONS

In Section 7–3 we discussed how in certain circumstances, unions could be used to conserve memory by storing different types of data in the same memory locations. We also indicated there that a programmer could easily forget the type of data currently stored in the union, resulting in hard-to-find errors. A union can be combined with a class to prevent these types of errors from occurring. There are many schemes that can be used. We shall present a simple one in this section.

Figure 8–9 contains a function embedded in a class. The class declaration is

```
class multi-var {                                    8–40a
    char check;                                      8–40b
    union {                                          8–40c
        float flt;                                   8–40d
        int in;                                      8–40e
        char ch;                                     8–40f
    };                                               8–40g
public:                                              8–40h
    void write_float(float);                         8–40i
    void write_int(int);                             8–40j
    void write_char(char);                           8–40k
    float read_float();                              8–40l
    int read_int();                                  8–40m
    char read_char();                                8–40n
};                                                   8–40o
```

There are two fields in this class: **check**, which stores a variable of type **char**, and the **union** field, which stores data of either type **float**, **int**, or **char**. The functions **write_float**, **write_int**, and **write_char** write data of type **float**, **int**, and **char** respectively into the union. The C++ compiler normally verifies that the types of the arguments of functions are correct. Thus, the compiler will report an error if the argument of any of these functions is of the wrong type. The argument of each of the functions is assigned to the appropriate variable of the union. In addition, a value is assigned to **check**. Note that **check** is assigned an 'f', 'i', or 'c' according to whether the data to be stored in the **union** is of type **float**, **int**, or **char**, respectively.

Now consider the functions that read the data. We shall discuss **read_float** as an example. If the value assigned to **check** is 'f', the value stored in the union is interpreted as being of type **float** and is returned by **read_float**. If the value assigned to **check** is not 'f', an error message is output, and 0.0 is returned. Note that the output of an error message is simply a representation of an error-handling process; other procedures could

FIGURE 8–9 ■ A **union** embedded in a class.

```
/* an example of structure and a union */
#include <stream.h>
class multi_var  {
    char check;
    union {
        float flt;
        int in;
        char ch;
    };
public:
    void write_float(float);
    void write_int(int);
    void write_char(char);
    float read_float();
```

```
        int read_int();
        char read_char();
};

void multi_var::write_float(float val)
{
        check = 'f';
        flt = val;
        return;
}

void multi_var::write_int(int val)
{
        check = 'i';
        in = val;
        return;
}

void multi_var::write_char(char val)
{
        check = 'c';
        ch = val;
        return;
}

float multi_var::read_float()
{
        if(check == 'f')return flt;
        else   cout << "\nerror wrong type\n";
        return 0.0;
}

int multi_var::read_int()
{
        if(check == 'i')return in;
        else   cout << "\nerror wrong type\n";
        return 0;
}

char multi_var::read_char()
{
        if(check == 'c')return ch;
        else   cout << "\nerror wrong type\n";
        return '\0';
}

main()
{
        multi_var x;
        x.write_char('a');
        cout << x.read_char();
        cout << "\n" << x.read_int();  // error message generated
        x.write_float(155.67);
        cout << "\n" << x.read_float();
        cout << "\n" << x.read_char(); // error message generated
        x.write_int(3);
        cout << "\n" << x.read_int();
        x.in = 99;  // nested union not private
        cout << "\n" << x.read_int();
}
```

be used. For instance, **exit()** could be called, in which case the program would terminate. Remember that, once the program is written properly, the data in the union will be correctly accessed. Relatively simple error-handling procedures, therefore, can be used.

The main program illustrates the use of the **multi_var** class. A variable **x** is declared to be of type **multi_var**. Data is entered and retrieved using the functions. Note that the program deliberately includes statements that are incorrect in that they use an improper function to read data from the union. For instance, **read_char** is called when the last data stored in the union is of type **float**. When these statements are executed, an error message is output.

The last lines of the program may be surprising. If a union is embedded within a **class**, that union is *not* private. Thus, the variables of the union can be accessed directly. In particular, the statement

$$x.in \; = \; 99; \hspace{4cm} \textbf{8–41}$$

is valid. If the class field variables can be accessed, then a measure of protection is lost. If the procedure that we have discussed is to prevent errors from occurring, the programmer must learn not to access the data directly.

Classes can, in turn, contain embedded classes and structures. The behavior in regards to privacy is the same as we have discussed for a union. That is, the embedded structure or class is not a private part of the class that lexically encompasses it.

8–7 ■ operator OVERLOADING

C++ allows the user to define *operators*. At least one of the operands of these operators must be the data of a class. The symbols used for the user-defined operators are the standard C++ operators. However, they are overloaded just as functions are overloaded, so that the compiler can choose the appropriate operator from its operand(s). We shall see that the definition of an operator is essentially the same as that of a function. Indeed, we can speak of *operator functions*.

The operators that can be used for overloading are the standard C++ operators, as listed in Table 8–1. No other symbols may be defined to be operators. Although the meaning of the operators can be defined by the programmer, the syntax of the operators is fixed. For instance, == is a binary operator; that is, it operates on two operands. The symbol !, on the other hand, represents a unary operator; that is, it has only a single operand. The operators **new** and **delete** are used to allocate and deallocate memory space. They are the only operators that do not have at least one operand that is of a class type. The following facts should be noted: the operators [] and () have

---

TABLE 8–1 ■ Operators Available for Overloading

+ − / * ! ^ & ~ ! : ( ) [ ] = % < >
+= −= *= /= %= ^= &= := << >>
<<= >>= == != <= >= && ++ −−
: : new delete

---

special meanings that we shall discuss subsequently. When − − and **++** are overloaded, the compiler cannot distinguish between their prefix and postfix operation. The hierarchy of the various operators is unchanged when they are overloaded.

An operator is defined by the programmer as a function, so it can be called an operator function. Operators are defined with the keyword **operator**. At least one operand of a user-defined operator must be a member of a class or structure. (Remember that a structure is a particular kind of class.) The declarations of operators must conform to a specific syntax. Let us consider the example of Figure 8–10. We shall work with the class **checking** that we have been discussing in this chapter. Now suppose that we define the operator **+** to function in the following way. Its first (left) operand is to be a number of type **float**, and its second (right) operand is to be the name of a variable of type **checking**. The operator is to cause the **balance** field of the second operand to be incremented by the amount of the first operand. The new **balance** is to be returned. For instance, if **depositor[i]** is a variable of type **checking**, and the value stored in its **balance** field is 1000.00, then the execution of

$$\text{account\_balance} \; = \; 500.00 \; + \; \text{depositor[i]}; \qquad \textbf{8–42}$$

causes the **balance** field of **depositor[i]** to store 1500.00, and the same number is assigned to **account_balance**. Note that **account_balance** is a variable of type **float**.

The **operator** function is declared in the body of the class **checking** as

$$\text{friend float operator +(float,checking\&)}; \qquad \textbf{8–43}$$

It is declared as a **friend** function; thus, it is not actually part of the class. We shall consider the reason for declaring it as a friend subsequently. An operator function is declared in the same way as an ordinary function, except that the word **operator** followed by the operator symbol replaces the name of the function. Note that in 8–43 there is no space between the word **operator** and the function symbol. This is a matter of choice, and a blank space can be included. The space should be included for the operators **new** and **delete**.

The **operator** function is actually a function. For instance, we shall see that the following statement can be used instead of 8–42:

$$\text{account\_balance} \; = \; \text{operator} +(500.00,\text{depositor[i]}); \qquad \textbf{8–44}$$

FIGURE 8–10 ■ An illustration of operator overloading. Only the modifications to Figure 8–8 are shown.

```
/* an illustration of operator overloading */

class checking {
     char name[81];
     int act_no;
     float balance;
     static float service_charge_amt;
public:
     int find_depositor(int);
     void make_deposit(int);
     void debit_check(int);
     void service_charge(int);
     checking* open_account(int);
     void output_data(int);
     void output_old_data();
     void set_service_charge_amt();
     friend float operator+(float,checking&);
     float operator-();
     checking();
     ~checking();
};

float operator+(float amount, checking& chk)
{
     chk.balance += amount;
     return chk.balance;
}

float checking::operator-()
{
     balance -= service_charge_amt;
     return balance;
}


main()
{

// declarations and statements ...
               case 'm':
                   cout << "\nenter amount deposited\n";
                   cin >> amount_deposited;
                   account_balance = amount_deposited + depositor[i];
                   cout << "\nnew balance is " << account_balance;
                   break;
               case 's':
                   account_balance = -depositor[i];
                   cout << "\nnew balance is " << account_balance;
                   break;

// statements ...

}
```

The body of the **operator +** function is

float operator + (float amount,checking& chk)	**8–45a**
{	**8–45b**
chk.balance += amount;	**8–45c**
return chk.balance;	**8–45d**
}	**8–45e**

Again note that the word **operator** followed by the operator symbol replaces the function name. In fact, the word **operator** plus the function symbol is the function name.

An **operator** function that overloads the unary operator minus is also defined in Figure 8–10. The single argument of this function is the address of a variable of type **checking**. In accordance with the syntax of C++ for pass by reference, the name of the variable, not its address, is the argument. This user-defined operator function subtracts the value assigned to **service_charge_amt** from the **balance** field of the argument. The declaration of the function is

float operator − ( );	**8–46**

Note that no argument is listed for the unary operator. Because this function is a member of class **checking**, the operator is assumed to operate on the variable of type **checking** that lies to its right. Thus, it is not necessary to list an argument. We have not explained how the compiler recognizes that this minus is a unary operator. We shall do this subsequently; for the time being, assume that the compiler recognizes this to be a unary operator.

A statement that uses the operator is

account_balance = −depositor[i];	**8–47**

When this statement is executed, the value of **depositor[i].balance** is reduced by the value of **service_charge_amt**, and the new **balance** is assigned to **account_balance**.

The actual function is defined as

float checking::operator − ( )	**8–48a**
{	**8–48b**
balance −= service_charge_amt;	**8–48c**
return balance;	**8–48d**
}	**8–48e**

This is written just as any other member function would be.

The C++ compiler distinguishes between a unary and a binary operator by the number of arguments each has, and by whether it is a **friend** or member function. If a **friend operator** function has one argument, then a unary operator is defined; if a **friend operator** function has two arguments, then a binary operator is defined. Conversely, if a member **operator** function has no arguments, then a unary operator is defined; if a member function has one argument, then a binary operator is defined. Note that the type of operator is determined by whether the **operator** function is a **friend** or a member, and by the number of arguments. Operators cannot have more than two operands.

In the program in Figure 8–10 we defined a binary operator as a **friend** and a unary operator as a member. Now let us do the converse. In the program in Figure 8–11, the binary + operator is defined as a member while the unary − is defined as a **friend**. The modifications in the functions are due to the fact that a **friend** has become a member and vice versa. The function **operator +** uses the scope-resolution operator in its definition, as do all member functions that are not defined within the body of the class declaration. Dot notation is no longer used in this function. Conversely, the **operator −** function no longer uses the scope-resolution operator in its definition, and dot notation is used in the body of the function to reference the field variables of **class checking**.

In the program in Figure 8–11, the order of the arguments of the + operator has been changed. For instance, to perform the operation of Statement 8–42 we would now write

$$\text{account\_balance} \; = \; \text{depositor[i]} \; + \; 500.00; \qquad \textbf{8–49}$$

When both arguments are specified for a binary operator (it is defined as a **friend**), then the order of the arguments can be arbitrarily specified by the programmer. Remember that at least one argument must be of a class type. When only one argument of a binary operator is specified, then the left operand must be of the implied class type. Thus, in 8–49, the variable of type **checking** must be the left operand.

The usage of user-defined operators must be unique. For instance, it is valid for a program to contain two definitions of the same binary operator as long as the compiler can distinguish them by usage. We will use + as defined in Figures 8–10 and 8–11 as an example; this discussion, however, applies to any binary operator. Suppose that the definitions of the + operator given in Figures 8–10 and 8–11 are both included in the same program. This would pose no problem because the compiler can distinguish between the two overloaded + operators. (The fact that the same operation is performed by the two operator functions is irrelevant.) In particular, if the usage is as in 8–42, then the + defined in Figure 8–10 is used because the left operand is of type **float** and the right operand is of type **checking**. On the other hand, if the usage is as in 8–49, then the + defined in Figure 8–11 is used. Suppose, however, that the definition of + in Figure 8–10 were changed so that the first argument was **checking&**, and the second argument was of type **float**. In this case, both operators would be called using the form of Statement 8–49, and the compiler would not be able to distinguish between them by usage. A compiler error would result in this case, and the program would not compile.

FIGURE 8–11 ■ A modification of the program of Figure 8–10.

```
/* an illustration of operator overloading */

class checking {
    char name[81];
    int act_no;
    float balance;
    static float service_charge_amt;
public:
    int find_depositor(int);
    void make_deposit(int);
    void debit_check(int);
    void service_charge(int);
    checking* open_account(int);
    void output_data(int);
    void output_old_data();
    void set_service_charge_amt();
    float operator+(float);
    friend float operator-(checking&);
    checking();
    ~checking();
};

float checking::operator+(float amount)
{
    balance += amount;
    return balance;
}

float operator-(checking& chk)
{
    chk.balance -= chk.service_charge_amt;
    return chk.balance;
}


main()
{
// declarations and statements ...


            case 'm':
                cout << "\nenter amount deposited\n";
                cin >> amount_deposited;
                account_balance = depositor[i] + amount_deposited;
                cout << "\nnew balance is " << account_balance;
                break;
            case 's':
                account_balance = -depositor[i];
                cout << "\nnew balance is " << account_balance;
                break;

// statements ..

}
```

8–8 ■ THE operator[ ] FUNCTION—SUBSCRIPTING

The operator [ ] sets up a function that is called by writing the class variable name followed by square brackets enclosing a value. The function then operates on the class variable using the specified value. For instance, suppose that we are working with the **checking** class that we have been discussing in this chapter, and that the following declarations are made:

checking person,depositor[10];   **8–50**

If a function named **operator[ ]** has been written to be a member of **class checking**, and that function takes an integer value, then two typical calls to that function are

person[22];   **8–51a**
depositor[5][27];   **8–51b**

In the case of 8–51a, the function **operator[ ]** operates on the variable **person** using the value 22. In the case of 8–51b, the function **operator[ ]** operates on the variable **depositor[5]** using the value 27. Note that although **[22]** and **[27]** appear to be subscripts, only **[5]** represents the actual subscript of an array. However, **[22]** and **[7]** are sometimes referred to as subscripts when used as in 8–57. The square brackets can contain either one or no arguments.

The program in Figure 8–12 illustrates these ideas. The function in question is called **operator[ ]**; it returns a value of type **float** and its argument is of type **float**. The function declaration is

float operator[ ](float);   **8–52**

Note that it is declared just as any other function. As defined in Figure 8–12, the function adds its argument to the **balance** field of the variable of type **checking** that appears in the function call. The function returns the new **balance**. The body of the function is

float checking::operator[ ](float amount)   **8–53a**
{   **8–53b**
balance += amount;   **8–53c**
return balance;   **8–53d**
}   **8–53e**

This function has the same form as an ordinary function that performs the same operations, but because its name is **operator[ ]**, the method of calling it is different from the usual function call.

The part of the program in Figure 8–12 that calls the function **operator[ ]** is listed in the figure. Remember that each element of the array **depositor** is of type **checking**. The function is called with the statement

account_balance = depositor[i][amount_deposited];   **8–54**

FIGURE 8–12 ■ An illustration of the use of **operator**[ ].

```
/* an illustration of operator[] */

class checking {
     char name[81];
     int act_no;
     float balance;
     static float service_charge_amt;
public:
     int find_depositor(int);
     void make_deposit(int);
     void debit_check(int);
     void service_charge(int);
     checking* open_account(int);
     void output_data(int);
     void output_old_data();
     void set_service_charge_amt();
     float operator+(float);
     friend float operator-(checking&);
     float operator[](float);
     checking();
     ~checking();
};

float checking::operator[](float amount)
{
     balance += amount;
     return balance;
}


main()
{


// declarations and statements ...
          case 'm':
               cout << "\nenter amount deposited\n";
               cin >> amount_deposited;
               account_balance = depositor[i][amount_deposited];
               cout << "\nnew balance is " << account_balance;
               break;

// statements ...


}
```

After 8–54 is executed, the **balance** field of **depositor[i]** will be increased by the value of **amount_deposited**, and the result will be assigned to **account_balance**.

Another example of the function **operator**[ ] is given in Figure 8–13. In that program the function **operator**[ ] allocates space for a pointer to a class type. Notice that the class **vars** is declared. It contains a character field, an **int** field, and a field containing an array of 20 characters.

FIGURE 8–13 ■ A further illustration of the use of **operator[]** and a memory-allocating subroutine.

```
/* an illustration of the use of operator[] and memory allocation */
#include <stream.h>
class vars   {
     char ch;
     int in;
     char name[20];
public:
     vars* operator[](long size);
};


     vars* vars::operator[](long size)   {
        void* v = new char[size*sizeof(vars)];
        if(v != 0)cout << "\nallocated size is " << size*sizeof(vars);
        else
            cout << "\nnot enough space for allocation";
        return (vars*)v;
     }
```

Suppose that, in the main program, we have the declarations

$$vars\ x;\qquad\qquad\text{8–55a}$$
$$vars^*\ x\_pt;\qquad\qquad\text{8–55b}$$

The pertinent function call is then

$$x\_pt\ =\ x[20]\qquad\qquad\text{8–56}$$

This reserves space for 20 variables of type **x** to which **x_pt** points. The function is of the form

vars* vars::operator[](long size)	8–57a
{	8–57b
void* v = new char[size*sizeof(vars)];	8–57c
if(v != 0)cout << "\nallocated size is "	
<< size*sizeof(vars);	8–57d
else	8–56e
cout << "\nnot enough space for allocation";	8–57f
return (vars*)v;	8–57g
}	8–57h

The variable **v** is declared to be a *pointer to **void***. It may seem as though a pointer to nothing is meaningless. However, a pointer to **void** is a pointer whose type can be cast to any other pointer type. In addition, any pointer type can be assigned to a **void** pointer. In general, in any one computer system, all pointers store the same form of data. That is, each pointer represents a particular memory location, independent of the type of the pointer. C++ uses different pointer types to enable the proper operation of pointer arithmetic. Note that

$$size*sizeof(vars) \hspace{3cm} 8–58$$

represents the total space required to store **size** variables of type **vars**.

The **new** operation does not always function properly. If you request more space than is available, *no space will be allocated*. In that case, the value 0 is returned for the pointer. When this happens, the function 8–51 causes a warning message to be output. In practice, this is *not* sufficient. The warning statement is listed in place of an error-handling routine. If sufficient memory cannot be allocated, the program cannot simply continue. The simplest operation is to call **exit()** and terminate operation. If it is possible that the program could function with less memory, the error-handling routine could reduce the request for memory and allow a reduced form of the program to continue.

The warning statement of 8–57f could be replaced by a function call to the error-handling routine. C++ provides a procedure for doing this automatically. There is a built-in variable called **_new_handler** that is a pointer to a function. (Pointers to functions were discussed in Section 5–9.) You can set this variable to point to your error-handling routine. C++ provides a function called **set_new_handler** that assigns the desired value to that variable. If the variable **_new_handler** has been set, and **new** fails to allocate memory, the function pointed at by **_new_handler** is called automatically.

The program of Figure 8–14 is a modification of Figure 8–13 that uses the built-in pointer **_new_handler**. The error-handling routine that we have written is called **out_of_memory**, and it is a member of class **vars**. The **typedef** statement is used as a convenience to make **ptf** a type that represents a pointer to a function. This is used in the declaration of **set_new_handler**. The **operator[]** function is

```
vars* vars::operator[](long size)                    8–59a
{                                                     8–59b
    set_new_handler(&vars::out_of_memory);           8–59c
    void* v = new char[size*sizeof(vars)];           8–59d
    return (vars*)v;                                 8–59e
}                                                     8–59f
```

Note that the error-handling routine has been removed from this function. Statement 8–59c causes the pointer **_new_handler** to point at the routine named **out_of_memory**. If **new** cannot allocate the memory, this routine will be called automatically. Note that **new** may *not* return 0 if **set_new-handler** has been called. However, this is not a problem because it is assumed that the error-handling routine performs the necessary tasks. Note that the error-handling routine in Figure 8–14 simply prints an output statement. Naturally, in an actual program more elaborate error handling, such as that discussed above, would have to be used.

FIGURE 8-14 ■ A modification of Figure 8-11 that uses different error-handling.

```
/* an illustration of the use of operator[] and memory allocation */
#include <stream.h>
typedef void (*ptf)();
extern ptf set_new_handler(ptf);
class vars  {
     char ch;
     int in;
     char name[20];
public:
     vars* operator[](long size);
     void out_of_memory();
};


     vars* vars::operator[](long size)  {
          set_new_handler(&vars::out_of_memory);
          void* v = new char[size*sizeof(vars)];
          return (vars*)v;
     }

void vars::out_of_memory()
{
     cout << "\n out of memory run ";
}
```

8-9 ■ THE operator() FUNCTION

As discussed in the last section, the **operator[]** function allowed a passing of zero or one argument to a function that was called by following the name of a variable of a class type with square brackets enclosing the argument. The **operator()** function is similar to **operator[]**, except that parentheses take the place of the square brackets, and the number of arguments is not limited to zero or one. The reader may question the need for **operator[]** if its operation can be performed by **operator()**. The availability of two different functions provides versatility. For instance, the programmer could write two different functions, neither one of which could overload the other because they have the same argument types. In addition, the use of square brackets could be reserved for functions that are related, in some way, to subscripts, thus providing a memory aid.

The use of **operator()** is illustrated in Figure 8-15, which is a modification of the program in Figure 8-12. Now two deposits are simultaneously added to a depositor's account. The **operator** function is declared with the statement

$$\text{float operator()(float,float)} \qquad \textbf{8-60}$$

The function's definition is listed in Figure 8-15. It adds the two arguments to the amount stored in the **balance** field and returns the new balance.

FIGURE 8–15 ■ An illustration of the use of **operator()**.

```
/* an illustration of operator() */

class checking {
     char name[81];
     int act_no;
     float balance;
     static float service_charge_amt;
public:
     int find_depositor(int);
     void make_deposit(int);
     void debit_check(int);
     void service_charge(int);
     checking* open_account(int);
     void output_data(int);
     void output_old_data();
     void set_service_charge_amt();
     float operator+(float);
     friend float operator-(checking&);
     float operator()(float,float);
     checking();
     ~checking();
};

float checking::operator()(float amount1,float amount2)
{
     balance += amount1;
     balance += amount2;
     return balance;
}




main()
{

// declarations and statements ...

          case 'm':
               cout << "\nenter amount of two deposits\n";
               cin >> amt_dep1 >> amt_dep2;
               account_balance = depositor[i](amt_dep1,amt_dep2);
               cout << "\nnew balance is " << account_balance;
               break;

// statements ...


}
```

The function is called using the statement

account_balance = depositor[i](amt_dep1,amt_dep2);   **8–61**

where **depositor[i]** is a variable of type **checking**, and **account_balance**, **amt_dep1**, and **amt_dep2** are variables of type **float**.

Remember that **operator()** and **operator[]**, as well as all operator functions, can be overloaded. The rules for their overloading follow those for ordinary overloaded functions.

8-10 ■ USER-DEFINED TYPE CONVERSION—ASSIGNMENT

A constructor function may be called when a class type is declared. In addition, constructors can be used for type conversion. Because classes are user-defined types, this is termed *user-defined type conversion*. The program in Figure 8–16 will be used in this discussion. That figure contains three constructors; they are declared as

checking(int);	**8–62a**
checking(int,float);	**8–62b**
checking(test);	**8–62c**

Note that **test** is a structure type whose fields include a character array, a type **int**, and a type **float**. The types of the fields of **test** are the same as the types of the fields of **class checking**.

The constructor functions are listed in Figure 8–16. Note that the constructor corresponding to 8–62a assigns a value to the **act_no** field; the constructor corresponding to 8–62b assigns values to the **act_no** and **balance** fields; the constructor corresponding to 8–62c assigns values to all three fields, and those values correspond to the values stored in the fields of a variable of type **test**.

In Section 8–2 we illustrated the use of constructors in declaration statements. In that case, the argument(s) of the constructor were listed in a parenthetical list following the variable name. The constructor can be called by writing it after an assignment sign. For instance, the following are equivalent:

checking account(77);	**8–63a**
checking account = checking(77);	**8–63b**

Either 8–63a or 8–63b defines a variable called **account** of type **checking**. The constructor with a single integer variable is called and assigns 77 to the account. If there is only a *single* argument, then the declaration can be abbreviated. In that case, 8–63b can be written as

checking account = 77;	**8–64**

Assignment

Class types can be used in assignments just as other types can. For instance, the variables **account** and **depositor** have been declared to be variables of **class checking** in the program in Figure 8–16. Suppose that the field variables of each have been assigned (different) values. A valid statement is

account = depositor;	**8–65**

FIGURE 8–16 ■ An illustration of class assignment and user-defined type conversion.

```
/* an illustration of user defined type conversion */
#include <stream.h>
struct test {
      char name[81];
      int numb;
      float total;
};
class checking {
      char name[81];
      int act_no;
      float balance;
public:
      void make_deposit(int);
      void debit_check(int);
      void service_charge(int);
      void open_account(int);
      void output_data(int);
      checking(int);
      checking(int,float);
      checking(test);
};

checking::checking(int acc_numb)
{
      act_no = acc_numb;
}

checking::checking(int acc_numb,float bal_start)
{
      act_no = acc_numb;
      balance = bal_start;
}

checking::checking(test tst)
{
      int i;
      for(i=0;i<81;i++)name[i] = tst.name[i];
      balance = tst.total;
      act_no = tst.numb;
}


main()
{
// declarations ...

      checking account=77;
      checking depositor = checking(120,6000.);
      account = depositor;
      account = 25;
      test jones;
      jones.name[0] = 'j';
      jones.name[1] = 'o';
      jones.name[2] = 'n';
      jones.name[3] = 0;
      jones.numb = 123;
      jones.total = 7000.0;
      account = checking(jones);

//statements ...

}
```

Now the field variables of **account** are assigned values equal to the values of the corresponding field variables of **balance**.

The constructors can be invoked as part of an assignment, even though the variable has been declared previously and the constructor was invoked previously. For instance, the execution of

$$\text{account } = \text{ checking}(77,1500.0) \qquad \textbf{8–66}$$

will cause the **act_no** field of **account** to be assigned 77, and the **balance** field of **account** to be assigned 1500.0. If there is a constructor with a single argument, then the abbreviated form illustrated in 8–64 can be used. For instance the execution of

$$\text{account } = \text{ 99}; \qquad \textbf{8–67}$$

results in 99 being assigned to **account.act_no**. Note that 8–67 is actually a function call. Of course, the arguments must be correct, and all the rules of overloading apply.

The structure **test** is defined in the program in Figure 8–16. A variable called **jones** is declared to be of type **test**, and values are stored in its fields. One of the constructors takes a variable of type **test** as its argument. The appropriate values are assigned to a variable of type **checking**. For instance, the execution of

$$\text{account } = \text{ checking}(\text{jones}); \qquad \textbf{8–68}$$

causes the fields of **account** to be assigned the values of the corresponding fields of **jones**. Note that 8–68 has the form of the ordinary C++ type conversion and, therefore, is called a user-defined type conversion. Because there is only a single argument for the constructor, the abbreviated form can be used, so that 8–68 can be written as

$$\text{account } = \text{ jones}; \qquad \textbf{8–69}$$

This also follows the form of type conversion for built-in variables. Of course, the appropriate constructors must be written if the type conversion is to work.

A word of caution is necessary. It is possible to call constructors many times for each variable. For example, statements of the form of 8–69 could be executed many times. However, the corresponding destructor will be called once when the variable goes out of scope. Thus, the constructor may be called more often than the destructor. Often this is not a problem, but the programmer should be aware that this type of operation does occur.

EXERCISES

Check any programs or functions that you write by running them on your computer. If necessary write a main program.

1. Write a structure that is called **classroom**. The structure should store the following data: a student's name, ID number, grades in up to 10 tests, total number of tests taken, average, and letter grade. The ID number and number of tests taken are to be of type **int**, and the other numerical data is to be of type **float**. There should be functions included in the structure that perform the following operations: enter the student's name and ID number; enter a student's grade in a single test and upgrade the total number of tests taken, using the student's ID number as a check; average a student's grade; compute a letter grade based on the average; and output the student's name, ID number, and grade. The letter grade is to be based on the following scale: A if the average is 90 or greater; B if the average is less than 90 and equal to or greater than 80; C if the average is less than 80 and equal to or greater than 70; D if the average is less than 70 and equal to or greater than 60; F if the average is less than 60.

   Write a program that declares three variables of type **classroom**. The data for three students should be entered and output to check the operation of your functions.

2. Repeat Exercise 1, but now use a class rather than a structure. All the data should be private to the class.

3. Modify the structure of Exercise 2. Now include a constructor that sets all the ID numbers to 0 and all the grades and averages to 0.0 whenever a variable of type **classroom** is declared.

4. Modify the constructor of Exercise 3 so that it assigns a new ID number as each variable is established. The ID number should be output to the screen.

5. Add constructors to the class of Exercise 4. They should output the ID number when they are invoked.

6. Write a constructor whose argument is an ID number. Overload it with the constructor of Exercise 5. Write a main program that tests this new constructor.

7. Repeat Exercise 6, but add a constructor that has two arguments, one for the ID number and the other for the name.

8. Write a main program that sets up an array of variables of type **classroom**. The program should allow the user to enter data for up to 10 students and output the name, ID number, and grade for each student.

9. Modify the program of Exercise 8. Now, when data is to be entered, the person running the program is to be prompted with the last-entered ID number.

10. Modify the class **classroom** so that a function called **reader**, that is not a member of the class, can read the data stored in variables of the class. The function should not be able to write to these variables.

11. Set up another class called **attendance** that stores a student's name, ID number, and number of absences. Write member functions to enter data, add absences and read data. Test the operation of the class **attendance**.

Now write a function that is a member of **classroom** that can read the data stored in variables of type **attendance**. Modify the class **attendance** so that this reading can take place.

12. Modify the main program of Exercise 9 so that the average of all the averages is obtained. Now modify **class classroom** so that this overall average is stored in each variable of the class. If the overall average is modified for one variable of the class, it should be automatically modified for all variables of the class.

13. Modify Exercise 10 of Chapter 7 so that only proper data can be read from the union, provided that the appropriate functions are used to read and write data.

14. Write a binary operator called + that takes two arguments. The first argument is a test grade, and the second argument is a variable of type **classroom**. The first argument is to be treated as an additional test grade. That is, it is to be stored in the appropriate array field of the second argument, and the array field representing the total number of tests is to be incremented. Check that there is enough room for the storage of the additional test grade. The average is to be recomputed based on the additional test. The new average is to be output. The **operator** function is to be a *friend*.

15. Repeat Exercise 14, but now make the **operator** function a *member*. Change the order of the operands if necessary.

16. Write a unary operator called ++ that increments the number of absences stored in a variable of type **attendance** (see Exercise 11). The operator function should be a friend.

17. Repeat Exercise 16, but now make the **operator** function a member.

18. Demonstrate that an **operator** function can be invoked with a standard function call.

19. Perform the function of Exercise 15, but now use **operator[ ]**.

20. Perform the function of Exercise 15, but now use **operator()**.

21. Write a constructor that allows data of type **attendance** to be assigned to a variable of type **classroom** that has been modified to store attendance data.

CHAPTER 9
Derived Classes

There are times when it would be very convenient if the capabilities of a class could be extended. For instance, in Chapter 8 we considered a class that might be used to process checking account information. Suppose that the bank decided to give each depositor a credit card. In that case, it would be desirable if the class representing a depositor could manipulate this additional data as well. Naturally, you could rewrite the original class, adding new features to it. However, rewriting the class is time consuming and provides an opportunity for the introduction of errors.

C++ includes the concept of a *derived class*. A derived class starts with an existing *base class* and builds upon it. For instance, a new class could be derived from the base class **checking** that was discussed in the last chapter. This new derived class would act as if it contained the base class. For instance, the derived class could use the public functions and variables of **checking** as if they were its own. Of course, the private fields and functions of the base class could be manipulated only through the public functions of the base class. If classes are written properly, the derived class can be used as though it is simply a larger class that has all the properties of the base class.

Derived classes are most often used to extend classes. However, they can also be used to provide an *alternative interface* to the class. The interface to a class is its public parts. For a particular application of a class, you may decide that additional functions or different functions should be available. A derived class can provide this additional feature without requiring that the class be rewritten.

9-1 ■ DERIVED CLASSES

Very often, a class has properties that almost, or partially, are those that match a new application. For instance, suppose that a class called department_store has been set up to store and manipulate the data relating to a department store that sells many products, but does not sell shoes. The existing class will have no data or functions relating to shoes, but will have all the other data relating to the operation of the store. Now suppose that the policy of the store is changed, and shoes are added to the list of available merchandise. Data concerning shoes and the functions to manipulate that data must be added to the class. It would be a waste of effort to rewrite the class completely. However, it would be very convenient if a new class, new_department_store, could be written that *inherited* all the properties of the original class. In that case, only the features of the new class would have to be written. The original class is called the *base class*, and the new class is called the *derived class*.

C++ allows the programmer to form derived classes from base classes. These operations are illustrated in the program in Figure 9–1. The base class is checking, the class that was introduced in Chapter 8. This class is used to process checking accounts for customers of a bank. (A complete banking operation is not represented here.) Now suppose that the bank provides each of its depositors with a credit card. Additional data and functions must be supplied to manipulate the credit card data. A new class called credit_card

FIGURE 9–1 ■ A program that uses a derived class. (pp. 254–259).

```
/* an illustration of a derived class */
#include <stream.h>
class checking {
     char name[81];
     int act_no;
     float balance;
     static float service_charge_amt;
public:
     int find_depositor(int);
     void make_deposit(int);
     void debit_check(int);
     void service_charge(int);
     checking* open_account(int);
     void output_data(int);
     void output_old_data();
     void set_service_charge_amt();
     void output_name(int);
     int get_id(int);
     float operator+(float);
     friend float operator-(checking&);
     checking();
     ~checking();
};

class credit_card : public checking {
     float credit_balance;
     static float service_charge_amt;
public:
```

```
        void output_data(int);
        void set_service_charge_amt();
        void service_charge(int);
        void credit_payment(int);
        void debit_purchase(int);
        credit_card();
        ~credit_card();
};

credit_card::credit_card()
{
        credit_balance = 0.0;
        cout << "\n########start######";
}

credit_card::~credit_card()
{
        cout << "\n######finish########";
}

void credit_card::output_data(int acc_numb)
{
        int act_number;
        act_number = get_id(acc_numb);
        if(acc_numb == act_number)  {
            cout << "\naccount number " << act_number << "\n";
            output_name(acc_numb);
            cout << "\ncredit card balance " << credit_balance;
        } // end if(acc_numb == act_number) start else
        else cout << "\nwrong depositor\n";
        return;
}


void credit_card::credit_payment(int acc_numb)
{
        int act_number;
        float amount;
        act_number = get_id(acc_numb);
        if(acc_numb == act_number)  {
            cout << "\nenter payment\n";
            cin >> amount;
            credit_balance += amount;
        } // end if(acc_numb == act_number) start else
        else cout << "\nwrong depositor\n";
        return;
}

void credit_card::debit_purchase(int acc_numb)
{
        int act_number;
        float amount;
        act_number = get_id(acc_numb);
        if(acc_numb == act_number)  {
            cout << "\nenter purchase amount\n";
            cin >> amount;
            credit_balance -= amount;
```

FIGURE 9–1 ■ *(continued)*

```
      } // end if(acc_numb == act_number) start else
      else cout << "\nwrong depositor\n";
      return;
}

void credit_card::set_service_charge_amt()
{
      cout << "\nenter service charge amount\n";
      cin >> service_charge_amt;
}

void credit_card::service_charge(int acc_numb)
{
      int act_number;
      act_number = get_id(acc_numb);
      if(acc_numb == act_number)credit_balance -= service_charge_amt;
      else cout << "\nwrong depositor";
}

void checking::output_name(int acc_numb)
{
      if(acc_numb == act_no)cout << name;
      else cout <<"\nwrong depositor\n";
      return;
}

int checking::get_id(int acc_numb)
{
      if(acc_numb == act_no)return act_no;
      else {
          cout << "\nwrong depositor\n";
          return 0;
      }
}

float checking::operator+(float amount)
{
      balance += amount;
      return balance;
}

float operator-(checking& chk)
{
      chk.balance -= chk.service_charge_amt;
      return chk.balance;
}

void checking::set_service_charge_amt()
{
      cout << "\nenter service charge amount\n";
      cin >> service_charge_amt;
}

checking::checking()
{
      balance = 0.0;
      cout << "\n***********initialized*********";
```

FIGURE 9–1 ■ *(continued)*

```
}
checking::~checking()
{
     cout << "\n**********finished*********";
}

int checking::find_depositor(int acc_numb)
{
     int ans=0;
     if(acc_numb == act_no)ans = 1;
     return ans;
}


void checking::make_deposit(int acc_numb)
{
     float amount;
     if(acc_numb == act_no)  {
             cout << "\nenter amount of deposit\n";
             cin >> amount;
             balance += amount;
     }  // end if(acc_numb == act_no)
     else cout << "\nwrong depositor\n";
     return;
}
void checking::debit_check(int acc_numb)
{
     float amount;
     cout << "\nenter amount of check\n";
     cin >> amount;
     if(acc_numb == act_no)balance -= amount;
     else cout << "\nwrong depositor\n";
     return;
}

void checking::service_charge(int acc_numb)
{
     if(acc_numb == act_no)balance -= service_charge_amt;
     else cout << "\nwrong depositor\n";
     return;
}

checking* checking::open_account(int acc_numb)
{
     float amount;
     if(acc_numb != 0)    {
         cout << "\check account number\n";
         return this;
     }  // end if(acc_numb !=0)
     cout << "\nenter account number\n";
     cin >> acc_numb;
     act_no = acc_numb;
     cout << "\nenter name\n";
     cin >> name;
     cout << "\nenter initial deposit\n";
```

FIGURE 9–1 ■ *(continued)*

```
     cin >> amount;
     balance = amount;
     return this;
}

void checking::output_data(int acc_numb)
{
     if(acc_numb == act_no)  {
         cout << "\naccount number " << act_no;
         cout << "\n" << name;
         cout << "\nbalance " << balance;
     } // end if(acc_numb == depositor>act_no) start else
     else cout << "\nwrong depositor\n";
     return;
}


void checking::output_old_data()
{
         cout << "\naccount number " << act_no;
         cout << "\n" << name;
         cout << "\nbalance " << balance;
     return;
}
main()
{
     extern void exit(int);
     const int total_depositors=10;
     int is_depositor = 0,i,actual_depositors=0,ender=0;
     credit_card depositor[total_depositors];
     checking* old;
     char ch;
     int account_numb;
     float amount_deposited,account_balance;
     while(ender == 0)  {
         cout << "\nenter account number\nenter 0 for new account";
         cout << "\nenter -1 to terminate program\n\n";
         cin >> account_numb;
         if(account_numb < 0)break;
         for(i=0;i<total_depositors;i++)  {
             if(account_numb == 0)break;
             is_depositor = depositor[i].find_depositor(account_numb);
             if(is_depositor == 1)break;
         } // end for(i=0;i<total_depositors;i++)
         if((is_depositor == 0)&&(account_numb != 0))continue;
         cout << "\nMenu\n";
         cout << "\nm make deposit";
         cout << "\nn credit card payment";
         cout << "\nd debit check";
         cout << "\ne debit credit card purchase";
         cout << "\ns checking service charge";
         cout << "\nt credit card service charge";
         cout << "\no open account";
         cout << "\nv set credit card servide charge for all depositors";
         cout << "\nw set checking service charge for all depositors";
         cout << "\nx output checking data";
         cout << "\ny output credit_card data";
```

FIGURE 9–1 ■ *(continued)*

```
      cout << "\nz end program\n";
      cin >> ch;
      switch(ch) {
          case 'm':
              cout << "\nenter amount deposited\n";
              cin >> amount_deposited;
              account_balance = depositor[i] + amount_deposited;
              cout << "\nnew balance is " << account_balance;
              break;
          case 'n':
              depositor[i].credit_payment(account_numb);
              break;
          case 'd':
              depositor[i].debit_check(account_numb);
              break;
          case 'e':
              depositor[i].debit_purchase(account_numb);
              break;
          case 's':
              account_balance = -depositor[i];
              cout << "\nnew balance is " << account_balance;
              break;
          case 't':
              depositor[i].service_charge(account_numb);
              break;
          case 'o':
              if(actual_depositors == total_depositors) {
                  cout << "\nnot enough space for new account\n";
                  break;
              }  // end if(actual_depositors == total_depositors)
              cout <<"\ndata for last new depositor is\n";
              if(actual_depositors > 0)old->output_old_data();
              old = depositor[actual_depositors].open_account(account_numb);
              actual_depositors++;
              break;
          case 'v':
              depositor[i].set_service_charge_amt();
              break;
          case 'w':
              depositor[i].checking::set_service_charge_amt();
              break;
          case 'x':
              depositor[i].checking::output_data(account_numb);
              break;
          case 'y':
              depositor[i].output_data(account_numb);
              break;
          case 'a':
              ender = 1;
              break;
          default:
              cout << "\nwrong entry\n";
              break;
      }  // end switch
  } // end while(ender == 0)
}
```

is written. This class is derived from the base class **checking**. The declaration of the derived class is

```
class credit_card : public checking {          9–1a
    float credit_balance;                       9–1b
    float service_charge_amt;                   9–1c
public:                                         9–1d
    void output_data(int);                      9–1e
    void set_service_charge_amt();              9–1f
    void service_charge(int);                   9–1g
    void credit_payment(int);                   9–1h
    void debit_purchase(int);                   9–1i
    credit_card();                              9–1j
    ~credit_card();                             9–1k
};                                              9–1l
```

The fact that this is a derived class is indicated on the first line. The name of the class is followed by a colon, :, the keyword **public**, and the name of the base class (**checking** in this case). The public parts of the base class are treated as though they were public members of the derived class **credit_card**. In particular the (public) functions that are members of **class checking** can be called as though they are members of **credit_card**. For instance, if there is the declaration

```
credit_card person;                             9–2
```

then the following are valid function calls:

```
person.credit_payment(account_numb);            9–3a
person.debit_check(account_numb);               9–3b
person.service_charge(account_numb);            9–3c
person.checking::service_charge(account_numb);  9–3d
```

The function call 9–3a is a call to one of the functions of **class credit_card**, while that of 9–3b is a call to one of the functions of the base class. Note that these calls have the same form. Although the field variables of the derived class (**credit_card**) consist of *both* its own variables and the field variables of the base class (**checking**), the (private) field variables of **checking** can be accessed only by the functions of **checking**. The base class and the derived class each have functions called **service_charge**, and each of these functions has integer arguments. Because the arguments are of the same type, these functions cannot be overloaded. Thus, we have used the de-referencing operator to designate that 9–3d refers to the function **service_charge** from **class checking**. Because **person** is of type **credit_card**, there is no need to use de-referencing in 9–3c. If the compiler could distinguish between the two functions because their arguments were different, then the functions could be overloaded, and there would be no reason to use de-referencing. We have deliberately picked function names in the derived class that are the same as those in the base class for illustrative purposes. However, it would be better not to do so. There is less likelihood of error if the functions have unique names.

The private variables in the base class cannot be directly accessed by the functions of the derived class. These variables are private to **checking** and can be accessed only through its functions. It might seem as though the variables of the base class should be directly accessible by the functions of the derived class. However, that would mean the private variables of a class could be made public simply by declaring a derived class. All the error prevention justifications for using privacy imply that the privacy of the base class should be maintained. Functions have been added to the base class that return or output the values of some of its field variables. These values can be read, but not changed, by these functions. If any of the variables of the base class are public, then they are directly accessible by the derived class. Their visibility is the same as for the public functions of the base class. That is, if a public variable of the base class has a name that is different from any variable of the derived class, then that base class variable can be referred to as if it were a member of the derived class. If the name of a public variable of the base class is the same as the name of a variable of the derived class, then the dereferencing operator and class name must be used to refer to that base class variable by functions of the derived class.

Note that constructors and destructors have been declared and written for the derived class. When a variable whose type is the derived class is declared, two constructors are invoked, one for the base class and one for the derived class. Similarly, when a variable whose type is the derived class passes out of scope, two sets of destructors are called. Constructors for derived classes can be written with arguments. The discussion in Section 8–2 applies to derived classes as well. The constructors and destructors of Figure 9–1 output text. Normally, this would not be done. It is done here for instructional purposes, to indicate when the constructors and destructors are called. The constructors for the base class are called before those of the derived class. Destructors are called in the reverse order. When the program in Figure 9–1 is run, 10 variables of type **credit_card** are established, one for each element of the **depositor** array. Ten pairs of constructors are called, one pair for each variable.

The keyword **public** in 9–1a causes the public functions of the base class **checking** to become public functions of the derived class. If the word **public** is omitted, then the public functions of the base class become private functions of the derived class. In this case the functions of the base class could be accessed only through functions of the derived class. In any event, the private variables and functions of the base class remain private. If your application does not require privacy, then structures can be used instead of classes.

There may be occasions when you want to change the *interface to a class*. The interface is the set of functions that is used to access the field variables. If a derived class is declared with the base class declared public, the interface is increased. That is, it consists of the public functions of the derived class plus the public functions of the base class. If the base class is not declared public, then the functions of the base class are not part of the interface to the derived class, and the interface of the derived class is the public functions of the derived class. In this case, a new interface to the class field variables has been established.

The functions of the derived class must be able to read the variables of the base class. This can be accomplished in one of several ways. The functions of the derived class could be made friends of the base class, thus enabling those functions to both read and modify the private field variables of the base class. Although this simple procedure is often used, it violates the rule that only the functions of a class should be able to change its private variables. An alternative procedure is to provide the base class with functions that return or output the values of the private variables, but do not modify them. In this way, the derived class, or the main program for that matter, could read and use the field variables of the class without being able to modify them directly. Two functions have been added to **class checking**. The function **get_id** returns the ID number of the instantiation corresponding to the integer index that is the function's argument. Note that an array of type **credit_card** called **depositor** is set up in the main program, and after the **for** loop is executed, the value returned by **get_id** is the ID number that corresponds to the current index of the depositor array. The function **output_name** outputs the **name** field of the instantiation of **credit_card** corresponding to the array index that is the function's argument. This function returns no argument because **name** is not used by any of the functions of the derived class, **credit_card**.

Consider case "o" in the main program. This has not been modified. The function **open_account**, which is part of the base class **checking**, is called here. The calling statement is

```
old = depositor[actual_depositors].open_account(account_numb);        9–4
```

The function **open_account** returns the pointer **this**. The variable **depositor** is of type **charge_account**, the derived class. Even though the function is in the base class, **this** points at **depositor[actual_depositors]**, a member of the derived class.

The complete program is listed in Figure 9–1. This is done so that all its details are presented. Although this is by no means a complete banking program, it does represent the basic ideas of derived classes.

9–2 ■ CLASS TREES—CLASS HIERARCHIES

In the last section we used **class checking** as the base class for **class credit_card**. A derived class can itself be the base class for another class, and so on. In addition, a base class can be the base class for more than one derived class. There are some rules that must be followed when there are several derived classes: a derived class can have only one base class; a class cannot be derived from itself or any class that was derived from itself. The following are a valid set of class declarations:

class banking { ... };	**9–5a**
class checking : banking { ... };	**9–5b**
class credit_card : checking { ... };	**9–5c**
class savings : banking { ... };	**9–5d**
class money_market : savings { ... };	**9–5e**
class investment : checking { ... };	**9–5f**

This set of classes is a generalization of the banking classes that we have discussed. We assume that **class banking** contains general information common to all types of banking, such as name, account number, and social security number. **Class checking** contains additional information that applies to checking accounts. **Class credit_card** is derived from **class checking** (see Section 9–1). Of course, each class contains the appropriate functions needed to access and process its data.

The declarations 9–5 can be said to represent a *hierarchy of class*. That is, **banking** has the highest hierarchy, and all classes can be traced back to it. This hierarchy can be represented diagrammatically as shown in Figure 9–2. This is called a *tree structure* or a *class tree*. All classes can be traced back to **banking**, which is called the *root* of the tree. Note that unlike a botanical tree, but like a family tree, Figure 9–2 has its root at the top of the diagram.

FIGURE 9–2 ■ A class tree.

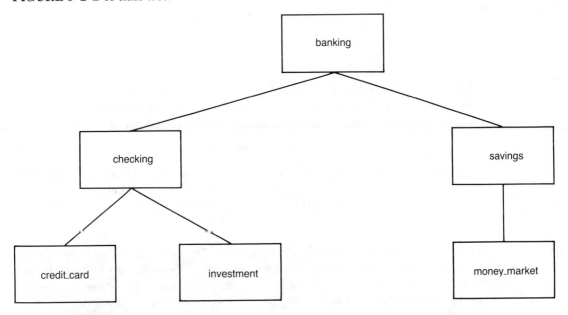

In the interest of brevity we have omitted the keyword **public** from 9–5, but it could be included there. Note that each class is derived from the other classes that lie along the same branch of the tree and are closer to the root. For instance, **class credit_card** is derived from **class checking**, which in turn is derived from **class banking**. Thus, all the public functions and variables of **class checking** and **class banking** are contained within **class credit_card**. Actually, the private variables and functions are also contained within **class credit_card**, but they must be accessed through the proper functions.

The tree diagram is a general representation of the forms of derived structures that can be built up in C++. Derived structures cannot be constructed in other forms such as loops. However, the tree structure is general enough for most applications.

9–3 ■ POINTERS AND DERIVED CLASSES

Pointers to derived classes can be declared and manipulated in the same way as pointers to base classes can. However, there are some additional considerations when working with pointers to derived classes. Suppose that we have a base class called **base_class** and a derived class called **pub**. These are declared as

$$\text{class base\_class}\{ \ \dots \ \}; \qquad \qquad \textbf{9--6a}$$
$$\text{class pub : public base\_class } \{ \ \dots \ \}; \qquad \textbf{9--6b}$$

Now suppose that in the main program we have the declarations

$$\text{pub aaa;} \qquad \qquad \textbf{9--7a}$$
$$\text{base\_class* bc\_pt;} \qquad \textbf{9--7b}$$

We can now write the statement

$$\text{bc\_pt } = \text{ \&aaa;} \qquad \qquad \textbf{9--8}$$

That is, a (declared) pointer to the base class can be assigned the value of the address of an instance of the derived class. Suppose that the derived class contains a public function called **dfn**. It could be called using

$$\text{bc\_pt} \to \text{pub::dfn();} \qquad \qquad \textbf{9--9}$$

The scope-resolution operator is needed here because **bc_pt** is a pointer to the base class, and the function **dfn** is a member of the derived class.

Statement 9–8 represents a mixed-mode operation in that an address of a variable of one type is assigned to a pointer of another type. However, no type conversion is needed here because the address of a derived class variable is being assigned to a base class pointer type. The converse is not true. A *cast*, or explicit type conversion, must be used in that case. Figure 9–3 illustrates some of the ideas that we have been discussing. Note that a cast is used to assign the address of a base class variable to a derived class pointer.

FIGURE 9–3 ■ Some pointer manipulations.

```
/* an illustration of some pointer manipulations */
#include <stream.h>
class base_class {
     char name[81];
     int act_no;
public:
     float balance;
};

class pub : public base_class {
    int abc;
public:
    void write_balance();
};

void pub::write_balance()
{
     cout << "\nbalance = " << balance;
}

main()
{
    pub aaa;
    pub* bbb;
    base_class bc;
    base_class* bc_pt;
    aaa.balance = 300.0;
    bc_pt = &aaa;
    bc_pt->balance = 200.00;
    aaa.write_balance();
    bc_pt->pub::write_balance();
    bbb = (pub*)&bc;
    bbb->balance = 700.0;
    bbb->write_balance();
}
```

We have been discussing a public base class. If the base class is private, the previous discussion must be modified. We shall see that some of the privacy rules can be overridden by use of pointers. In general, *such operations are dangerous and should not be performed*. We present these ideas mainly to stress that, although possible, they are not recommended. The program in Figure 9–4 illustrates this discussion. The same base class is used in Figures 9–3 and 9–4. Note that the base class has a public variable called **balance**. In the program in Figure 9–3, the base class is public, and, therefore, **balance** is a public variable of the derived class as well. In the program in Figure 9–4, the base class is private to the derived class **xyz**. Thus, **balance** has become a private variable for **class xyz**.

The main program has the declarations

<table>
<tr><td>xyz aaa;</td><td>9–10a</td></tr>
<tr><td>base_class* bc_pt;</td><td>9–10b</td></tr>
</table>

FIGURE 9–4 ■ Some pointer manipulations that should not be used.

```
/* an illustration of some pointer manipulations */
#include <stream.h>
class base_class {
     char name[81];
     int act_no;
public:
     float balance;
};

class xyz : base_class {
     int abc;
public:
     void write_balance();
};

void xyz::write_balance()
{
     cout << "\nbalance = " << balance;
}

main()
{
     xyz aaa;
     base_class* bc_pt;
//   aaa.balance = 300.0;  will not compile with this statement
     bc_pt = (base_class*)&aaa;
     bc_pt->balance = 200.00;
     aaa.write_balance();
}
```

Thus, **aaa** is a variable of type **xyz**, and **bc_pt** is a pointer to the base class. The statement

$$\text{aaa.balance} = 300.0; \qquad\qquad \textbf{9–11}$$

will not compile because it attempts to assign a value to a private variable.

Suppose that the base class pointer is assigned the value of the derived class variable. The previous discussion indicates that this could be done with the statement

$$\text{bc\_pt} = \&\text{aaa}; \qquad\qquad \textbf{9–12}$$

However, an error results in this case. A base class pointer *cannot* simply be assigned a derived class address if the base class is *private* to the derived class. This is a measure of protection, but it can be broken easily enough because a cast is allowed. Thus, the statement

$$\text{bc\_pt} = (\text{base\_class}^*)\&\text{aaa}; \qquad\qquad \textbf{9–13}$$

will compile. Now the derived class variables can be addressed with a base class pointer. The variable **balance** is public in the base class. Thus, it can be changed directly from the main program with a base class pointer. This is accomplished with the statement

$$\text{bc\_pt} - >\text{balance} = 200.00 \qquad \textbf{9-14}$$

The value assigned to **balance** has been changed by a simple statement in the main program. Remember that **balance** is a field in the derived class variable **aaa**, and is private. Thus, the privacy has been circumvented.

Although there are times when privacy can be broken, it should not be done. If you are the only programmer working on a program, very nasty bugs can develop. If several programmers are working on a program, you can destroy their work. It cannot be emphasized too strongly that you should never circumvent the privacy of a class.

9-4 ■ virtual FUNCTIONS

Sometimes a related operation is performed on both a derived class and on its base class. For instance, suppose that the data for a person's account is to be output in the program in Figure 9-1. In that program, all accounts were of type **credit_card**. Although we used two functions to output the data, it would be a simple matter to write a function to output all the data for a variable of type **credit_card**. Suppose, however, that there were some people who had only checking accounts and others that had both checking accounts and credit card accounts. Using the classes of Figure 9-1, the variables representing persons with only checking accounts would be of type **checking**, while those variables representing people with both kinds of accounts would be of type **credit_card**.

Now suppose that we want to output the data for both types of people. It would be convenient to use the same name for the function that outputs data for each type of account. The program in Figure 9-5 illustrates how this could be done. (For the time being ignore the word **virtual** in the declaration of the function **output_all** in **class checking**.) The function **output_all** in **class checking** outputs the **act_no**, **name**, and **balance** for the instantiation that calls it. The function **output_all** in **class credit_card** calls the function **output_all** in **class checking** and then outputs **credit_balance**. Thus, all four items of data will be output when **output_all** in **class credit_card** is called. Now suppose that we have the following declarations:

$$\text{checking check;} \qquad \textbf{9-15a}$$
$$\text{credit\_card cred;} \qquad \textbf{9-15b}$$

The following function calls will have the desired result:

$$\text{check.output\_all();} \qquad \textbf{9-16a}$$
$$\text{cred.output\_all();} \qquad \textbf{9-16b}$$

FIGURE 9–5 ■ An illustration of a **virtual** function.

```
/* an illustration of a virtual class */
#include <stream.h>
class checking {
    char name[81];
    int act_no;
    float balance;
    static float service_charge_amt;
public:
    int find_depositor(int);
    void make_deposit(int);
    void debit_check(int);
    void service_charge(int);
    checking* open_account(int);
    void output_data(int);
    void output_old_data();
    void set_service_charge_amt();
    void output_name(int);
    int get_id(int);
    virtual void output_all();
    float operator+(float);
    friend float operator-(checking&);
    checking();
    ~checking();
};

class credit_card : public checking {
    float credit_balance;
    static float service_charge_amt;
public:
    void output_data(int);
    void set_service_charge_amt();
    void service_charge(int);
    void credit_payment(int);
    void debit_purchase(int);
    void output_all();
    credit_card();
    ~credit_card();
};

void checking::output_all()
{
        cout << "\naccount number " << act_no;
        cout << "\n" << name;
        cout << "\nbalance " << balance;
    return;
}

void credit_card::output_all()
{
        checking::output_all();
        cout << "\ncredit card balance " << credit_balance;
    return;
}
```

Overloading causes 9–16a to call the **output_all** in class **checking**, and 9–16b to call the **output_all** in class **credit_card**.

The functions of Figure 9–5 seem to have resolved the problem. Indeed, in this simple case, they have. However, there are circumstances under which simple overloading will not suffice. Consider that pointers to the *base* type (**checking***) are used to represent all the class variables. For instance, suppose that variables representing all the bank's customers are to be stored in an array. Remember that only a single data type can be stored in an array. Every variable of type **checking** or of type **credit_card** can be represented by a pointer of type **checking*** because pointers to the base class can be used as pointers to all types derived from the base class (see Section 9–3). Thus, there can be a single array of pointers of class **checking*** that can reference both types of customers. If we simplify this to the two variables that we have used as an example, we can write

checking* pt1;	**9–17a**
checking* pt2;	**9–17b**
pt1 = ✓	**9–17c**
pt2 = &cred;	**9–17d**

Suppose that **output_all** is called using these pointers. That is, the statements

pt1 − >output_all( );	**9–18a**
pt2 − >output_all( );	**9–18b**

are executed. Now overloading will not suffice because both pointers are of the same type, **checking***, and the **output_all** in type **checking** will be called by both statements. Thus, the program will not function properly because 9–18b should be a call to **output_all** in type **credit_card**. If the compiler kept track of the type of variable to which the pointer points, then 8–19b would function properly. However, if the compiler did this for all pointers, the compilation would become unduly complex. Fortunately, the compiler will keep track of those pointers that are used in the call of a particular type of function called a *virtual function*. The virtual function is declared in the base class by preceding its declaration with the keyword **virtual**. The body of the function is written in the same way as is any other function. Note that function must be written for the base class. The derived class(es) simply declare the **virtual** function in the usual way. In particular, the word **virtual** is *not* used in the declaration(s) in the derived class(es). The declaration in the derived classes must be the same as the declaration in the base class, i.e., the returned type and arguments must be the same as in the base class. It is not necessary for all derived types to declare the **virtual** function. The function **output_all** is declared to be **virtual** in Figure 9–5 with the declaration

virtual void output_all( );	**9–19**

Now Statements 9–18a and 9–18b will function properly. That is, 9–18a calls **output_all** from **class checking**, and 9–18b calls **output_all** from **class credit_card**, because the compiler keeps track of the actual type of **class** to which the pointer of type **checking*** points.

There are other techniques besides **virtual** functions that can resolve the problem. However, they usually are cumbersome. For instance, an extra field that stores a letter could be added to each class. The letter stored in that field indicates the class type. This technique is similar to that used in Figure 8–9 to keep track of the data type stored in a union. In that case, the field called **check** stored either an 'f', 'i', or 'c' to represent data of type **float**, **int**, or **char**, respectively. In the present case a field called **check** could be added to each class to store either a 'c' or an 'r' to indicate that the particular instantiation was of **class checking** or of **class credit_card**. Only one **output_all** function would be written and stored in the base class **checking**. This function would have two branches. The appropriate branch would be chosen by the value of the **check** field. This technique has several drawbacks: there is another value to keep track of, and thus, another chance for error. In addition, the base class must be modified each time that a new derived class is added. When **virtual** functions are used, the base class has to be neither modified nor recompiled when new derived classes are added.

9–5 ■ GENERIC CLASSES

There may be occasions when many classes of the same form are to be generated. For example, consider the banking system that we have been discussing. The data stored for a savings customer might be account number, name, and balance. Similar data might be stored for a checking account customer, and so forth. (Again we have oversimplified the banking business to keep our examples simple.) You might then write several classes that have the same overall form. C++ provides a built-in header file called **generic.h** that contains macros that help you write *generic classes*. A generic class is itself a macro that generates classes that all have the same general form. In the case of the banking system, you would write one generic class for the banking system, and this macro would be used to generate all the required classes.

The program in Figure 9–6 will be used in this discussion. As previously mentioned, the file **generic.h** contains a number of macros that aid in the writing of generic function macros. We shall consider several of them. Consult this file and your system manual to determine all the macros supplied in your **generic.h**. The macro **name2**, defined in **generic.h**, takes two arguments and **concatenates** them (strings them together). For instance,

name2(tom,jones)   **9–20** expands to **tomjones**. The macro **name3** functions in a very similar way, except it takes three arguments and strings them together. The macro that we use to set up the classes is called **set_up_banking**. Its form is

```
#define set_up_banking(type)   class name2                         \   9–21a
                         (banking_,type)     {                     \   9–21b
        int act_no;                                                \   9–21c
        float balance;                                             \   9–21d
    public:                                                        \
        void name3(type,_,add_to_balance)                          \
                              (float amount)                       \   9–21e
        {                                                          \   9–21f
            balance += amount;                                     \   9–21g
        }                                                          \   9–21h
        void name3(type,_,output)()                                \   9–21i
        {                                                          \   9–21j
            cout << "\nbalance  =  " << balance;                   \   9–21k
        }                                                          \   9–21l
    };                                                             \   9–21m
```

FIGURE 9–6 ■ An illustration of a generic class.

```
/* an illustration of a generic class */
#include <stream.h>
#include <generic.h>

#define set_up_banking(type) class name2(banking_,type)    {     \
     int act_no;                                                  \
     float balance;                                               \
public:                                                           \
     void name3(type,_,add_to_balance)(float amount)             \
     {                                                            \
         balance += amount;                                       \
     }                                                            \
     void name3(type,_,output)()     {                           \
         cout << "\nbalance = " << balance;                       \
     }                                                            \
};                                                                \


set_up_banking(savings)

set_up_banking(checking)

main()
{
    banking_savings smith;
    banking_checking jones;
    smith.savings_add_to_balance(2000.50);
    jones.checking_add_to_balance(5000.30);
    smith.savings_output();
    jones.checking_output();
}
```

When it is expanded, its argument, **type**, is replaced by the argument of the macro call. Note the backslashes (\) at the end of each line of the macro. They indicate that the macro is continued onto the next line. With many preprocessors, the first line of the macro definition must contain more than just the macro name and the first line to be expanded. That is, the first line, 9–21a, could *not* contain only

```
#define set_up_banking(type)              \
```

The macro is called twice with the lines

set_up_banking(savings)	9–22a
set_up_banking(checking)	9–22b

There will be two classes set up, **banking_savings** and **banking_checking**. For instance, the expansion of 9–22a results in **type** being replaced by **savings** in the expansions of **name2** and **name3**. The resulting function is

class banking_savings {	9–23a
int act_no;	9–23b
float balance;	9–23c
public:	9–23d
void savings_add_to_balance(float amount)	9–23e
{	9–23f
balance += amount;	9–23g
}	9–23h
void savings_output	9–23i
{	9–23j
cout << "\nbalance = " << balance;	9–23k
}	9–23l
};	9–23m

Note that **name3** did not have to be used in the macro; we could have used **name2** throughout. We used **name3** for illustrative purposes.

The class name (**checking** or **savings**) has been appended to each of the functions of the corresponding class. This is done for illustrative purposes. All the functions in each class could have the same name, and the compiler would distinguish between them because of overloading.

The example of a generic class in Figure 9–6 is not a derived class. Of course, derived classes can be generated in this way as well. A colon, possibly the word **public**, and the base class name would be included in the macro in that part of the macro that generated the class name.

9–6 ■ LINKED LISTS: SOME GENERAL COMMENTS

In this section we shall consider the implementation of a *list*. In addition, we shall make some general comments about classes and object-oriented programming. The list is a commonly used form of data storage. In this section we consider a particular form of list called a *linked list*. Text is stored in each element of the list as a single word with no whitespace. The size of the words and the size of the list are not specified beforehand. The list is to be stored in the minimum amount of space. Because the list is not specified beforehand, space for the list must be allocated dynamically.

A program that implements the list is shown in Figure 9–7. A class called **list** is declared. This class stores two items of data: a pointer to a string that

FIGURE 9–7 ■ An example of list manipulation. (pp. 273–275).

```
/* an example of list manipulation */
#include <stream.h>
class list {
     char* data;
     list* next;
public:
     void add_to_list();
     void read_list();
     list* find_last();
     char* car();
     list* cdr();
     list();
};


list::list()
{
     data = 0;
     next = 0;
     return;
}


void list::add_to_list()
{
     char string[81];
     int length=0,i;
     list* new_element;
     cout << "\nenter one word\n";
     cin >> string;
     /* get length of string */
         while (string[length] != 0)  {
         if(length > 80)break;
         length++;
     }  // end while(string[length] != 0)
     length++;
     cout << "\nstring length is " << length;
     /* if element is not first element of empty list generate new element */
     if(data != 0) {
         /* generate new element of list */
         new_element = new list;
         next = new_element;
     } // end if(data != 0) start else
     else new_element = this;
     /* allocate space for string */
     new_element->data = new char[length];
     for(i=0;i<length;i++) *((new_element->data)+i) = string[i];
     return;
}
```

FIGURE 9–7 ■ *(continued)*

```
list* list::find_last()
{
     list* hold;
     if(next == 0)return this;
     hold = next->find_last();
     return hold;
}
void list::read_list()
{
     cout << "\n" << data;
     if(next == 0)  {
          return;
     }   // end if(next == 0)
     next->read_list();
}

char* list::car()
{
     return data;
}

list* list::cdr()
{
     if(data == 0)return 0;
     return next;
}
main()
{
     list item;
     list* pt;
     list* rest;
     char ch;
     char* ch_pt;
     int ender = 0;
     while(ender == 0)     {
          cout << "\n\nmenu\n";
          cout << "\na add to list";
          cout << "\ne rest of list";
          cout << "\nf first element of list";
          cout << "\nr read list";
          cout << "\nz end program\n";
          cin >> ch;
          switch(ch)    {
          case 'a':
               pt = item.find_last();
               pt->add_to_list();
               break;
          case 'e':
               rest = item.cdr();
               if(rest != 0)rest->read_list();
               else cout<< "\nnil";
               break;
          case 'f':
               cout << "\nthe first element is\n";
               ch_pt = item.car();
               cout << "\n" << ch_pt;
               if(ch_pt == 0)cout <<"nil";
               break;
```

```
    case 'r':
        item.read_list();
        break;
    case 'z':
        ender = 1;
        break;
    default:
        cout << "\nwrong entry\n";
        break;
    } // end case
 } // end while(ender == 0);
}
```

stores the single word of each element of the list, and a pointer to the next instantiation of the class. By definition, the last instantiation of the class points at 0, which we shall call *nil*. Figure 9–8 is a representation of a linked list that stores the list "the book is on the table". The rectangles represent instantiations of the class list. Each instantiation is called a *cell*. One pointer points at one of the words of the list, and the other pointer points at the next cell in the list. The exception is the last cell in the list; its second pointer points to nil.

The declaration of the class is

class list {	**9–24a**
char* data;	**9–24b**
list* next;	**9–24c**
public:	**9–24d**
void add_to_list();	**9–24e**
void read_list();	**9–24f**
list* find_last();	**9–24g**
char* car();	**9–24h**
list* cdr();	**9–24i**
list();	
};	**9–24j**

Thus, **data** is a pointer to a word of the list and **next** is a pointer to the next cell. Note that the constructor (see Figure 9–7) initializes both pointers to 0.

Now consider the function **add_to_list** (see Figure 9–7). The function prompts for the entry of a single word. Note that the function could be easily modified to accept the word as an argument. This word is stored in the array

FIGURE 9–8 ■ A representation of a linked list.

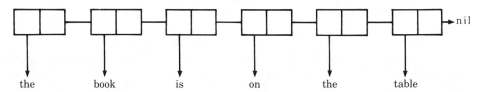

string. The integer variable named **length** is set equal to the length of the string, including the 0 terminator. The next segment of the function is

```
if(data != 0) {                                              9-25a
    new_element = new list;                                  9-25b
    next = new_element                                       9-25c
} // end if(data != 0) start else                            9-25d
else new_element = this;                                     9-25e
/* allocate space for string */                              9-25f
new_element->data = new char[length];                        9-25g
for(i = 0;i<length;i++)*((new_element->data)+i)
                        = string[i];                         9-25h
return;                                                      9-25i
```

This function is called in the main program. Suppose that the instantiation of the first cell is declared in the main program and is called **item** (see Figure 9-7). The function call is

$$pt->add\_to\_list(); \qquad 9-26$$

The first cell is called **item**. In 9-26, **pt** is a pointer to the last cell. Each time that a cell is established, its two pointers are set equal to 0. A single cell, both of whose pointers are assigned 0, is called an *empty list*. When the first word is added to the list, space need be set up only for that word. When the second and each subsequent word is added to the list, a new instantiation of type **list** must be established, and space must be set up for the word. If the data field stores 0, then the list is empty. Thus, if the condition of 9-25a is true, the list is not empty. A new instantiation of **list** is set up using **new** (see 9-25c). The pointer **new_element** will point to this new instantiation. The **next** field in the cell, which was the last cell until the new instantiation of list was created, will be changed from 0 to **new_element**. Thus, it points at the newly created cell. If the condition of 9-25a is not true, then the first word is being entered. In this case, **new_element** is set equal to **this**. Thus, **new_element** points at the existing first cell. Space for the word is set up using 9-25g, and the data is read into this space using 9-25h.

A pointer to the last cell of the list must be found. This is done with the function **find_last**. It is called using the statement

$$pt = item.find\_last(); \qquad 9-27$$

Remember that **item** is the first cell in the list. The function is

```
list* list::find_last()                                      9-28a
{                                                            9-28b
    list* hold;                                              9-28c
    if(next == 0)return this;                                9-28d
    hold = next->find_last();                                9-28e
    return hold;                                             9-28f
}                                                            9-28g
```

This is a recursive function call. If **next** is equal to 0, the last cell has been found, and thus, the pointer to that cell is returned. If **next** is not equal to 0, then 9–28e is executed. This is a recursive call to **next − >find_last**. Thus, the second cell will be tested to determine if it is the last cell in the list. This operation continues until the last cell is found.

The list data is output by the function **read_list**. This is also a recursive function. The data field for the first cell is output, and then the function is called recursively, using the **next** cell pointer, until the last word is output.

The function **car** returns a pointer to the first item of data in the list. The function **cdr** returns a pointer that points at the second item in the list. In effect, it returns a new list that is the old list with the first item removed. If the list has only one item, then **cdr** returns 0.

There is no destructor in the class **list**. When class instantiations are generated using **new**, C++ does not guarantee that **delete** will be called when these variables pass out of scope. If the memory were to be freed using **delete**, the pointers to the various instantiations would have to be used in conjunction with specific calls to **delete**.

The main program consists of a menu and **switch-case** construction. It illustrates the use of the various functions that we have discussed.

Some General Comments

Classes can be used to implement what is called *object-oriented programming*. This was mentioned in the introduction to Chapter 8. Now, after considering classes in detail, let us reconsider some of these ideas. An *object*, which is usually a class, is written. The class consists of the private variables and the public functions. We assume that it is fully debugged. This class is provided to all programmers, who manipulate the variables through the functions of the class. Let us consider some of the advantages of this. The main programs that use the classes are usually very simple. Consider the main programs that we have written, such as those in Figures 9–1 and 9–7. They are mostly menus and **switch-case** constructions. The actual programs consist primarily of function calls. Admittedly, these programs are relatively simple, but they are not trivial. Once the programmer receives a well-written object, the programming tasks are greatly simplified.

The data can be manipulated only by the functions of the class. This usually eliminates many errors. This is especially true in large complex programs that may be written by a team of many programmers. The requirement that the variables be assigned values only by the functions of the class implies that some degree of order will be maintained. Of course, it is assumed that the functions of the class maintain this order. For instance, in the program in Figure 9–7, an item cannot be added to the list without setting the next field of the cell that previously was last to point at the new last cell, and setting the next field of that new last cell to 0. If these fields were assigned from the main program, the programmer would have to keep track of the details. If an error were made, data could be lost, or the program might attempt to read or write from the wrong area of memory. This could crash the computer or result in a bug that would be very difficult to locate.

Object-oriented programming does not free programmers from the details of programming. First and foremost, the objects must be written. The functions of the objects consider all the details, and the programmer must contend with them. If the object (class) is not well-written and error-free, then it can be worse than useless. Most objects will not contain functions to deal with every possible detail. Thus, the programmer who uses the object must contend with some of those details. Of course, classes can be extended (derived) so that the details in the main program can be kept to a minimum. Remember that well-written objects can certainly make the programmer's job simpler and allow him or her to write complex programs more rapidly and with fewer errors.

EXERCISES

Check any programs that you write by running them on your computer. Write main programs to test any functions that you write.

1. Add a derived class to the class of Exercise 2 of Chapter 8. The derived class is to be called **classroom_lab**. The derived class is to contain the class **classroom**, plus an additional array that stores the grades of four laboratory experiments, the average of these grades, and the total average. The total average is to be obtained by considering that the average in the laboratory grades is weighted as a single test grade; that is, the total average is the average of all the test grades and the average of the laboratory grades. Include public functions that provide for the entering of the laboratory grades, computing the average of the laboratory grades, obtaining the total average, and the output of the letter grade based on the total average. The grade criteria are in **class classroom**. Write a main program that tests all features of this program.

2. Include a constructor in the class of Exercise 1 that sets all variables of the derived class to 0.0.

3. Modify the main program of Exercise 1; now use pointers in the function calls.

4. Demonstrate how pointers can be used to circumvent the privacy provisions of a derived class whose base class has a public variable. Why should the use of these procedures be avoided?

5. Add functions to the base class and to the derived class of the class **classroom_lab** of Exercise 2. That function should output all the test grades. All the grades should be output with a single function call.

6. Repeat Exercise 5, but now use a **virtual** function call. The function should be called in the main program using pointers to the base class type.

7. Write a macro that sets up a *generic class* of the general form of type **student**, as it is defined in Exercise 2 of Chapter 8.

8. Write a macro that sets up a generic class of the general form of the class **classroom_lab** that is defined in Exercise 1 of this chapter. The base class should be **classroom**.

9. Add a function to the class **list** (see Figure 9–7). The function should have two arguments. One argument is a single word, and the other is the name of a variable that references the first word in a list of words. The function should return 0 if the first argument is not in the list or, if the first argument is a member of the list, the integer corresponding to the position of the word in the list.

10. Write a list that stores an arbitrary number of floating-point numbers. Write functions that are analogous to those in the class **list** of Figure 9–7. In addition, write a function that averages all the numbers in the list.

11. What is meant by *object-oriented programming*? What constitutes a well-written object?

12. Discuss the advantages of object-oriented programming.

CHAPTER 10
Streams

We have been using streams for the input and output of data and text. In this chapter we shall extend these ideas. Techniques for using streams in conjunction with user-defined types, as well as the important topic of files, will be discussed. In addition, some general aspects of C++ shall be considered.

Streams are not actually part of C++. However, most C++ systems supply a header file called **stream.h** that defines the fundamental stream classes. It is those classes that we have been using for input/output.

10-1 ■ OUTPUT STREAMS—USER-DEFINED TYPES— OUTPUT REDIRECTION

We discussed the output of standard C++ types in Section 3–2. We shall extend that discussion now, and extend stream output to user-defined types. Output to the screen will be primarily considered in this section. We shall consider other forms of output, such as output to a disk file, later in this chapter. In Section 3–2, we discussed the unformatted and formatted output of data. We assume here that the reader is familiar with that discussion.

A stream can be directed toward various types of output devices such as the screen, a data port, or a disk file. There are two standard outputs provided with the C++ system: they are *standard output* and *standard error*. The standard output stream is designated as **cout**. The standard error stream is designated as **cerr**. If **cerr** simply is substituted for **cout** in the programs that we have written, no difference in the output would be observed. C++, like C, has the ability to *redirect the output* from the screen to a specified file. Actually, in a general sense, a device such as a printer or a communications port can be treated as a file. This redirection is done on the line that is used to invoke the program. For instance, suppose that the program is invoked by typing **test** followed by RETURN. Assume that the output is of the form that we have considered. Furthermore, suppose that the program **test** contains the statements

cout <<"\nthis is the output of test";	**10–1a**
cerr <<"\nthis output cannot be redirected";	**10–1b**

When **test** is run normally, the strings

this is the output of test	**10–2a**
this output cannot be redirected	**10–2b**

are output. Now suppose that the program is invoked by typing

test > FILENAME	**10–3**

The output that is directed to the standard output is redirected to the disk file named FILENAME; it will not appear on the screen. However, the output to **cerr** is not redirected, and instead, is output on the screen. Note that 10–3 consists of the word that invokes the program, followed by the greater-than sign, >, and a file name.

The standard error stream is useful when you want only a portion of the output to be redirected. Usually, when redirection is used, almost all the output is redirected. Exceptions to this are *error messages*. For instance, suppose that a program allocates memory using **new**. If sufficient memory is not available, an error-handling routine (see Figures 8–13 and 8–14) should be called. In general, the output of the error-handling routine should appear on the screen so that the person running the program knows what has occurred. If all the output were redirected, this would not happen. For this reason, error-handling routines often direct their output to standard error.

FILENAME in 10–3 can be any valid file name. Consult your operating system manual to determine what constitutes a valid file name. FILENAME can also represent a device such as a printer because, in many operating systems, devices can be represented by file names. Again, consult your operating system manual to determine the file names that represent devices.

The file **stream.h** sets up various classes. One that deals with output is called **ostream**. The overloaded **operator<<** functions are defined in **class ostream**. There is one **operator<<** defined for each built-in data type. For instance, the declaration for the output of types **long** and **double** are

ostream& operator<<(long);	**10–4a**
ostream& operator<<(double);	**10–4b**

There are similar declarations for the other overloaded **operator<<** functions. Note that the standard form of each operator returns an address of type **ostream**.

Programmers can overload their own **operator<<** functions to output user-defined data types. The functions in **stream.h** interact with the operating system to produce the desired output. However, programmers do not have to be concerned with the details of the operating system when they write **operator<<** functions. This is one of the advantages of classes and object-oriented programming. The user-defined **operator<<** functions can be written in terms of the public functions that are in **class ostream**. We shall illustrate this with an example. There are two advantages here. First, the programmer does not have to become involved with the details of the operating system. Furthermore, programs written this way will be portable. If your program worked with a particular operating system, and it contained routines that interact with that operating system, it would not run on another system. However, if you use the functions in **class ostream**, then the program can be recompiled on a C++ system written for a different operating system; it should then compile and run successfully.

An example of a user defined **operator<<** function is given in Figure 10–1. This is a modification of the program in Figure 9–7 where user-defined stream output is used to output a variable of type **list**. The declaration of the operator is:

friend ostream& operator<<(ostream&,list);   10–5

The function definition is

ostream& operator<<(ostream& x,list y)	**10–6a**
{	**10–6b**
x << "\n" << y.data;	**10–6c**
if(y.next == 0)return x;	**10–6d**
operator<<(x,*(y.next));	**10–6e**
}	**10–6f**

Statement 10–6c represents the output of a standard type; both "\n" and the memory pointed at by **y.data** are strings. Thus, the functions defined in **class ostream** are used to output this data.

If **y.next** is equal to zero, then the end of the list has been reached, and operation terminates. If the end of the list has not been reached, **operator<<** is called recursively. The second argument is then *(y.next). Remember that **next** is a pointer to the next cell. Note that this function's operations are essentially the same as those of the function **read_list** (see Figure 9–7).

The function returns **x**, and **x** is the first term in the formal parameter list. Actually, as it is used in the program, the function could return **void**. However, each **operator<<** function returns a reference to its particular **ostream** type so that it can be applied to another **ostream** operation. For instance, 10–6c has two **ostream** operations.

The Function put

When a **char** is output using the standard stream function **operator<<**, the numerical representation of the character is output. Typically, that output representation is the ASCII code. If the actual character is to be output, the function **put** (that is, part of class **ostream**) is used. For instance, if **ch** has been declared to be of type **char**, then the character representation of the ASCII code stored in **ch** will be output by

$$\text{cout.ostream::put(ch);}\qquad\qquad\textbf{10--7}$$

In 10–7 the output has been directed to the standard output. If another output destination is desired, then **cout** should be replaced. For instance, it could be replaced by **cerr**.

FIGURE 10–1 ■ An example of stream output of a user-defined **operator**$\ll$ function. Only the pertinent functions are listed.

```
/* an example of a user-defined operator<< function */
#include <stream.h>
class list {
     char* data;
     list* next;
public:
     void add_to_list();
     void read_list();
     friend ostream& operator<<(ostream&,list);
     list* find_last();
     char* car();
     list* cdr();
     list();
};


ostream& operator<<(ostream& x,list y)
{
     x << "\n" << y.data;
     if(y.next == 0)return x;
     operator<<(x,*(y.next));
}


main()
{
     list item;
     list* pt;
     list* rest;
     char ch;
     char* ch_pt;
     int ender = 0;
     while(ender == 0)     {
          cout << "\n\nmenu\n";
          cout << "\na add to list";
          cout << "\ne rest of list";
          cout << "\nf first element of list";
          cout << "\nr read list";
          cout << "\nz end program\n";
          cin >> ch;
          switch(ch)     {
```

```
                    case 'a':
                        pt = item.find_last();
                        pt->add_to_list();
                        break;
                    case 'e':
                        rest = item.cdr();
                        if(rest != 0)cout << *(rest);
                        else cout<< "\nnil";
                        break;
                    case 'f':
                        cout << "\nthe first element is\n";
                        ch_pt = item.car();
                        cout << "\n" << ch_pt;
                        if(ch_pt == 0)cout <<"nil";
                        break;
                    case 'r':
                        cout << item;
                        break;
                    case 'z':
                        ender = 1;
                        break;
                    default:
                        cout << "\nwrong entry\n";
                        break;
                } // end case
            }   // end while(ender == 0);
        }
```

10–2 ■ INPUT STREAMS—USER-DEFINED TYPES— INPUT REDIRECTION

The file **stream.h** contains a class called **istream** that is used for stream input. This class is to input what **ostream** is to output. Class **istream** overloads the **operator>>** functions for all the built-in types. Two typical declarations of **operator>>** in **istream** are

$$\text{istream\& operator>>(long\&);} \qquad \textbf{10–8a}$$
$$\text{istream\& operator>>(double\&)} \qquad \textbf{10–8b}$$

Note that in 10–8, the arguments are *addresses*. This must be the case for all user-defined **operator>>** functions.

The **operator>>** functions are written essentially as other functions are. An illustration is shown in Figure 10–2. Here we have used a derived class. The **operator>>** function accesses variables in both the base class and in the derived class. Thus, it has been made a **friend** to both classes. (Note that we have a forward reference situation here so that the statement **class pub** is included before the base class.) The declaration of the **operator>>** function is

$$\text{friend istream\& operator>>(istream\&,pub\&);} \qquad \textbf{10–9}$$

FIGURE 10–2 ■ An example of stream input and output of a user-defined type.

```
/* an illustration of stream input and output */
#include <stream.h>
class pub;

class base_class {
    char name[81];
    int act_no;
public:
    float balance;
    friend istream& operator>>(istream&,pub&);
    friend ostream& operator<<(ostream&,pub);
};

class pub : public base_class {
    int abc;
public:
    void write_balance();
    friend istream& operator>>(istream&,pub&);
    friend ostream& operator<<(ostream&,pub);
};

istream& operator>>(istream& x,pub& y)
{
    x >> y.abc;
    x >> y.balance;
    x >> y.act_no;
    x >> y.name;
    return x;
}

ostream& operator<<(ostream& x,pub y)
{
    x << "\nabc = " << y.abc;
    x << "\nbalance = " << y.balance;
    x << "\nact number = " << y.act_no;
    x << "\n" << y.name;
    return x;
}

void pub::write_balance()
{
    cout << "\nbalance = " << balance;
}

main()
{
    pub aaa;
    cout << "\n enter abc,balance, account number, name\n";
    cin >> aaa;
    cout << aaa;
}
```

The actual **operator** >> function is

istream& operator>>(istream& x,pub& y)	**10–10a**
{	**10–10b**
x >> y.abc;	**10–10c**
x >> y.balance;	**10–10d**
x >> y.act_no;	**10–10e**
x >> y.name;	**10–10f**
return x;	**10–10g**
}	**10–10h**

Note that the **operator>>** functions provided in **stream.h** have been used to implement the function 10–10.

The program in Figure 10–2 also contains an **operator<<** function that is used to output the derived class data. The main program is shown in Figure 10–2 as well. Note that the user-defined **operator<<** and **operator>>** are used in the main program just as the built-in functions are.

The program in Figure 10–2 uses a single function to access both the base class and the derived class. An alternative procedure is to write two **operator>>** functions; one inputs the variables of the base class, and the other inputs variables of the derived class. Such a program is shown in Figure 10–3. The **operator>>** for the derived class inputs the variables for the complete derived class. As such, it utilizes the **operator>>** function for the base class.

The **operator>>** function for the base class is similar to 10–10 except that the second term in the formal parameter list is of type **base_class&**, and 10–10c is not present because **abc** is a derived class field variable. The derived class **operator>>** is

istream& operator>>(istream& x,pub& y)	**10–11a**
{	**10–11b**
base_class* ba_pt;	**10–11c**
ba_pt = &y;	**10–11d**
x >> y.abc;	**10–11e**
x >> *ba_pt;	**10–11f**
return x;	**10–11g**
}	**10–11h**

Here, after **ba_pt** is declared to be a pointer to the base class, it is assigned the address of **y**. Thus, when 10–11f is executed, the base class **operator>>** function is overloaded because ***ba_pt** is of type **base_class**. We have not rewritten the output function, but the **operator<<** functions could be rewritten so that one was used for the base class and the other for the derived class. It should be noted that operator functions that are members of a class can be declared as **virtual**. In addition, constructors and destructors can be written for operators that are members of a class.

FIGURE 10-3 ■ An example of stream input and output with a derived class.

```
/* an illustration of stream input and output */
#include <stream.h>
class pub;

class base_class {
    char name[81];
    int act_no;
public:
    float balance;
    friend istream& operator>>(istream&,base_class&);
    friend ostream& operator<<(ostream&,pub);
};

class pub : public base_class {
    int abc;
public:
    void write_balance();
    friend istream& operator>>(istream&,pub&);
    friend ostream& operator<<(ostream&,pub);
};

istream& operator>>(istream& x,base_class& y)
{
    x >> y.balance;
    x >> y.act_no;
    x >> y.name;
    return x;
}

istream& operator>>(istream& x,pub& y)
{
    base_class* ba_pt;
    ba_pt = &y;
    x >> y.abc;
    x >> *ba_pt;
    return x;
}

ostream& operator<<(ostream& x,pub y)
{
    x << "\nabc = " << y.abc;
    x << "\nbalance = " << y.balance;
    x << "\nact number = " << y.act_no;
    x << "\n" << y.name;
    return x;
}

void pub::write_balance()
{
    cout << "\nbalance = " << balance;
}

main()
{
    pub aaa;
    cout << "\n enter abc,balance, account number, name\n";
    cin >> aaa;
    cout << aaa;
}
```

In Section 10–1 we discussed output redirection by including a > sign and a file name on the command line. In a similar way, the input from the standard input can be redirected. Note that the standard input is the keyboard and is designated by **cin**. The standard input can be redirected by entering the name that invokes the program, a less-than sign, <, and the file name; for instance,

$$\text{test} < \text{FILENAME} \qquad \textbf{10–12}$$

Now, the program takes its standard input from the file called FILENAME. As we discussed in Section 10–1, FILENAME can represent a device.

The file must contain the input in the correct form. For instance, the program of Figure 10–3 requires the input of an integer, a floating-point number, an integer, and a string, in that order. Thus, the file might contain

$$11\ 5000.00\ 22\ \text{smith} \qquad \textbf{10–13}$$

Any whitespace can separate the data. For instance, each item could be entered on a separate line. At this time, we have discussed writing of files by redirection of the output. We shall consider more versatile file-handling procedures later in this chapter.

Both the standard input and the standard output can be redirected. For instance, if **test** is invoked from the command line

$$\text{test} > \text{FILE2} < \text{FILE1} \qquad \textbf{10–14a}$$

then the standard input will be taken from FILE1, and the standard output will be directed to FILE2. The order of writing the input and output is unimportant. For instance, the following command line is equivalent to 10–14a:

$$\text{test} < \text{FILE1} > \text{FILE2} \qquad \textbf{10–14b}$$

10–3 ■ STREAM STATES

We have thus far assumed that all input and output proceeds without error. However, errors do occur. For instance, a character can be entered when a numerical response is expected. Even more serious errors can occur when streams are used for file input and output. We shall consider those in the next section. Each stream has a *state* associated with it. The state can be used to detect if an error, or some other condition, has occurred. There are four *stream states*; they are represented by the integers 0, 1, 2, and 3. These are in turn represented by an *enumerated type* that is defined in the file **stream.h**. The enumerated type is

$$\text{enum stream\_state}\{\ \_\text{good}=0,\ \_\text{eof}=1,\ \_\text{fail}=2,\ \_\text{bad}=3\}\,; \qquad \textbf{10–15}$$

FIGURE 10–4 ■ A program that uses the stream state in an error-handling routine.

```
/* a program that uses the stream state to test for an error */
#include <stream.h>
main()
{
    int a;
    cout << "\nenter an integer\n";
    cin >> a;
    if(cin.rdstate() != _good)    {
        cout << "\nwrong type entered - program terminating\n";
        exit(0);
    } // end if(cin.rdstate() != _good)
    cout << "\nprogram completed successfully";
}
```

Some C++ systems may use different definitions for the enumerated type 10–15; the enumerated type may also be called by a somewhat different name. The stream states **_good** and **_eof** generally represent successful transfer of data. For the type of input and output that we have been considering, if the data is input or output properly, the stream state will be **_good**. If the input calls for an integer and a character is entered, an error occurs, and the stream state is **_fail**. The stream state **_eof** indicates that the end of a file has been reached. There is often no specification for the length of a file. The file is read until the end is reached. When the end of the file is reached, the stream state becomes **_eof**. This state can be used to terminate reading appropriately. Both **_fail** and **_bad** indicate that an error has occurred. The differences are important only to those programmers who write low-level stream operations; they will not be discussed here.

The file **stream.h** contains a function called **rdstate** that returns the current state of the stream. Figure 10–4 is a program that illustrates using the stream state in a simple error-handling routine. The user is prompted to enter an integer, which is then assigned to the variable **a**. Note that **a** is declared to be of type **int**. The condition portion of the **if** statement is

$$\text{cin.rdstate() } != \text{ \_good} \qquad \textbf{10–16}$$

Remember that both the function **rdstate** and the enumerated type **stream_state** are contained in **stream.h**. If an integer is entered, the stream state is **_good** and "program completed successfully" is output. If a character is entered in response to the prompt, **_fail** is returned by **cin.rdstate()**, and 10–16 is true. Now "wrong type entered—program terminating" is output, **exit(0)**; is executed, and the program terminates.

Figure 10–4 is an example of a very simple error-handling routine. Of course, more complicated ones can be written. The program in Figure 10–4 will not prevent all types of errors. For instance, on some C++ systems, if a number of type **float** is entered in response to the prompt, the number will simply be converted to an integer, and the system state is **_good**.

10–4 ■ FILES

The data that a program generates usually must be saved and reused at a later time. It would be impractical to keep a single program running for weeks or months at a time if it were used only infrequently. In other circumstances, the computer may not be able to store all the data. For instance, most computers could not store all the data for every one of a bank's depositors. To overcome these difficulties, the data should be stored in a file on either a *floppy disk* or a *hard disk*. When there is a very large amount of data to be stored, *magnetic tape* can be used to store it. For instance, in the first case discussed above, the program would be run and the data stored in a disk file, at which point the execution of the program would terminate. When the program is run at a later date, the data stored in the file would be read back into the memory, and the program would proceed using the stored data and other new data. In the case of the bank's depositors, the data for all the depositors would be stored on tape or on a large hard disk. Only the data for the depositor whose record was being processed would be read into memory.

We shall consider the writing and reading of files stored on a disk. The operating system keeps track of these files. Each file has a name that the operating system uses to identify it. (In addition, the operating system must keep track of other things, such as where the file is stored and its size.) The operating system name is the one that appears in the directory listing.

Whenever a file is written or read, an area of memory called a *buffer* is set up to speed the file operations. Suppose that the data consists of a sequence of characters. Instead of transferring one character at a time to and from the file, a sequence of characters is stored in the buffer and transmitted to the file as a group or, conversely, a sequence of characters is transferred from the file to the buffer. Each input or output stream must be associated with a buffer. Two procedures are involved in this process. First the buffer must be established, and then it must be associated with the appropriate stream. The file **stream.h** contains a class type called **filebuf**. When a variable of type **filebuf** is declared, the appropriate memory allocation is made. The buffer is identified by the declared variable name. For instance, the following statement declares that a variable called **file_buf1** is of type **filebuf** and also establishes a buffer that is referred to by the name **file_buf1**.

filebuf file_buf1;   **10–17**

The operating system name for the file also must be associated with the appropriate buffer. In addition, you must declare whether the file is to be written to or read from (we shall consider other procedures, subsequently). This is accomplished by the function called **open** that is part of the class **filebuf** defined in **stream.h**. A statement that opens a file whose directory name is **c:test.text** for reading is

file_buf1.open("c:test.txt",input);   **10–18**

Note that this follows the usual rules of dot notation. The file named **c:test.txt** is related to the buffer whose variable name is **file_buf1**. The first argument of **open** is the directory name of the file. It can be literally specified as it is in 10–18, or it can be represented by a string variable. The second argument is either **input**, **output**, or **append**. (Not all systems implement **append**.) A file that is opened for **input** is read; a file that is open for **output** is written to. Only an existing file can be opened for **input**. However, if a previously nonexistent file is opened for **output**, then that file will be created. If an existing file is opened for **output**, all its data will be erased before it is written to. That means that if you open an existing file for **output**, all the old data in that file will be lost. When a file is opened in the **append** mode, the file is opened for **output** but the old data is not lost; instead, the new data is added to the end of the file. For instance, the following statement opens a file called **c:new.dat** for writing to:

file_buf2.open("c:new.dat",output);   **10–19**

where **file_buf2** has been declared to be of type **filebuf**. The allowable form of the file name varies with the operating system. Consult your operating system manual to determine the specification of valid file names.

The function **open** returns a pointer of type **filebuf*** if the file is opened successfully. If the file is not opened successfully, **open** returns 0. It is important to always determine whether the file has been opened successfully. Failure to open a file may occur for a number of reasons. A failure in an attempt to open a file for reading may be due to the specification of a nonexistent file name. An error when a file is opened for writing may be due to a lack of sufficient space available on the disk; in either failure, the disk drive may be inoperative. If a program fails to open a file, and simply proceeds without interruption, unpredictable results can occur and data may be lost. Thus, you must always test to see if files are opened properly. If they are not, a suitable error-handling routine should be called. In general, such routines do not permit computation to proceed unless some corrective measures, such as entering a correct file name, are taken. The following statement opens a file and checks for success:

if(file_buf2.open("c:new.dat",output) == 0)error_handler();   **10–20**

If **open** returns 0, the error handler will be called; otherwise the program proceeds.

If you are writing a file, a variable of type **ostream** must be declared. If the writing is to the standard output, a predeclared variable called **cout** is used. As an example, we shall declare a variable called **to** of type **ostream**. This stream variable must be related to the buffer. This is automatically done by the **ostream** constructor. The argument of the declared variable is the address of the stream variable. Thus, for the example that we are using, the declaration of **to** would be

ostream to(&file_buf2);   **10–21**

Note that there is no significance to the variable name **to**; any valid variable name could be used.

In a similar way, we must declare a stream variable of type **istream** for reading from a file. This can be done with the statement

istream from(&file_buf1);   10–22

Again there is no significance to the name **from**. Any valid variable name could be used.

Once the stream has been opened, it can be used just as we have used **cin** and **cout**. For instance, we can write to the stream **to** using the statement

to << x;   10–23

where **x** is a variable of standard type or of a type whose **operator**<< has been overloaded. When 10–23 is executed, the value stored in **x** is written to the stream designated by **to**. Thus, it will be written to the file specified in the **open** statement. Similarly, we can write

from >> y;   10–24

Now the input will be taken from the file and assigned to **y**. When data is stored in a disk file, each item must be delimited (separated) by whitespace so that it can be read properly. When data is written to a file, you must ensure that the proper whitespace is written into the file. We shall illustrate this subsequently. If a sequence of characters is stored on a file, the characters do not need to be delimited because the system can recognize the single characters. For instance, the sequence of characters **xyz** represents an "x," a "y," and a "z." On the other hand, the numerical sequence **10110** could represent many numbers, such as the single number 10110, or the numbers 101 and 10, or 10 and 110, etc. Note that input of data from a file follows the principles of data input from the keyboard.

When a data item of type **char** is written to a file with a statement such as 10–23, the numerical representation of the character is stored just as it is when you write to **cout**. If you want to write a character to a file as a character, rather than as its numerical representation, then the function **put** should be used. If a single character is to be read from a stream, the function **get** can be used.

Figure 10–5 is a program that reads characters from a file and writes them to another file. In an actual program, the data would probably be processed after it is read, and before it is output. The statements that we have discussed are used in the program.

The function **error_handler** is called when a file is not opened properly. The function outputs a suitable error message and then terminates operation. Thus, the program cannot proceed unless the files have been opened properly.

Note that the specific file names used in 10–18 and 10–19 have been replaced by string variable names **input_file** and **output_file**. The person

FIGURE 10–5 ■ A program that reads and writes a file of characters.

```
/* an example of file input and output */
#include <stream.h>
extern void exit(int);
void error_handler(char* s)
{
    cerr << "\n cannot open " << s;
    cerr << "\nprogram terminating";
    exit(1);
    return;
}
main()
{
    filebuf file_buf1;   // set up file buffers
    filebuf file_buf2;
    char* input_file;
    char* output_file;
    char ch;
    const unsigned STORE_SIZE=1000;
    char store[STORE_SIZE];
    int real_size=0;
    int i;
    input_file = new char[81];
    output_file = new char[81];
    cout << "\nenter input file name\n";
    cin >> input_file;
    cout << "\nenter output file name\n";
    cin >> output_file;
    /* read file */
    if(file_buf1.open(input_file,input) == 0)error_handler(input_file);
    istream from(&file_buf1);   // variable from declared
    while(from.get(ch) != 0)  {
        store[real_size] = ch;
        real_size++;
        if(real_size >= STORE_SIZE)break;
    }
    /* file data could be processed here */
    /* write file */
    if(file_buf2.open(output_file,output) == 0)error_handler(output_file);
    ostream to(&file_buf2);   // variable to declared
    for(i=0;i<real_size;i++)to.put(store[i]);
}
```

running the program is prompted for the directory file names, and these are stored in these two variables.

The character data is sequentially read into the variable **ch**. Each character is then stored in an array of type **char**, called **store**. The data is read using the statement

while(from.get(ch) != 0) {	10–25a
store[real_size] = ch;	10–25b
real_size++;	10–25c
if(real_size >= STORE_SIZE)break;	10–25d
}	10–25e

When the end of file is reached, **get** returns 0; thus, the **while** loop reads the complete file. Because STORE_SIZE is the dimension of the array store, 10–25d prevents too much data from being written into the array.

The data is written into the output file with the statement

$$\text{for}(i = 0; i < \text{real\_size}; i + +)\text{to.put(store[i])};$$ **10–26**

Note that **real_size** is assigned the actual amount of data stored in **store**. Thus, all the input data will be written to the output file.

The program in Figure 10–6 is similar to that in Figure 10–5, except that the data is now of type **float**. The standard operators are used here. For instance, the statement that is equivalent to 10–25a is

$$\text{while(from} >> \text{numb} != 0) \; \{$$ **10–27**

Here **numb** is a variable of type **float**. Note that the operation **from** $>>$ **numb** returns 0 if the end of file has been reached. In the last section we discussed the stream state **_good**. Because **_good** is different from **_eof**, **_good** can also be used to test for end of file and to ensure that the reading is proceeding properly. However, the procedure used here has the advantage of combining several steps without being hard to read.

The statement in Figure 10–6 that corresponds to 10–26 is:

$$\text{for}(i = 0; i < \text{real\_size}; i + +)\text{to} << \text{store[i]} << \text{"\textbackslash n"};$$ **10–28**

Again, note that the streams **from** and **to** are used with files in the same way that **cin** and **cout** are used with standard input and standard output. Note that 10–28 writes a newline after each entered number to serve as whitespace. Statement 10–28 causes characters to be written to the file, just as they are written to standard output. That is, the floating-point data is stored in its character representation. Thus, the floating-point numbers that are stored in the array **store** are converted to their character representations and are then output. In a similar way, when 10–27 is executed, the characters stored in the file are converted to their floating-point representations and stored in **numb**.

In general, it takes more bits, or space on a file, to store a number as a string of characters than as its binary representation. The advantage of using a string of characters to represent the data is that standard input and output and file input and output have the same form, and all the features of streams can be used. In addition, such files can usually be read and written by most word processors. Some systems do provide procedures for the writing of data in its binary representation. Consult your system manual to see if your system implements such a feature.

When a program opens a file for writing, it must close the file as well. This allows the operating system to upgrade the directory information. In addition, as we discussed, each item of data that is written to the buffer is not immediately written to the file; it is stored in the buffer. When the buffer fills, the group of data stored there is written to the file. There is a danger that the last items of data in the buffer may not be written to the file. However,

FIGURE 10–6 ■ A program that reads and writes data of type **float**.

```
/* an example of file input and output */
#include <stream.h>
extern void exit(int);
void error_handler(char* s)
{
     cerr << "\n cannot open " << s;
     cerr << "\nprogram terminating";
     exit(1);
     return;
}
main()
{
     filebuf file_buf1;   // set up file buffers
     filebuf file_buf2;
     char* input_file;
     char* output_file;
     float numb;
     const unsigned STORE_SIZE=100;
     float store[STORE_SIZE];
     int real_size=0;
     int i;
     input_file = new char[81];
     output_file = new char[81];
     cout << "\nenter input file name\n";
     cin >> input_file;
     cout << "\nenter output file name\n";
     cin >> output_file;
     /* read file */
     if(file_buf1.open(input_file,input) == 0)error_handler(input_file);
     istream from(&file_buf1);   // variable from declared
     while(from >> numb != 0)  {
          store[real_size] = numb;
          real_size++;
          if(real_size >= STORE_SIZE)break;
     }
     cout << "\nfile size = " << real_size << "\n";
     for(i=0;i<real_size;i++)cout << " " << store[i];
     /* file data could be processed here */
     /* write file */
     if(file_buf2.open(output_file,output) == 0)error_handler(output_file);
     ostream to(&file_buf2);   // variable to declared
     for(i=0;i<real_size;i++)to << store[i] << "\n";
}
```

when the file is closed, any data left in the buffer is automatically written to the file. The buffer is said to be *flushed*. We did not explicitly close the files because **istream** and **ostream** have destructors that automatically flush the buffer and close the file. Files that are opened for reading can also be closed. However, it is usually not critical in this case. In the programs in Figure 10–5 and 10–6, the files were written at the end of each program so that they were automatically closed immediately after they were written. If program writes a file and then performs much additional computation without a subsequent writing to the file, it is wise to explicitly flush the buffer and close the file. This protects against a loss of data in case the program terminates abnormally. The buffer is flushed with the statement

$$to.flush();$$ **10–29**

while the file is closed with the statement

$$file\_buf2.close();$$ **10–30**

Note that **flush** is a member of **ostream**, while **close** is a member of **filebuf**.

We have discussed that devices can be represented by files. For instance, if **con** is the file name that represents the console on your operating system, then if that file name is given as the input file name for the program in Figure 10–5 or Figure 10–6, the program will take its input from the console rather than from a disk file. In a similar way, if **prn** represents the printer, and if the output file name is given to the program as **prn**, the output will be directed to the printer. Of course, you must use the file names that are appropriate for your system. For instance, if **prn** did not represent the printer, then the output would be written to a file called **prn**. Check your operating system manual to determine the file names corresponding to the various devices.

10–5 ■ COMPILER DIRECTIVES

We have already discussed the **#include** and **#define** compiler directives. In this section we shall consider some additional compiler directives.

There are times when a **#define** compiler directive is used for a particular portion of a program, but it would be desirable if the compiler could forget about that definition in the remainder of the program. The compiler directive **#undef** performs that function. For instance, if the following sequence occurs in a program:

$$\#define\ FOO\ 20$$ **10–31a**
.
.
.
$$\#undef\ FOO$$ **10–31b**

then after line 10–31b, FOO will have no special significance to the compiler. In particular, it will not be replaced by 20.

When a program contains a syntax error, the compiler outputs an error message and indicates a line number. At times, it is convenient to change the numbering in part of the program to help isolate such an error. This can be done with the **#line** compiler directive. One form of its use is

$$\#line\ 100$$ **10–32**

For purposes of error diagnostics, the next line in the program will be numbered 100. The following line will be numbered 101, etc. Actually, the **#line** directive is more general than we have indicated. Its general form is

#line constant_expression "filename"   10–33

The **constant_expression** is a constant expression that can be evaluated to an integer during compilation. The optional **filename** changes the name of the file from which the compiler is currently reading the program.

Conditional Compilation

Compiler directives can be used to control the compilation, in that the compiler can be made to ignore certain lines of the program, based on some condition. The three related compiler directives **#if**, **#else**, and **#endif** are used as indicated here:

#if constant_expression	**10–34a**
statements_a	**10–34b**
#else	**10–34c**
statements_b	**10–34d**
#endif	**10–34e**

The **constant_expression** is the usual form of constant expression that can be evaluated during compilation. If the **constant_expression** does not evaluate to 0, i.e., it is true, then **statements_a** will be compiled, and **statements_b** will be ignored. On the other hand, if **constant_expression** evaluates to 0, i.e., it is false, then **statements_a** will be ignored, and **statements_b** will be compiled. The **#else** is optional; that is, 10–34c and 10–34d can be omitted from the construction of 10–34.

The **#if** compiler directive can be replaced by either **#ifdef** or **#ifndef**. The form of their use is

#ifdef identifier	**10–35a**
#ifndef identifier	**10–35b**

where **identifier** represents any identifier. If the identifier has been defined with a **#define**, then 10–35a is equivalent to the **constant_expression** in 10–34a being non-zero (true); if the identifier has not been defined, then 10–35a is equivalent to the **constant_expression** in 10–34a being 0 (false). Thus, **#ifdef** checks to see if the identifier has been defined. Conversely, **#ifndef** checks to see if the identifier is undefined.

Conditional compilation can be used to change the workings of programs, because different parts can be compiled based on some value. One common use of conditional compilation is to ensure that the same file is not included more than once. For instance, suppose that the file **test.h** has a line containing

#define FOO   10–36

Now suppose that this file is to be included in a program that is made by combining several separate files into one large file, which is then compiled. It is possible that several of the files could **#include** the file **test.h**; this would result in an error. However, the following sequence can be used to prevent multiple includes of **test.h**:

$$\#\text{ifndef FOO} \qquad\qquad \textbf{10--37a}$$
$$\#\text{include } <\text{test.h}> \qquad \textbf{10--37b}$$
$$\#\text{endif} \qquad\qquad\qquad \textbf{10--37c}$$

If **test.h** was previously included, then 10–37b is ignored by the compiler, because FOO has been defined. On the other hand, if **test.h** has not been included, and FOO has not been defined elsewhere, then 10–37b is evaluated. Thus, the desired result has been achieved.

EXERCISES

Check any programs that you write by running them on your computer. If you write a function, write a main program to check it.

1. Write an **operator**$<<$ function that outputs all the data for the class of Exercise 2 of Chapter 8. Include suitable explanatory statements in the output.

2. Write an **operator**$<<$ function that outputs all the data for the derived class of Exercise 1 of Chapter 9. Include the base class data in the output. Include suitable explanatory statements in the output.

3. Write an **operator**$>>$ function that inputs all the data for the class of Exercise 2 of Chapter 8.

4. Write an **operator**$>>$ function that inputs all the data for the derived class of Exercise 1 of Chapter 9. Include the base class data in the input.

5. Repeat Exercise 2, but now write one **operator**$<<$ function that outputs the base class variables, and another **operator**$<<$ function that calls the first one and then outputs the variables of the derived class.

6. Repeat Exercise 4, but now write one **operator**$>>$ function that inputs the base class variables, and then write another **operator**$>>$ function that calls the first one and then inputs the derived class variables.

7. Demonstrate that two different **operator**$<<$ functions that you write can be used in the same statement.

8. Write a program that includes statements that test the *state* of the input and output stream.

9. Redirect the output of a program to a file.

10. Redirect the input of a program to be from a file.

11. Redirect the output of a program to the printer.

12. Write a program that inputs 10 integers from the keyboard, and then stores the square of each of the integers in a disk file. Include a suitable error-handling routine in your program.

13. Write a program that reads the file generated in Exercise 10 and outputs the results. Include a suitable error-handling routine in your program.

14. Modify the programs of Exercises 12 and 13 so that numbers of type **double** are processed.

15. Use *compiler directives* to write a program that either multiplies or adds three numbers, but not both. The choice should be made by changing one number in the program prior to compilation.

16. Study the file **stream.h** that comes with your system. Now write a set of statements that will include **stream.h** if it has not been included previously.

INDEX